The Beginner's Guide to Opera Stage Management

The Beginner's Guide to Opera Stage Management is the first book to cover theatrical stage management practices specifically for opera productions, providing an invaluable step-by-step guide.

Beginning with a brief history of opera and detailing its difference from theater, the book covers stage management best practices through prep, rehearsals, tech, performance, and wrap up. From the moment a manager accepts a contract, right through to archiving paperwork, this essential toolkit covers each step of a stage manager's journey. Working with a score, reading music, working with singers, conductors, and musicians, basic duties of a stage manager versus an assistant stage manager, and other tasks specific to opera are also included in this comprehensive guide. This book is full of tips and tricks, as well as the good, bad, and ugly stories from opera stage managers, sharing both their experiences and mistakes.

This is the perfect how-to book for the professional or emerging stage manager looking to work in opera, or to expand their existing stage management skillset.

Danielle Ranno has worked in opera for over a decade, both regionally and internationally. Credits include Lincoln Center, Seattle Opera, The Glimmerglass Festival, Opera Columbus, On-Site Opera, International Summer Opera Festival of Morelia, Lakes Area Music Festival, Brevard Music Center, Opera Grand Rapids, Tri-Cities Opera, and The Castleton Festival. She also regularly works on Broadway plays and musicals, including the Tony Award winning play, *The Lehman Trilogy, Six,* and *&Juliet.* Danielle has a BA in Communications, with a concentration in Public Relations from Florida Gulf Coast University and an MFA from Mason Gross School of the Arts at Rutgers University in Stage Management. She is a proud member of The Actors Equity Association and American Guild of Musical Artists.

The Beginner's Guide to Opera Stage Management

Gathering the Tools You Need to Work in Opera

Danielle Ranno

Routledge
Taylor & Francis Group

NEW YORK AND LONDON

Cover image: © Rebekah Bruce

First published 2023
by Routledge
605 Third Avenue, New York, NY 10158

and by Routledge
4 Park Square, Milton Park, Abingdon, Oxon, OX14 4RN

Routledge is an imprint of the Taylor & Francis Group, an informa business

Library of Congress Cataloging-in-Publication Data
Names: Ranno, Danielle, author.
Title: The beginner's guide to opera stage management : gathering the tools
you need to work in opera / Danielle Ranno.
Description: [1.] | New York, NY : Routledge, 2022. | Includes index.
Identifiers: LCCN 2022024310 (print) | LCCN 2022024311 (ebook) |
ISBN 9780367497934 (hardback) | ISBN 9780367497927 (paperback) |
ISBN 9781003047391 (ebook)
Subjects: LCSH: Opera--Production and direction. | Stage management.
Classification: LCC MT955 .R34 2022 (print) | LCC MT955 (ebook) |
DDC 792.602/3--dc23/eng/20220523
LC record available at https://lccn.loc.gov/2022024310
LC ebook record available at https://lccn.loc.gov/2022024311

ISBN: 9780367497934 (hbk)
ISBN: 9780367497927 (pbk)
ISBN: 9781003047391 (ebk)

DOI: 10.4324/9781003047391

Typeset in Times New Roman
by KnowledgeWorks Global Ltd.

Contents

Foreword

It's high time for a book of this caliber and guidance to be written, and, in my mind, it has been written by the perfect person.

I first met Danielle in a production of *Il barbiere di Siviglia* I was directing at Opera Naples in 2014. Now in 2021, we've done countless productions together with several in the future, and if I had my choice, she would get packed in my suitcase for every job I have.

The Beginner's Guide To Opera Stage Management is a clear, and concise guide for any young stage manager, director, administrator, or singer to understand the job description and level of commitment needed for stage management. It's truly a step-by-step pathway to success. The comparisons between theater and opera are beyond valuable and I honestly feel it should be mandatory reading for any *artist* that enters a rehearsal room.

I have the utmost respect for the stage managers of the world and they are often the last to be thanked. Always the first to arrive and the last to leave. Often expected to miss nothing, and be two steps ahead of everyone. Sometimes a traffic cop, and sometimes a stand-in actor who already knows the blocking. Caregiver fits for me. Especially when I'm told I need water instead of coffee. They are the treasure of our industry.

I've watched Danielle teach her "craft" of stage management to many young interns over the years and each of them has grown, prospered, and valued her on so many levels. I admire her attention to detail, her work ethic, her ability to manage just about everything in the room, including me. We both believe our matching "Virgo" tendencies befit our calling and are well suited for this industry. We are in tune to the point that she often finishes my sentences or has already written down a note before I even speak. But what wraps up everything about Danielle is her spirit and kindness. I'm humbled, honored, and grateful to work alongside her, and mostly, to call her my dear friend.

Dean Anthony
Director of Opera,
The Janiec Opera Company of the Brevard Music Center

Preface

o·pe·ra

/ˈäp(ə)rə/

As defined by Merriam-Webster

Noun

A drama set to music and made up of vocal pieces with orchestral accompaniment and orchestra overtures and interludes.

BUT OPERA?

Many people are turned off by working in opera because they think that if they do not know how to read music, they cannot do it. Not true! Music can be intimidating, especially when you first look at a full orchestra score, but it does not have to be. If you are willing to take the time, you can learn. Another often-mentioned concern is not knowing the language. Most stage managers that I have crossed paths with, myself included, do not speak fluent Italian, Spanish, French, German, or Czech. Although it might be helpful, it is not a deal breaker. It simply means you will have to get your hands on a great translation, such as a Castel.

In reality, there is nothing that you need to know ahead of your first opera other than basic stage management skills, such as how to be present in a rehearsal room, take notes, put together paperwork, and run a show, either on the deck or as a calling stage manager. Sure, the paperwork may differ, but there is nothing you cannot learn on the job. Most companies and stage managers use their own templates and will make an old version of the show accessible. Study these templates, and replicate them with the information pertaining to your own show. When I started at the Castleton Festival, I was the least experienced assistant stage manager on the team. Any extra time that I had was spent dissecting old paperwork and replicating it. I got to know the music really well by listening to it over and over again, both on its own and while following in the score and ensured I knew the story well enough by going through the English libretto. Although it was a lot of work for me to catch up on, it was not impossible.

EVERYTHING I KNOW ABOUT OPERA I LEARNED FROM CARTOONS

Little did we know at the time, but opera has been a part of our lives since we were very young. If you grew up on cartoons such as the *Pink Panther,* you've probably heard the beginning of Beethoven's Fifth, that is until Pink

Panther started playing Henry Mancini's theme. If you grew up with Bugs Bunny and Elmer Fudd, you were introduced to *The Barber of Seville* in *Rabbit of Seville*, and *Die Walküre* from Wagner's Ring Cycle in *What's Opera Doc?* Most millennials will remember *What's Opera Arnold?* from Nickelodeon's *Hey Arnold,* where Arnold, Helga, and their classmates performed tunes from *Carmen, Pagliacci,* and *Die Walküre.* Fans of *The Simpsons* probably remember when Homer became an opera singer after an accident in season 19 and sang the role of Rodolfo in Puccini's *La Boheme.* And who can forget Robin Williams singing Figaro's famous aria *Largo al factotum* from *The Barber of Seville* at the start of one of his beloved movies, *Mrs. Doubtfire?* Similar to what music did for silent films, the addition of these operatic music bits not only kept the scene moving, but also lent a hand in the storytelling to make it more enticing and memorable by strengthening the emotions they evoke.

Acknowledgments

This project came out of an observation that nothing of its kind existed. I first made this comment at my grad school interview, to which I was told that I should write it. Without hesitation, I told them that I was expressing a need I saw in our industry, not that I was here to *fill* it. But then I realized if all we do is voice our needs and never *actually* do something about them, nothing will ever get accomplished. In large part, I have been self-taught. In my early days of opera stage management, I dug high and low for some sort of reference guide, wishing I had something to thumb through when I had questions or needed to be reminded what a "*Who, What, Where*" was. I was surprised that nothing of the sort existed, despite how vibrant the opera stage management community is. This book has probably been the most difficult, daunting, yet rewarding project I have worked on to date. What attracted me to write this book was my love of mentoring, and the ability to pass along all the tips and tricks that I wish I knew when I was starting out. Thank you, Leslie Lyter Ferrari, for not only planting the seed, but also for all your support and encouragement as I began this journey.

One thing that I love most about working in the performing arts is the community. Working in opera, similar to working in theater or dance, is based on collaboration. It takes a village to make something great, and this book contains just that. Thank you to all who lent their voice, their art, and their perspective. Among those people are: Cindy Hennon Marino, Dean Anthony, Andrea Boccanfuso, Ian Silverman, Sarah Stark, Zoë Kim, Tláloc López-Watermann, Cara Consilvio, Alex W. Seidel, Kayla Uribe, Bobby Bradley, Elana Deutch, Tyler Micoleau, Alison Pogorelc, Bethanie Wampol Watson, Jackie Mercer, Jimmy Rotondo, Meghan Crawford, Peter J. Davison, Shoko Kambara, Mikaela Baird, Eileen Downey, Michael Ching, Tri-Cities Opera, Brevard Music Center, Lakes Area Music Center and Manhattan School of Music. I extend my gratitude to you and all the other voices contained within these pages.

The intention of this book is to help stage managers wrap their head around everything there is to know about working their first opera. This beginner's guide will illustrate that opera is not scary! The reason so many stage managers shy away from it is because they simply do not know what it is. The skill set is the same, just with a different set of lingo. I hope this book is a fun adventure you never thought you would go on. If the mention of *opera* has you thinking of running in the opposite direction, I hope that this guide is the fork in the road that redirects you toward the music.

Introduction

This book is an important contribution to Stage Management training that has been missing from the conversation. I have taught Stage Management using several amazing textbooks over the years. Still, I have advised Stage Managers who want to break into the Opera world to work under a well-seasoned Opera PSM to learn the nuancing and intricacies necessary for Opera Stage Management success. Finally, this book gives you a concrete roadmap for Opera Stage Management. It is a manual Opera Stage Managers can follow to navigate their way through their first opera or hone their skills on their twentieth opera and beyond. More than that, this book illuminates Stage Management as an art form.

The Stage Manager is an artist in their own right; balancing practical needs, artistic temperaments, and the heartbeat of the show—and making it all appear effortless. This book is a window into the Stage Manager's soul.

Through this book, Danielle invites you into her process. She coaches you through manageable and well-illustrated steps, just as I have seen her prepare apprentice ASMs working a summer for the Brevard Music Center's Janiec Opera Company. Her work demonstrates a command of the full breadth and depth of everything that is an Opera Stage Manager. I am grateful that through this book, her expertise will reach a wider audience and influence the next generation of Opera PSMs. The Opera industry will be enhanced through this textbook offering.

On a personal note, I have worked with Danielle for many years and have always been fascinated by her innate ability to craft positive group dynamic among her Stage Management team and by extension, hold space for limitless creativity in the rehearsal room. She understands that warm, supportive, professional energy allows those in the room to relax and put attentions on the effort of creating art. She is the person you always want in the room with you as there is no doubt that she is in complete unassuming control of every aspect of the production.

DOI: 10.4324/9781003047391-1

To every aspiring Opera Stage Manager: please read, absorb, and put into action the wisdom and compassion poured into this book. Use the information like a trusted guide as you forge the path to make Opera Stage Management your own.

Andrea Boccanfuso, MFA

Director of Production, Brevard Music Center

Associate Professor of Theatre – Design/Technology, Brevard College

Opera Background

WHAT IS OPERA?

The English word *opera* is an abbreviation of the Italian phrase *opera in musica* ("work in music"). It is a story told strictly to music, mainly sung from beginning to end. What makes opera so powerful is the combination of words and music to transmit emotions in a play. In opera, you can find the same emotion that we experience in our daily lives, such as love, jealousy, betrayal, friendship or conflict. By identifying ourselves with the characters and situations presented on stage, we recognize in them part of our own character. The large emotional impact is what makes opera a source for such powerful, intense enjoyment, which leads so many people to fall in love with this great performing art. Opera is not dying, it is just evolving.

BRIEF HISTORY

You thought you could get away from those theatrical Greek tragedies by moving into opera, but they are back! Opera was born in Italy over 400 years ago, during the Renaissance. One day in Florence, a small group of artists known as the Florentine Camerata decided to recreate the storytelling of Greek drama through music. Say hello to Jacopo Peri, composer of *La Dafine* (the myth of Daphne and Apollo), which, first appeared in 1598, is considered by many to be the first opera. In the 1600s, Peri presented *Euridice*, which was performed at Pitti Palace as a wedding gift to the new Queen, Maria de Médius. The ending was altered for the wedding celebration. A figure named Tragedy addressed the audience with, "usually I make face of the crowd brim with pity." Instead, she sang, "I temper my song with happier notes." Rather than Eurydice returning to hell, both she and Orpheus ascend safely into a happy future.

A few years later, in 1607, Claudio Monteverdi presented his version of *Orfeo* at the court of Mantua where he was in residence. He too altered the story to have a happy ending. Although his final operas were considered examples of

DOI: 10.4324/9781003047391-2

early baroque opera, that period did not truly develop until the late 17th and early 18th century (1600–1750). One of the well-known and great composers of Italian Baroque opera was Georg Frideric Handel (1685–1759), who wrote over 40 Italian operas, such as Giulio *Cesare* (Julius Casear), *Rinaldo*, and *Serse*. Unlike some composers, Handel was not a revolutionary in opera. He worked off of the forms that he found but embellished them with his own inimitable genius. The subject matter of his operas are conventional, drawn from history, mythology, or romantic legend.

Although opera seria, pieces for the royalty that attended and sponsored them, and opera buffa, also known as comedies, were both products of the 18th century, they did not really reach their zenith until the time of Wolfgang Amadeus Mozart. Mozart mainly wrote during the social movement known as the Enlightenment, which changed how people saw music. Composers felt they had a moral obligation to provide fine music for the common people. Rather than presenting gods and the nobility, Mozart brought to the stage relatable, everyday people. He wrote in both opera seria and opera buffa, and sometimes even mixed the two, such as he did in *Don Giovanni*. Opera buffa survived Mozart and continued to be composed by Gioachino Rossini *(The Barber of Seville, La Cenerentola)* and Gactanno Donizetti *(Don Pasquale)* in the first part of the 19th century. They (Rossini and Donizetti) also composed more serious operas and developed a style known as the Italian bel canto movement, which translates to "beautiful singing." This style was all about the vocal brilliance and ornamentation bolstered by a simpler harmonic structure. In addition to Rossini and Donizetti, the third composer to round out the bel canto trio was Vincenzo Bellini (*Norma, La sonnambula*).

Opera facts! 🎼

Opera seria was characterized by serious, historical dramas targeted toward royalty and noble audiences, and led by two opera singing voices—prima dona (leading lady) and castrato (male hero). Opera seria followed an A-B-A pattern, where the first section presented a musical theme, the second section presented a new one, and the third section repeated the first theme. Opera buffa was inspired by the acrobatic, parodic ensemble comedy of the popular Italian theatrical tradition of *commedia dell'arte*. Similarly, conversational plots, stock characters, and physical humor all made an appearance. Opera buffa first got its footing as a one act comedic section of an opera seria to bring some light relief to the serious/tragic opera. But, by popular demand, it soon became a genre of its own.

Opera continued to get bigger in scope and longer in duration during the Romantic period (1830–1900). This is when the phrase "grand opera" made its way into the culture. Grand opera, meaning exactly what it sounds like, was known to have four to five acts and large casts and orchestras, as well as lavish designs and effects. Another feature of grand opera that was developed in Paris through the 1830s was the presence of ballet, which appeared at or near the beginning of the second act. Although it was not required, it was mainly to satisfy the demands of the opera's wealthy and aristocratic patrons. In contrast, in the present day, if a company is performing an opera that had a ballet, it often ends up being cut due to overall length and time.

The 19th century was dominated by two larger-than-life composers, both born in 1813: the Italian, Giuseppe Verdi and the German, Richard Wagner. Verdi was known as a composer who understood the human voice and character. The most-loved Verdi pieces include *Rigoletto, La Traviata,* and *Il Trovatore.* In Germany, Wagner took the opera scene by storm and singlehandedly changed the culture of opera performance. He is credited with the creation of leitmotifs, literally meaning "leading motives." These musical figures would arise naturally as expressive vocal phrases sung by characters and would be developed by the orchestra as "reminisces" to express the dramatic and psychological development. In short, leitmotifs, or "carriers of feeling" as Wagner referred to them, are played whenever a specific character or object appears onstage in order to portray a specific emotion. His best-known music is his fifteen-hour, four-opera *Ring* cycle: *Das Rheingold, Die Walküre, Siegfried*, and *Götterdämmerung.* Wagner is the first composer to demand the total unity of all the elements of a production, controlling the music, libretto, costumes, scenery, and singers to ensure the dramatic and visual cohesiveness of the opera.

The early 20th century was conquered by another Italian composer, Giacomo Puccini. He wrote popular works in the Italian grand opera tradition with a new emphasis on realism, also known as "verismo." His works include *La Bohème* (which *Rent* is based off of), *Tosca, Madama Butterfly,* and *Turandot.* Other composers from the 20th century that made names for themselves are Dmitri Shostakovich with *Lady Macbeth* (1934), Benjamin Britten with *Peter Grimes* (1945), and John Adams with *Nixon in China* (1987).

Opera facts!

Ruggero Leoncavallo's *I Pagliacci* is considered a verismo opera, although it uses the commedia dell'arte style for the "play within a play" in Act II. However, it is a dramatic device, not a stylistic element, of the opera.

We are currently in a renaissance of opera. Whereas in the past, there were a handful of composers writing and having their operas performed, we now see a burst of composers' works making it to the stage. Opera is becoming more accessible to a larger span of audience. Not only are more and more pieces surfacing in English, but they are also covering topics and events that are either current or within recent history, such as *The (R)evolution of Steve Jobs* (Mason Bates), *Scalia/Ginsburg* (Derrick Wang), *Anna Nicole* (Mark-Anthony Turnage), and *Dead Man Walking* (Jake Heggie).

TOP TEN OPERAS TO KNOW

If you want to start familiarizing yourself with the most popular operas, where do you start? When learning a new language, you start with the alphabet. The same goes for opera. Begin with the ABCs; *Aida, La Bohème,* and *Carmen.* Below is a list of the most frequently produced operas in North America.

1. *Aida* (Verdi)

2. *La Bohème* (Puccini)

3. *Carmen* (Bizet)

4. *The Barber of Seville [Il barbiere di Siviglia]* (Rossini)

5. *Cinderella [La Cenerentola]* (Rossini)

6. *Hansel and Gretel* (Humperdinck)

7. *Madama Butterfly* (Puccini)

8. *The Magic Flute [Die Zauberflöte]* (Mozart)

9. *The Marriage of Figaro [Le nozze di Figaro]* (Mozart)

10. *La Traviata* (Verdi)

You might ask, why do I need to know all this history in order to stage manage? All opera singers, directors, designers, and music staff must learn the history and roots of their craft and of the individual show that they are working on. As you have gathered from this chapter, and will grapple with throughout this book, opera is steeped in tradition that has continued to be passed down since its inception. If you are not aware of the history of the show that you are working on or even the art form itself, it is not as easy to be a part of the conversation. The knowledge allows you to voice your opinion and to understand why something is done a certain way. It will help you be a more effective opera stage manager. Knowing the style of music may suggest what a piece is called, or why certain instruments are used. If you know where to look, you will find the clues hidden within the score.

Document Design

Stage managers may not be on stage singing their lungs out, mixing colors behind the light board, or building a skirt they designed. We do, however, show our creativity in our paperwork. Picking a "show font," for example, can be a fun little exercise where you get to select a visual representation of the show, or the overall theme. It will end up in all your headers, callboards, and anything else associated with the show. That being said, we still want to make sure the schedule, or document is still easy to read, and the necessary information that is needed gets across to the reader.

The rule of thumb that I like to follow is this: reserve any decorative fonts for the title of the show only. When it comes to the body of text, try to use a more neutral font, such as Ariel, Cambria, or Times New Roman. As for color, try to limit it when and where possible. You want the reader to be focused on the information you are sharing, not get distracted by an art project.

WHO IS THE DOCUMENT GOING TO?

When creating a document, you want to first ask yourself, *who will be receiving this information and how? Who is my audience?* Knowing the answers to these two questions will help determine the importance of the information being presented and how to best format it. Something that may be posted on a callboard, such as a sign-in sheet or notice, may need a larger and bolder font so it catches the attention of cast members or can be seen from a distance. A deck or costume run sheet can have a slightly smaller font but should still be large enough that it can easily be deciphered in partial darkness or at a quick glance. I have found that it is best to use a table format when providing paperwork to a large group of individuals who are not as familiar with the production. It makes it easier to organize activities and duties within a table to make it clearer for an individual to see what happens and when. Tastefully using CAPS, underlining, *italics*, and

DOI: 10.4324/9781003047391-3

highlighting within paperwork so keywords, phrases, or actions stand out can also help get the information across. Just do not forget to add a key so the reader knows what everything means.

As heard on headset...

Do not get too attached to your paperwork. Remember the paperwork that you are creating is to help make the show run smoothly. It is for the crew. If they prefer the paper to be formatted in landscape instead of portrait so they can fold it easier, then do it. If the stage right run crew prefers to not have all of stage left's track part of their run sheet, then take it out. Tech is too short to negotiate paperwork with the crew.

—*Cindy Hennon Marino, Freelance Stage Manager*

HOW IS MY DOCUMENT PREPARED AND WHERE IS IT STORED?

The majority of stage managers will stick with Microsoft Office (Word and Excel) since it is the most common platform, although that is not to say that iWork (Pages and Numbers) is to be ruled out completely. There are ways to export Pages or Numbers documents into Word or Excel, although formatting sometimes becomes an issue. Something that looks a certain way in Numbers may not open and format correctly in Excel. A nice common ground that I see more people leaning towards is Google Docs and Sheets. These are both free to use and share as long as you have a Google account; keep in mind, though, that there may be some minor formatting discrepancies if you are downloading files to Microsoft Word/Excel. This has never been a huge roadblock for other stage managers that I have worked with. We have all been able to access and work on our paperwork with few or no issues. It is, however, something to be aware of.

Sharing and updating paperwork on a daily basis within the team has become a lot easier than in years past. We can thank two most used platforms, Dropbox and Google Drive. Both platforms have their pros and cons, but overall, the benefit is that all your files can be saved in the same area and everyone on the team can have access to them. The biggest difference between the two platforms is that documents that are saved and opened within Google Drive (this is working online) can have multiple people working on the same document at the same time, whereas with Dropbox, you have to download the document (unless you have Dropbox for your desktop) and only one person at a time can work on said document. If the file is open on one computer and simultaneously on another, a conflicted copy will then be made. Both platforms offer a certain amount of free storage before you have to start paying for additional space. Keep in mind that there are other file-sharing platforms out there, Google Drive and Dropbox are the most common and used with companies and team members.

Tips from the toolkit…

Another feature that I love about Dropbox and Google Drive is that you can access your documents from any computer! Gone are the days of having to carry back and forth a flash drive. If you are working at a company that has a desktop computer directly hooked up to the printer, just sign into your account and you'll have full access to all your documents! Just be careful with formatting, fonts, or photos. They may not download correctly if the processing system and programs are not the same as your personal computer. To avoid this, save the document as a PDF to avoid document jumble!

—DR

COLOR AND SHADING

When displaying a lot of information, sometimes we need a way to direct the eyes toward specific information, the same way a lighting designer will help guide the eye of the audience on stage. Some examples where the addition of color or highlighting may come in handy are:

- Displaying a change in a schedule
- Adding a singer to a rehearsal session
- A change in casting
- Getting across important information
- Bringing attention to crew/staff a quick change for costumes/props/scenery
- Highlighting new score cuts that might have been added to an already published cut list
- Shading on alternate rows to help breakup black text against white space

Colors are fun and make things pretty, but we have to remember the number one rule of thumb: *Will I have easy access to a colored printer?* Because of the volume of things that get printed—between scores, and various versions of paperwork—access to a colored printer or copier is not always easy to come by.

La Cenerentola

Tech Schedule

Director: Crystal Manich
Conductor: Craig Kier
Stage Manager: Danielle Ranno

TIME	WHAT	WHERE	WHO
	MONDAY, JULY 09, 2018		
9:30a-12:30p	Orchestra Read #1	Scott Concert Hall	Orchestra, Maestro
12:30-1:00p	Cue lights installed	Scott Concert Hall	Ben
12:30p	Wireless headsets available / Headset check	Scott Concert Hall	Justin
1:00p	Piano moved to pit / Piano tuned	Scott Concert Hall	
1:00-5:00p	Cuing on stage	Scott Concert Hall	Tláloc, Crystal, Stage Management
2:00p	Harpsicord delivered		
2:00-5:00p	Candide Rehearsal	Morrison Playhouse	JOC
	Lindsay in pit to work with harpsichord	Scott Concert Hall	Lindsay *If possible
3:00p	SM Tech Request Completed By	Scott Concert Hall	
5:00p	Piano/Harpsichord sound check [QUIET TIME IN THEATER] / SM Walk through	Scott Concert Hall	Sound, Maestro, Lindsay
	Dinner delivered to Porter Center		For Stage management (5)
5:30p	Crew Called	Scott Concert Hall	Rachael, Lisa, Elana, Meghan, Justyn
6:00-11:00p	Spacing Rehearsal	Scott Concert Hall	JOC
11:00-11:30p	Production Meeting	Scott Concert Hall	Designers, Stage Management, Production
11:30p-2:00a	Overnight Work on stage	Scott Concert Hall	Carpentry, Paints

1   SUBJECT TO BE CHANGED   As of July 05, 2018 dmr

Figure 2.1   An example of the use of shading with different colors.

Shading or bolding is a great substitution to achieve the same goal. Most black and white printers can still produce some sort of shading, as long as it is not too dark that it will come out black. Sticking with light shades of gray tend to be a safe bet.

Figure 2.1 is a tech schedule that was made for *La Cenerentola*. Within this document, shading of three different colors was used to help information stand out. All dates are shaded in a darker grey so each section/day of event stood out. All meals were shaded in blue that were provided by company management. The final color you see is tan, which represents all piano/harpsichord and sound checks. These needed to stand out for two reasons. First, the piano and harpsichord tuner serviced all the pianos in the festival, and it was imperative that the opera department made it onto their schedule due to our tight tech schedule. Second, it was necessary to alert the rest of the team that tuning was taking place and that the theater needed to be free of extraneous noise. Since this document was mainly accessed electronically, having the ability to print mass copies in full color was not a huge issue.

Figure 2.2 is another example of the effectiveness of shading. This character/ scene breakdown for *Don Pasquale* was done in Microsoft Excel. To make it

Brevard Music Center 2017 — As of 06/19/2017 — Version: D dmr — **Don Pasquale** — Character/Scene Breakdown — Director: David Gately — Conductor: Mo. Caleb Harris — Stage Manager: Danielle Ranno

			Act I: 40:19			Act II: 33:45			Act III: 41:15		
Scene		Overture	Sc. 1-1	Sc. 1-2	Sc. 1-3	Sc. 2-1	Sc. 2-2	Sc. 2-3	Sc. 3-1	Sc. 3-2	Sc. 3-3
Description			Hotel Lobby	Pasqu. Office	Norina BedR	Brothel	Pasqu. Office	Hotel Lobby	Hotel Lobby	Pasqu. Office	Garden
Pages		1-7	8-27	27-43	44-74	75-83	84-99	100-150	151-183	186-206	206-231
Duration		6:20	11:40	7:03	15:05	7:50	9:50	16:10	16:10	11:05	14:00
CHARACTER	ARTIST										
Don Pasquale	Steven Condy		X (6:00)	X			X (7:30)	X	X (0:00)	X	X
Malstesta	August Bair		X (7:30)		(29:30)		X (9:00)	X		X	X
Norina	Chelsea Helm				X (24:00)		X (9:00)	X	X (0:00)		X
Ernesto	Piotr Buszewski		X (15:00)	X		X (0:00)	X		X (14:00)	X	X
Notary	Ian Bolden						(presents)	Notary	Tradesman (0:00)		Notary
Hop Sing	Blake Ellege		X (6:00)	X			X (7:30)	X	X (0:00)		X

Figure 2.2 A character scene breakdown of *Don Pasquale* with shading, created by the author.

Brevard Music Center 2017 — As of 06/19/2017 — Version: D; dmr — **Don Pasquale** — Character/Scene Breakdown — Director: David Gately — Conductor: Mo. Caleb Harris — Stage Manager: Danielle Ranno

			Act I: 40:19			Act II: 33:45			Act III: 41:15		
Scene		Overture	Sc. 1-1	Sc. 1-2	Sc. 1-3	Sc. 2-1	Sc. 2-2	Sc. 2-3	Sc. 3-1	Sc. 3-2	Sc. 3-3
Description			Hotel Lobby	Pasqu. Office	Norina BedR	Brothel	Pasqu. Office	Hotel Lobby	Hotel Lobby	Pasqu. Office	Garden
Pages		1-7	8-27	27-43	44-74	75-83	84-99	100-150	151-183	186-206	206-231
Duration		6:20	11:40	7:03	15:05	7:50	9:50	16:10	16:10	11:05	14:00
CHARACTER	ARTIST										
Don Pasquale	Steven Condy		X (6:00)	X			X (7:30)	X	X (0:00)	X	X
Malstesta	August Bair		X (7:30)		(29:30)		X (9:00)	X		X	X
Norina	Chelsea Helm				X (24:00)		X (9:00)	X	X (0:00)		X
Ernesto	Piotr Buszewski		X (15:00)	X		X (0:00)	X		X (14:00)	X	X
Notary	Ian Bolden						(presents)	Notary	Tradesman (0:00)		Notary
Hop Sing	Blake Ellege		X (6:00)	X			X (7:30)	X	X (0:00)		X

Figure 2.3 The same character scene breakdown with the shading taken away.

easier to read all at once, the sheet was reformatted so everything could fit on one page (page layout set to tabloid). You can see that the top section, which lists the act, scene, location, pages, and time is of a slightly darker shade of grey than the breakdown proper. Since there is a lot of information listed, and a lot of area filled with text, the shading is altered between white and gray. You will notice how much easier it is to quickly glance at and read in Figure 2.2 because the white space is broken up. In contrast, in Figure 2.3 with the shading removed, there is the appearance of an overabundance of information, leaving you unsure of where to start.

On the following pages, Figures 2.4 and 2.5 show an original and then revised daily schedule that went out to the cast. Everything that was changed is red and bolded so that specific information stands out. Since the schedule was emailed, the red would show up regardless of the platform on which it was viewed. Although the printer in the SM office was a black and white printer, once printed, the same information was just highlighted so it still showed differentiation.

WHAT'S IN A NAME?

How we name our documents are very important, especially if there are going to be multiple versions and updates. The worst thing that can happen is that

**TR|CITIES
O|PERA**

**HANSEL &
GRETEL**

Daily Call

TUESDAY, NOVEMBER 1, 2016

NAME	ROLE	CALLLED	
Mary Beth Nelson	*Hansel*	2:00-2:45p	7:00-10:00p
Stacey Geyer	*Gretel*	1:30-2:15p	7:00-10:00p
Jordan Schreiner	*Witch*	4:00-4:45p	7:00-10:00p
Abigail Smith	*Mother*	3:00-3:45p	7:00-10:00p
Scott Purcell	*Father*	Not Called	7:00-10:00p
Lianne Aharony	*Dew Fairy*	6:15-6:45p	7:00-10:00p
Lauren Silberstein	*Dew Fairy*	Not Called	7:00-10:00p
Christina Russo	*Sandman*	Not Called	7:00-10:00p
Karima Jibril	*Sandman*	Not Called	7:00-10:00p
Children's Chorus		Not Called	Not Called

AGENDA:

TIME:	WHAT:	CALLED:
1:30-2:15p	Coaching (Red Room)	Ms. Geyer, Mo. Iftinca, Mr. Elam
2:00-2:45p	Coaching (Red Room)	Ms. Nelson, Mo. Iftinca, Mr. Elam
3:00-3:45p	Coaching (Red Room)	Ms. Smith, Mo. Iftinca, Mr. Elam
4:00-4:45p	Coaching (Red Room)	Mr. Schreiner, Mo. Iftinca, Mr. Elam
4:30-4:45p	Fitting	Ms. Rutkovsky
5:00-7:00p	*Dinner Break*	
5:00-6:00p	Hair & Make-up meeting	Ms. Vaughn, Ms. Consilvio, Stage Management
6:15-6:45p	Coaching (Red Room)	Ms. Aharony, Mo. Iftinca, Mr. Elam
7:00-7:30p	Coaching (Red Room)	Ms. Jibril, Mo. Iftinca, Mr. Elam
7:00-7:30p	Sightline staging	Tutti Principals, Ms. Consilvio
7:30-10:00p	Work Through	ADD: Ms. Jibril, Mo. Iftinca, Mr. Elam
10:00p	*End of rehearsal*	

Conductor: Vlad Iftinca

Director: Cara Consilvio   Page 1 of 1

SM: Danielle Ranno

Figure 2.4   The first version of a daily schedule for *Hansel & Gretel* that went out to the cast and company.

someone is working on a different or older version than the rest of the team. Some important information to include in your document naming:

- **Title of show:** A lot of companies and designers are either running in rep or prepping for another/multiple shows while working on yours. Having the title listed in the document name will help organize paperwork and avoid any confusion as to what people are about to open.

**TR|CITIES
O|PERA**

**HANSEL &
GRETEL**

Daily Call

TUESDAY, NOVEMBER 1, 2016 (UPDATED AS OF OCT.30 AT 10:30p)

NAME	ROLE	CALLLED	
Mary Beth Nelson	Hansel	2:00-2:45p	7:00-10:00p
Stacey Geyer	Gretel	1:30-2:15p	7:00-10:00p
Jordan Schreiner	Witch	Not Called	7:30-10:00p
Abigail Smith	Mother	3:00-3:45p	7:30-10:00p
Scott Purcell	Father	Not Called	7:30-10:00p
Lianne Aharony	Dew Fairy	6:15-6:45p	7:30-10:00p
Lauren Silberstein	Dew Fairy	Not Called	7:30-10:00p
Christina Russo	Sandman	Not Called	7:30-10:00p
Karima Jibril	Sandman	Not Called	7:30-10:00p
Children's Chorus		Not Called	Not Called

AGENDA:

TIME:	WHAT:	CALLED:
1:30-2:15p	Coaching (Red Room)	Ms. Geyer, Mo. Iftinca, Mr. Elam
2:00-2:45p	Coaching (Red Room)	Ms. Nelson, Mo. Iftinca, Mr. Elam
3:00-3:45p	Coaching (Red Room)	Ms. Smith, Mo. Iftinca, Mr. Elam
3:00-4:00p	Fitting	Ms. Rutkovsky
5:00-7:00p	*Dinner Break*	
5:00-6:00p	Hair & Make-up meeting	Ms. Vaughn, Ms. Consilvio, Stage Management
6:15-6:45p	Coaching (Red Room)	Ms. Aharony, Mo. Iftinca, Mr. Elam
7:00-7:30p	Sightline staging	Ms. Nelson, Ms. Geyer, Ms. Consilvio
7:30-10:00p	Work Thru	Tutti Principals, Mo. Iftinca, Mr. Elam
10:00p	*End of rehearsal*	

Conductor: Vlad Iftinca

Director: Cara Consilvio

Page 1 of 1

SM: Danielle Ranno

Figure 2.5 The revised daily schedule for *Hansel & Gretel* that went out to the cast and company showing the changes in red.

- **Title of the document:** Is this a rehearsal report, or is it a daily call?
- **Date or version of the document:** This will help differentiate the last time said document was updated.

Preferably, I like to try to fit this all in one line, so it does not get cut off in the preview of the document name. If an email containing said document is also going out, that is how I will also subject the message.

Tips from the toolkit!

You want to be careful with the type of punctuation you use when saving files. Preferably, you want to stick to letters and numbers. Dots, or periods tend to be problematic because a "." is considered a metacharacter (a character that has special meaning to a computer program), whereas underscores and letters are not. The last thing you want to happen is that you send an important document, and no one can read or open it.

Figure 2.6 is an example of an email subject for a rehearsal report about to go out. "RJ" is a shortened acronym for *Romeo et Juliette*. Having acronyms such as these help shorten the name of the document or email subject. Rule of thumb: You want to pick one acronym and stick with it, rather than have a subject line full of them. If you choose to shorten *Romeo et Juliette* to RJ, then you should try not to also use RR or PR for rehearsal or performance report. If I had typed out the full name: RomeoetJuliette RehearsalReport#6_061619, not only would it be too long and difficult to read, but also likely to be cutoff in the preview of the email name. Our eyes are trained to read sentences with spaces between words as well as punctuation. Shortened names or nicknames—but only if everyone on the team understands them—can help simplify long titles. Personally, when sending out reports, and sometimes even daily schedules, I like numbering them, so the files are organized in order, but this is not necessary. As long as the name and date are listed so consumers are aware of what they are looking at, you should be fine.

When it comes to paperwork, choosing to list the version or the date the document was last updated is up to you. If it does not make the title too long, then I may consider doing both. I have found though, that when saving the document, listing the date makes it easier to spot rather than the version label (letters or numbers are used). Not sure how you should name your document? Try listing your document in multiples way and see what looks the cleanest and easiest to read.

Figure 2.6   One example of how to subject a production-related email.

Tips from the toolkit!

In Dropbox and Google Drive folders, I always like to add an "old version" folder and label it "z_old" so it saves at the end of all my documents. I can throw past versions of various paperwork in this folder and keep my most recent version in the main folder. This type of organizing makes it simpler to access your documents quickly rather than scrolling through multiple saved documents and avoids possibly trashing or permanently deleting something.

THE BREAKDOWN ON HEADERS AND FOOTERS

Headers and footers (Figures 2.7 & 2.8) carry a lot of information, but they should not overpower your document in any way. Remember that show font we talked about earlier? This would be the appropriate place to use it as the show title. Everything else should be in a neutral font that is easy to read.

Common information that should be in your header:

- Title of show
- Name of document
- Logo of company—if available
- Score: publisher and plate number
- Name of the director
- Name of the conductor
- Version letter or date of last update

Common information that should be in your footer:

- Page number (can be listed as page of page, or just a single number)
- Any keys needed to decipher the document
- Version or date if not listed in header
- Creator's initials

Although this is one way of setting up your header and footer, it is not the only way. Some companies or stage managers may have a different way of listing header and footer information. As with many types of paperwork, the information is all the same; it may just be in a different order or layout.

Company Logo Score: [publisher/plate #]	**[TITLE OF SHOW]** DOCUMENT NAME	Director: NAME Conductor: NAME Version [letter] dmr

Figure 2.7 An example of a document header. The layout would be the same if the document was a horizontal layout.

EXAMPLE 1:

Highlighted=Possible paged curtain if help is needed   2 of 9   Version FINAL
                                                                                               Updated: 08.02.19 MCC

EXAMPLE 2:

Italics denotes a costume acting as a prop   **1 of 5**
* denotes consumables   Version FINAL
Bold denotes a repeating prop from a previous scene   Updated: 08.04.19 MCC
ALL CAPS denotes a furniture piece
Highlight denotes lighting

EXAMPLE 3:

VERSION: Piano Dress #1   1 of 7   As of 12/07/19 dmr

Figure 2.8 Three examples of footers taken from three different pieces of paperwork created by ASM Meghan Crawford and the author. They each have different keys, based on the type of paperwork shown.

CONTINUITY

Continuity as a stage manager is one of the most important aspects of the job. Not only do you want continuity in how you do your job, but also in how you communicate in emails and paperwork. Once you choose a font, set your headers and footers, even name characters, props, costumes, etc., you must stick with it. You will be putting into place a vocabulary and a way for others to receive information—even the slightest change may confuse them or cause an important piece of information to go unnoticed.

Page breaks are also important to keep in mind and can be your best friend when keeping information in paperwork grouped together and organized. Just as you would not want a break in mid-sentence, you insert page breaks when information gets split up between two pages due to length. Page breaks not only break up your pacing but can also interrupt the overview of the entire picture or thought. The same goes for your paperwork. For example, you do not want to have a page break in the middle of a large scene shift because it might cause a crew member to only do part of the shift. Both Figures 2.9 and 2.10 display

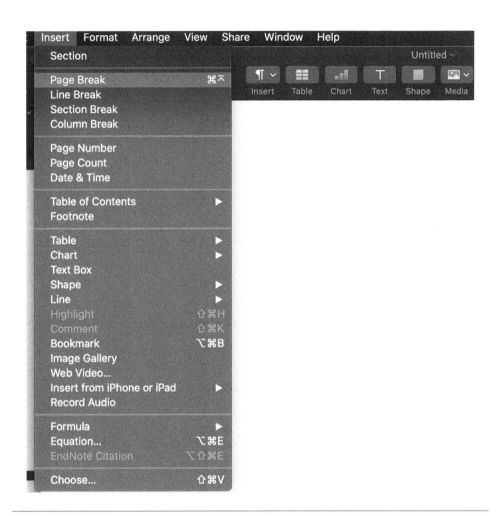

Figure 2.9 How to add a page break in Pages.

Figure 2.10 How to add a page break in Word.

how you can easily add a page break in Pages and Word. If you add them and then end up going back and editing that document, just note that you may need to redo or move your page breaks so information is not split between multiple pages by accident.

> **Tips from the toolkit!**
>
> It is both preferred and safer to have half a page of blank space than to have a shift or a preset between two pages. Figures 2.11 and 2.12 are examples of how to split up a preset with a page break. To make sure the crew is aware that the shift was listed on the next page, **TURN PAGE** with an arrow was written in all caps and bolded to draw attention to it.

NORINA ARIA

Props in scene:
- Book (Lexi enter with)
- Makeup
- Hair towel
- TABLE
- CHAIR

TURN PAGE→

OPERA SCENES
Scene Presets & props

NOZZE

Props in scene:
- Notebook & pencil (Melvin enter with)
- Yard stick (Melvin enter with)
- Measuring tape (Melvin enter with)
- Hand mirror
- Veil
- TABLE
- X2 CHAIRS

Figure 2.11   A run sheet with page breaks.

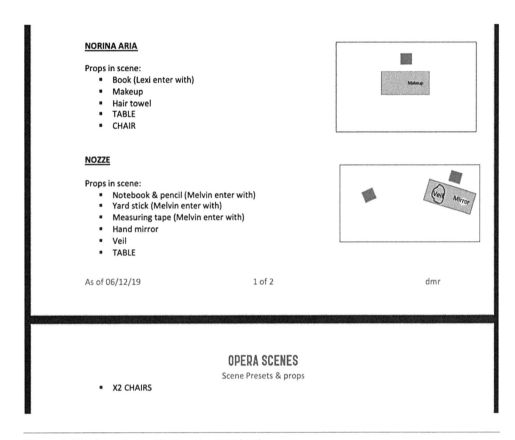

Figure 2.12   A run sheet without proper page breaks.

TO PDF OR NOT TO PDF, THAT IS THE QUESTION?

Are you publishing or sending something out to a group of people, such as the cast, production staff, or designers? By turning your document into a PDF (portable document format), you are preserving it as it. Not only will this avoid people from making unknown changes to your work, but it will also ensure that any formatting that you have incorporated into the document remains consistent, regardless of the program or computer it is opened on. Almost every computer server (Mac and PC) comes with a viewing program that can open PDFs. If the computer does not have it, there that are free downloads such as Acrobat Reader or Preview. Once you have converted your file, you can easily attach or embed it into an email, upload it to the web, or print it. If the document is remaining within the stage management team and you know that it is still being worked on or edited, then skip the PDF save until it has hit a finalized, or close to a finalized, version.

Now that we have some tips and tricks as to how to start and save our documents, we are ready to dive into the different stages of production, beginning with Prep Week. In the following chapters, we will unpack duties divided amongst the team, paperwork to work on, and the people you will come into contact with as you make your way through your opera journey.

CHAPTER 3

Prep Week

The length of a prep week can differ from company to company. At smaller regional companies, it can be a few days before the first rehearsal; in other larger companies, it can last for up to two weeks. The prep for summer festivals, where staff arrive at least a week before singers show up, can also vary in the number of weeks. Sometimes prep is done remotely, and other times is it done on site with the full team.

The hiring process for opera companies can have some similarities and differences with the hiring process for regional theater companies. They [opera companies] are known to have their seasons laid out a few years in advance, and singers tend to be booked anywhere from two to five years ahead. As for stage management, the contract could be offered anywhere from eight to twelve months out. Similar to when working in theater, stage managers in opera may have a say in who their assistants may be. Although many companies tend to have resident assistant stage managers or a group of them that rotate throughout the season, it never hurts to ask.

It is always great to start to familiarize yourself with the opera prior to arriving on site. Everyone has a different level of comfort in terms of how well they want to know a piece, or even in re-familiarizing themselves with the opera if they have not done it in a while. If you are not able to get your hands on the score or pull a score from the last time to you worked on the piece, listen to the music. Get it into your bones, even if you cannot understand what they are singing!

As heard on headset...

My first summer stock was at The Castleton Festival. I was assigned to work on Otello (Verdi) as the second assistant stage manager. Because I was still fairly new to opera, I did a lot of prep before my contract began to familiarize myself with the piece. The public library had a movie recording of the opera available, and lucky me, with the same

DOI: 10.4324/9781003047391-4

> conductor! I watched the movie, got my hands on a recording, and read
> the libretto. Because of the time I spent learning the score and familiar-
> izing myself with the music, I was able to focus on learning the ins and
> outs of being an opera ASM.
>
> —DR

RESOURCES TO BEGIN WITH

Here are a few resources that are commonly used:

- **International Music Score Library (IMSL):** This is a great resource
  for getting your hands on a version of the score to look at before the
  company provides you with a copy. This is a database that has all public
  domain scores available to download. Once you search for what you are
  looking for, you then have to dig through to find the best quality/scan
  available. Be sure to pick the vocal or piano score. This will be the closest
  to the one you will use in rehearsal.

- **Spotify/Apple iTunes/Amazon Music:** These are some of the more popular
  music sites and apps, but pretty much any resource where you can get
  ahold of a recording of the piece so you can start to listen to it will
  work. A handful of recordings will come up. If there is a recording with
  the same conductor you are working with, try to go with that one. If
  not, choose any one of them. The goal is to familiarize yourself with the
  music.

- **Libretto:** Most of the time, a version of the libretto, or text of the opera,
  can easily be found online. A great site where the majority of opera
  libretti can be found is DM's opera site (www.murashev.com). You will
  then choose the composer of said opera and go from there. Composers
  found on this site range in year from 1756 (Mozart) to 1953 (Kálmán).
  You can also do a search with words such as *Don Giovanni Libretto* or
  Don Giovanni English Libretto.

- **Castel:** These publications (word for word translation from its original
  language into English) are not easily found online but are one of the best
  resources because they give a word-for-word translation.

- **Good Old-fashioned Library:** Almost all of the above can be found either
  at a school or public library. Many public libraries still have CDs available
  (look for sections labeled *classical music* or *opera*), and if the piece you are
  working on is well known, at least one recording should be available. As
  for a score, search sections labeled *score music books, piano vocal scores*, or
  try searching by composer and then narrow your search from there.

- **Wikipedia or Google Search** (or whatever your preferred online search
  engine is): Simply search the title and read the synopsis. This will at least
  give you an idea of what the story line is and who the characters are.

- **YouTube:** Try to watch a few clips of the opera. You may even get lucky and find the full piece to watch. Although the staging or concept, or sometimes even the language, may be different than your production, the story line will still be the same. Another good resource is MET TV (The Metropolitan Opera), although a subscription may be needed.

I am not saying that you have to go out and check all these resources off. Your level of familiarity and how comfortable you are with it will dictate how much prep on your own you want to do prior to arriving at the company. I like to get my hands on a recording and will just listen while on the subway or while doing house chores. I found that having it play even when only partially listening to it helped get the music in my bones. Everyone will figure out what is best for them over time. What works for me, may not work for everyone.

As heard on headset…

My first calling SM job with a traditional opera was Madame Butterfly at Opera Santa Barbara. I had done a number of operas before and had my master's degree in stage management, so I thought I knew what I was doing! I walked into rehearsal that first day with all my minis in, my score highlighted, my props, costume and scenic paperwork, ready to go. What I hadn't done though is familiarize myself with what a traditional Butterfly is. Suddenly, they were saying "Let's go from O Kami! O Kami" and I just sat there staring because I had no idea what that meant. Or "let's pick up at the aria." Ok, I knew what an aria was, but how was I supposed to know what THE aria was? And because I had not actually watched a production of it (or knew the history), I didn't know how important the altar was or why the child's name (which can be translated differently) mattered. From then on out I told myself I would learn the music AND the piece well enough to be able to flip to that page when needed in rehearsal and to understand everything that "always happens" in the opera.

—Cindy Hennon Marino, Freelance Stage Manager

WHO DOES WHAT

You know your team, you know the opera you will spend the next few weeks working on, so now how do you know what to prep? Your stage manager, or sometimes even the company, will put together a breakdown, also known as a "Who Does What," which breaks down what department each team member will be a liaison to. This will also list what side of the stage each assistant stage manager will be assigned to and the paperwork they are responsible for. If the team has an assistant director (AD) and/or production assistant (PA), their duties will also be listed on the Who Does What.

Who Does What

PSM	AD	ASM SL	ASM SR	PA
Welcome Letter	Char/Scene Breakdown	Compile Props List	Costume List	Compile Welcome Packets
Artists Calendar	Director's Rehearsal	Reh Prop Requests	- by scene, if necessary	Contact Sheets
Media Info Sheet	Schedule	Props Run Sheets	Reh Costume Requests	Wallet card
Move to Opera Hs Letter	Master Blocking book	Coro Contact Liaison	Costume Run Sheets	Directions to rehearsal,
Prod. Meeting Agenda		Copy minis	Super Contact Liaison	theater, fittings
AV Request	"Train schedule" for tech	Artist "Facebook"	Photo Book	Print Media Info Sheet?
Cue Lights Request	along w/ PSM			Keep track of Artist Hours
Score Timings		Create Sign-In Sheets	Coro/Supers Fitting Schedule	
Dress Rm Assignments	Critical Coro Sheet	Coro Name tags	Lightwalker Request	Tape Rehearsal Hall
Publish Daily Schedule	Critical Super Sheet	Produce Synopsis for Supers	Super & Children Name Tags	Make Valuable Bags
Rehearsal Reports	Critical Children Sheet	Assist Skylar w/ packets	Assist PA w/packets	
Running Times Sheet	Cover Staging	Tape Rehearsal Hall	Tape Rehearsal Hall	Callboard setup:
Prompt Book	Bow list			Daily Schedule
TOA Checklists		Secure set model	Costume display	Next Calls
Deck Sheet		Follow up on prop notes	Follow up on W/M-U Notes	Check sign-in sheets
Measure Ground-plans		AV Run Sheet - if needed	First Entrances List	Distribute daily and notes
Tape Rehearsal Hall		Coffee setup and takedown	Dressing Room Signs	Originate W/W/W
FOH Info Sheet		Assist with cover staging	Coffee setup and takedown	Coffee setup and takedown
(by Orch Tech 1)			Assist with cover staging	Assist with cover staging
"Train schedule" for tech				Cover both ASMs
along w/ AD		STAGE LEFT	STAGE RIGHT	
		SL ASM Preshow Checklist	SR ASM Preshow Checklist	Assist PSM updates to
Performance Reports		W/W/W – updates	W/W/W – updates	crew sheets in cueing
W/W/W – tech cues				Assist in tracking blocking
				changes in piano techs
				Collect valuables
				Programs for singers

Figure 3.1 Who Does What version 1.

Figures 3.1–3.3 display three different versions of a Who Does What. Although the layout may be different or responsibilities may be swapped, overall, the information is the same. Also, depending on the type (and sometimes size) of show, different kinds of paperwork may be called for. The team may be smaller and consist of only one ASM instead of two. Or there may be no AD staffed for the production. In the end, there is no one right way.

Company Logo
Show Title

SM Who Does What

Page 1 of 1

NAME PSM	NAME AD	NAME ASM	NAME ASM
Carps Liaison	Director's Daily Rehearsal	Props Liaison	Wardrobe Liaison
Daily Sched w/ AD	Schedule		Super Contact Liaison
Measure ground plans		Act I Timings into Score	
Originate W/W/W	Char/Scene Breakdown	Show Contact Sheet	Act II Timings into Score
	Master Blocking book	Festival Casting Breakdown	Artists Calendar
Rehearsal Reports		Props List	Costume bkdown by scene
Prompt Book	"Train schedule" for tech along	Reh Prop Requests	Reh Costume Requests
Deck Running Sheet	with PSM	Create Sign-In Sheets	First Entrances List
		Coro/Super Name tags	Running Times Sheet
"Train schedule" for tech along	Key Supers Substitute plan	Produce Synopsis for Supers	Costume display for first day
with AD	Key Coro Substitute plan		
		Props Run Sheets	Costume Run Sheets
Performance Reports	Bow list	AV Run Sheet - if needed	take coro/super blocking as needed
		take coro/super blocking as needed	reset as needed during rehearsal
		reset as needed during rehearsal	
			STAGE LEFT
		STAGE RIGHT	SL ASM Preshow Checklist
		SR ASM Preshow Checklist	Callboard - sign-in sheets
		W/W/W – updates	W/W/W – updates
		Assist in cover stagings	Assist in cover stagings

Figure 3.2 Who Does What version 2.

Stage Manager [Name]	Assistant Director [Name]	1st Assistant Stage Manager (SR) [Name]	2nd Assistant Stage Manager (SL) [Name]

Advance w/   *Director, Designers, Music Staff*
 Scene Breakdown w/ AD
 Daily Schedule Requests w/ AD
 Rehearsal Notes
 TIMINGS:
   Show Timing Sheet
 SCENERY:
   Measure ground plans
 Dressing Room Assignments
 Scenery / Props Transfer Requests
 Train Schedule w/ AD
 Hair & Makeup Call Times
 Production Book & Calling Score
 Performance Reports
 Brush-up Rehearsals
 Cover Staging Rehearsals
 End of Show Archival
	Advance w/ *Director, Designers, Music Staff*
	 Scene Breakdown w/ SM
	 Daily Schedule Requests w/ SM
	 Text Changes / Cuts List
	 Train Schedule w/ SM
	 Blocking Book
	 Cover / Brush-up Rehearsal Request
	 Brush-up Rehearsals
	 Cover Staging Rehearsals
	 Critical Staging Sheet
	 Performer Tracking Sheets (if needed)
	 Bow List
		Contact Sheet
		 Artist Overview Calendar
		 Master Run Sheet (Scenery / Props)
		 SCENERY:
		   Mini ground plans
		   Rail Cue Sheet
		 PROPS:
		   Props List
		   Rehearsal Props + Request
		   Spike Measurements
		 A/V Monitor Plot
			Sign-in Sheets
			 Dressing Room Signs
			 TIMINGS:
			   30-second Timings
			 Copy & Distribute Timed Scores
			 COSTUMES:
			   Costume Breakdown / QC Sheet
			   Rehearsal Costumes + Request
			   Wardrobe/HMU Running Sheet
			 WIGS & MAKEUP:
			   First Entrance Timings

TEAM ASSIGNMENTS: Tape Floor / Rehearsal Room Setup Who/What/Where Mail Distribution Save FINAL Paperwork	TEAM ASSIGNMENTS: Save FINAL Paperwork (via SM) Scan AD blocking book for archives	TEAM ASSIGNMENTS: Tape Floor / Rehearsal Room Setup Sweep / Mop Floor (as necessary) Who/What/Where Save FINAL Paperwork	TEAM ASSIGNMENTS: Tape Floor / Rehearsal Room Setup Sweep / Mop Floor (as necessary) Who/What/Where Mail Distribution Save FINAL Paperwork

* *Italics* are shared items
**Please use the headers in the Template Folder and Arial - 10 pt. font as standard for all paperwork.
***Please save all FINAL versions of production files by the last performance with the following name: [SHOW CODE] [YY] [File Name] FINAL.

Figure 3.3 Who Does What version 3.

Who is listed:

- The Production Stage Manager (PSM also listed as SM)
- The Assistant Director (AD)
- 1st Assistant Stage Manager (ASM)
- 2nd Assistant Stage Manager (ASM)
- Production Assistant/Intern (PA — usually with a SM background)

In their own words...

Describe the responsibilities of the following:

Production Stage Manager (also listed as the stage manager or SM):
The PSM is the hub of communication for a production and the line of communication between the design team and rehearsal room.
           —*Alex W. Seidel, Freelance Stage Manager*

Assistant Stage Manager: *The ASM supports the production by running a side of stage; cueing principal artists, chorus, supernumeraries and dancers onto the stage during the performance; and communicating the shows running needs to their assigned departments by creating the necessary paperwork. The ASM shares in the overall responsibility of the staging staff team to maintain the artistic integrity of the production.*
           —*Alex W. Seidel, Freelance Stage Manager*

Assistant Director: *The role of the Assistant Director is to help the director in the best way they can. Most often, the AD is responsible for recording the blocking or staging to be used for reference later in the process or for future remounts. The AD will take notes for the director during run throughs allowing the director to focus on the action. The AD will also help be a liaison between the director and cast distributing notes as well as the director and stage management, making sure rehearsal reports are accurate. Usually, the AD is responsible for preparing the covers, especially in the event that a cover would have to perform. They also maintain other paperwork such as the bow lists, critical chorus staging and text change documents.*

—Ian Silverman, Freelance Director/Assistant Director

Production Assistant: *I worked as a stage management intern at the Glimmerglass Festival. Some of my responsibilities were: show timing sheet (timing how long each act was), create the show specific contact sheet, name tags, stock the rehearsal First Aid kit, create the show face page, valuable bags, hospitality supplies. Since Glimmerglass runs in rep and the ASMs are bouncing back and forth between shows, the SM interns act as ASM subs and cover ASM tracks in rehearsals. Once the show was up and running and the backstage flow was solidified, we then shadowed the ASMs on each of their tracks to ensure that we could take over for them if they had to call out.*

—Kayla Uribe, Freelance Stage Manager

Do not be mistaken—although both assistants are liaisons to a department, there should always be open communication with the PSM so they know what is going on and what conversations are being had. All notes still go through the PSM when it comes to listing them in the report or giving them to designers. If a larger problem arises, before you try to solve it, bring it to the SM's attention. The last thing you want to do is go over their head or resolve matters behind their back. When it comes down to it, the props/wardrobe ASMs head all props or wardrobe paperwork. If a singer has a note or concern about a specific item, they would most likely pass it along to the ASM who would then pass it along to the PSM. Also, if anything new comes into the room, such as a new hand prop or rehearsal costume, said ASM will be in charge of learning how the item is used from the designer and then in turn, introduce it to the singer using or wearing it.

In the next few sections, we will cover in further detail the duties that each team member listed on the Who Does What should prepare prior to the start of rehearsal. The demands may change depending on the type of production the company is mounting, whether it be fully staged, semi-staged, a concert version, or have a traditional versus modern view. The space in which the performance takes place may also call for different, or out-of-the-box paperwork. We will begin as if we were mounting a fully staged production.

PSM PREP

We will go in more depth about the PSM paperwork when we talk about tech, but here are some of the templates and prep paperwork the PSM will need to work on:

- Overview Schedule
- Daily Schedule
- Rehearsal Reports
- Character/Scene Breakdown (CSB)
- Blocking Key
- Measure Ground Plans for Taping

OVERVIEW SCHEDULE

The first version of the overview schedule will most likely come from the director, but, in some cases, it could come from the assistant director. This version will outline what is planned to be achieved per day and who is needed. Not all overview schedules from directors are as detailed. If there is an assistant director, a lot of times they will aid with breaking each session down. Other times, the stage manager will step into that role. From this, the PSM will put together a version that will be sent out to the company. Many times the director does not want to send out their full detailed schedule in the event that things change and will leave it to the daily schedule to have the full breakdown. Below (Figure 3.4) is one example of the director's overview, which was made to share with the company and staff. Figure 3.5 is an example of the stage manager's overview that went out.

Opera facts!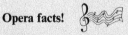

For union houses, it is usually the responsibility of the AD and PSM to keep track of everyone's hours. As soon as the director makes the schedule available, the SM and AD will go through each day and make sure hours per day and breaks do not go over. Depending on the contract, this will include covers as well.

Whether the stage manager puts together the overview in a calendar format versus a list is a matter of preference. The company may also have a standard template that they prefer to use. What it comes down to is the amount of information you need to distribute and the easiest way to do it. If you are strictly

Opera Columbus
Barber of Seville
Rehearsal and Tech Week Schedule
12/30/19 SUBJECT TO CHANGE

<u>**Monday January 20, 2020**</u>   *Room 1*
      1p-2p   Director/design Presentation
      2p-5p   Music rehearsal
      5p-6p   **Production Meeting**

<u>**Tuesday January 21, 2020**</u>   *Room 1 unavailable after 5*
      10a-11a   Pg. 13-18 (Count)
      11a-12p   Pg. 29-41 (Count, Figaro – Count release early)
      12p-1p   *Lunch*
      1p-2p   Pg. 41-49 (Count, Figaro)
      2p-3p   Pg. 49-54 (Count, Figaro, Rosina, Bartolo, Berta)
      3p-5p   Pg. 54-74 (Count, Figaro)

<u>**Wednesday January 22, 2020**</u>   *Room 1*
      10a-11:30a   Pg. 75-82 (Rosina – at 11, add Berta)
      11:30a-1p   Pg. 86-95 (Bartolo, Basilio)
      1p-2p   *Lunch*
      2p-49   Pg. 95-107 (Figaro, Rosina)
      4p-5p   Pg. 107-123 (Rosina, Bartolo)
      5:30p-7p   Rehearse with CORO boyband folks (Pg. 13-18)

<u>**Thursday January 23, 2020**</u>   *Room 1*
      1p-2:30p   Pg. 107-123 (Rosina, Bartolo)
      2:30p-4p   Pg. 125-140 (Berta, Count, Bartolo, Rosina)
      4p-5p   *Lunch*
      5p-5:45p   Pg. 140-146 (Berta, Count, Bartolo, Rosina, Basilio)
      5:45pp-8p   Pg. 146-201 (Berta, Count, Bartolo, Rosina, Basilio, Figaro)

<u>**Friday January 24, 2020**</u>   *Room 1*
      12p-3p Pg. 125-201 (Berta, Count, Bartolo, Rosina, Basilio, Figaro)
      3p-4p   *Lunch*
      4p-7p   Pg. 13-18 (Count & CORO Boyband)

<u>**Saturday January 25, 2020**</u>   *Room 1*
      11a-2P   Workthrough of act 1 (all principals)
      2p-3p   *Lunch*
      3p-6p   Workthrough of act 1 (all principals)

<u>**Sunday January 26, 2020**</u>
      Day Off   *No Xiaomeng Zhang*
      (Mary= 1-4 Development event)

Figure 3.4   Overview schedule from director.

listing blocks of rehearsal and that's it, then maybe lean towards the calendar so it can be seen as a whole and on a single sheet. If rehearsal blocks are going to be broken down into sections (by times) and specify who will be called and where, then going for a list style might be your best bet.

REHEARSAL REPORT AND DAILY SCHEDULE

These are templates that you will prep before the start of rehearsal. Some companies have a template that they prefer to use and will share these with you. This makes it much easier for them since their staff will be used to the format

OPERA COLUMBUS

The Barber of Seville
January/February Calendar

Director: Mary Birnbaum
Conductor: Ma. Kathleen Kelly
Stage Manager: Danielle Ranno

Sunday	Monday	Tuesday	Wednesday	Thursday	Friday	Saturday
	20 January 1:00-2:00p Director/Design Presentation 2:00-5:00p Music Rehearsal 5:00-6:00p Production Meeting	21 10:00a-12:00p Staging 12:00-1:00p Lunch 2:00-5:00p Staging	22 10:00a-1:00p Staging 1:00-2:00p Lunch 2:00-7:00p Staging w/ Coro	23 1:00-4:00p Staging 4:00-5:00p Lunch 5:00-8:00p Staging	24 12:00-3:00p Staging 3:00-4:00p Lunch 4:00-7:00p Staging w/Coro	25 11:00a-2:00p Staging 2:00-3:00p Lunch 3:00-6:00p Staging
26 DAY OFF	27 12:00-3:00p Staging 3:00-4:00p Lunch 4:00-7:00p Staging w/ CORO	28 10:00a-12:00p Staging 12:00-1:00p Lunch 1:00-5:00p Staging	29 12:00-3:00p Staging 3:00-4:00p Lunch 4:00-7:00p Staging w/ Coro	30 1:00-4:00p Staging 4:00-5:00p Lunch 5:00-8:00p Staging	31 12:00-3:00p Staging 3:00-4:00p Lunch 4:00-7:00p Staging w/Coro 5:00-7:30p Orchestra Read	1 February 11:00a-2:00p Staging 2:00-3:00p Lunch 3:00-6:00p Staging
2 DAY OFF	3 11:00a-12:00p Production Meeting 12:00-3:00p Review 3:00-4:00p Lunch 4:00-7:00p Review w/ CORO	4 10:00a-12:00p Staging TBA 12:00-1:00p Lunch TBA 1:00-5:00p Run Through 5:00-6:00p Dinner 6:00-9:00p Cover Rehearsal	5 12:00-3:00p TBA Work 3:00-4:00p Lunch TBA 4:00-7:00p Designer Run	6 1:00-4:00p TBA Work 4:00-5:00p Lunch 5:00-8:00p TBA Work	7 7:00-10:00p Piano Spacing Onstage	8 7:00-9:00p Piano Tech with costumes
9 DAY OFF	10 7:00-9:30p Orchestra Tech/Wandel (no costumes) 9:30-10:30p Production Meeting	11 5:00p Hair& Makeup call 7:00-9:30p Orchestra Dress 9:30-10:30p Production Meeting	12 5:30p Hair& Makeup call 7:30p Final Dress	13 DARK DAY	14 5:30p Hair& Makeup call 7:30p Performance #1	15 DAY OFF
16 12:00p Hair& Makeup call 2:00p Performance #2						

As of 01/13/20 dmr   **SUBJECT TO CHANGE**   Page 1 of 1

Figure 3.5   Overview schedule calendar.

and know exactly where to look for information. If they do not have their own template, then you are free to use your own. If this is the case, be sure it is simple, easy to follow and not too distracting. There is no right or wrong way to laying out a report, as long as it gets the information across clearly. We will go more into detail on templates and take a look at different examples in Chapter 5.

Tips from the toolkit...

If you are using your own template, check with the company if there are any non-traditional pieces of information they want to see in the daily report such as lateness of singers (especially if they are union) or a detailed breakdown of the day's schedule with breaks.

CHARACTER/SCENE BREAKDOWN

Purpose: The character/scene breakdown (CSB) gives a rundown of the full show listing the act, scenes, timing per scene, and who's on and off stage. This information is collected by going through the score, although it may vary, depending on the director's concept. They may have chorus on stage in a scene that traditionally does not, or a character may be in a scene even though they are not singing. In a traditional theater or musical theater piece, these details are under the stage manager's umbrella. But in opera, if the team has an AD on board, putting together the initial CSB and updating it, will fall on their plate. Figures 3.6 & 3.7 are two examples of character/scene breakdowns.

Other helpful uses of the character/scene breakdown are:

- Assists with scheduling
- Identifies costume or quick changes if a performer is singing multiple roles
- Identifies who may or may not be available if scene changes are choreographed within the opera

How to: The easiest way to organize all the information needed is in a table format. Whether it is done in Word or Excel is based on the preference of the creator.

Key items listed on the breakdown:

- Performer name
- Character name or role
- Covers (if any)
- Scene number
- Scene name or location
- Titles or musical numbers within the scene
- Pages (important to list the score and plate number)
- Scene length and/or start and end times of the scene
- A key defining and symbols or shortcuts used

Il Trovatore / sep 8/13/21 FINAL	II-1	II-1	II-1	II-1	I-1	I-2	II-3	II-3	II-3	II-3
Scene Name	Nomad Camp	Nomad Camp	Nomad Camp	Nomad Camp	Nomad Camp	Castle Luna	Convent	Convent	Convent	Convent
ACTS ONE/TWO Title	"Or del giorno i giorni albori?"	"Stride la vampa"		"Soli or siamo" "Condotta ell'era in ceppi"	"Non son tuo figlio?" "Mal ragionan" "L'usato mezzo Rui" "Perpitani ancor languarete"	"Aferra! Aferra!" "Di che fipl visea piatre beein" "E il padre?"	"Che pui fuiresti" "Tacea la notte placida"	"Tutto è diuanto" "il belen dei suo sentso"	"Quoi scono" "Anfri Andiam"		"Noi giammai" "E doggio a posso credolo?"
Ricordi 42315	p61-68	p68-68		p66-67, 67-75	p70-79, 79-83, 84-91	p14, 5-12, 13-20	p21-23, 23-33	p92-93, 93-95	p96-97, 97-107	p115-116	p116-117, 118-136
Scene Length		4:00		1:00, 4:65	1:45, 2:00, 3:36	2:00, 4:24, 3:06	1:54, 3:52	1:58, 3:08	0:30, 1:30	2:05	0:24, 3:09
Start/End Time	0:00-1:30		1:30-5:30	5:30-11:25	11:25-19:46	19:46-29:16	29:16-37:03	37:02-41:40	41:40 -43:40	43:40 - 45:45	45:45-49:17
ROLES										
Count Di Luna — Michael Mayes							Di Luna	Di Luna		Di Luna
Manrico — Gregory Kunde		Manrico		Manrico	Manrico					Manrico
Leonora — Latonia Moore									Leonora	Leonora
Azucena — Raehann Bryce-Davis	Azucena	Azucena	Azucena	Azucena		Leonora				Azucena
Ferrando — Peter Morgan					Ferrando		Ferrando	Ferrando		Ferrando
Nomad/Fate — Amanda Castro	Nomad/Fate	Nomad/Fate	Nomad/Fate	Nomad/Fate						Nomad/Fate
CHORUS - 3 women/4 men										
Coro — Lisa Marie Rogali	Nomad Coro	Nomad Coro	Nomad Coro			(QC 17m) Nun			Nun	Nun
Coro — Mary-Hollis Hundley	Nomad Coro	Nomad Coro	Nomad Coro			(QC 17m) Nun			Nun	Nun
Coro- Ines — Stephanie Sanchez	Nomad Coro	Nomad Coro	Nomad Coro			(QC 17m) Ines- Nun			Ines	Ines
Coro- Ruiz — Spencer Hamlin	Ruiz- Nomad	Nomad Coro	Ruiz- Nomad		(QC 13:00) Militia Coro					Ruiz- Nomad
Coro — Kameron Lopreore	Nomad Coro	Nomad Coro	Nomad Coro		(QC 13:00) Militia Coro		Militia Coro	Militia Coro		Militia Coro
Coro — Armando Contreras	Nomad Coro	Nomad Coro	Nomad Coro		(QC 13:00) Militia Coro					Nomad Coro
Coro — Ron Dukes	Nomad Coro	Nomad Coro	Nomad Coro		(QC 13:00) Militia Coro		Militia Coro	Militia Coro		Militia Coro

Il Trovatore / 7/8/21	III-5	III-5	IV-1	IV-1	IV-2	IV-3	IV-3	IV-3
Scene Name	Nomad Camp	Nomad Camp	Nomad Camp	Nomad Camp	Outside Cell	Holding Cell	Holding Cell	Holding Cell
ACTS THREE/FOUR Title	"Quale d'armi fragor" "Ah! Si, ben mio"	"La zingara vien!" "Di quella pira"	"Siam giunti" "D'amor sull'ali rosee"	"Miserere d' un'alma"	"Udsita?" "Mira, di acerba lagrime"	"Mâdre, non dormi?"	"Oh! Non mingamra..." "Parter mia/s nulol?"	"Ti scosta!" Finale
Ricordi 42315	p167-168, 169-173	p173-175, 175-183	p184-185, 185-189	p189-198	p206-209, 209-223	p223-233	p234-238, 238-244	p244-262
Scene Length	1:28, 3:25	1:00, 1:39	1:51, 3:30	2:30	1:40, 4:00	7:30	1:00, 7:30	4:38
Start/End Time	49:17-04:12	54:10-58:49	58:49-1:02:10	1:02:10-1:04:30	1:04:30-1:10:10	1:10:10-1:17:46	1:17:40-1:21:10	1:21:10-1:25:38
ROLES								
Count Di Luna — Michael Mayes					Di Luna		Di Luna	Di Luna
Manrico — Gregory Kunde	Manrico	Manrico				Manrico	Manrico	Manrico
Leonora — Latonia Moore	Leonora		Leonora	Leonora	Leonora		Leonora	Leonora
Azucena — Raehann Bryce-Davis		Azucena		Azucena	Azucena	Azucena	Azucena	Azucena
Ferrando — Peter Morgan		Ferrando		Ferrando	Ferrando		Ferrando	Ferrando
Nomad/Fate — Amanda Castro	Nomad/Fate	Nomad/Fate	Nomad/Fate	Nomad/Fate	Nomad/Fate	Nomad/Fate	Nomad/Fate	Nomad/Fate
CHORUS - 3 women/4 men								
Coro — Lisa Marie Rogali						Nun	Nun	Nun
Coro — Mary-Hollis Hundley						Nun	Nun	Nun
Coro- Ines — Stephanie Sanchez						Ines	Ines	Ines
Coro- Ruiz — Spencer Hamlin	Ruiz- Nomad	Ruiz- Nomad	Ruiz- Nomad	(Off Stage Vocal)		Ruiz- Nomad	Ruiz- Nomad	Ruiz- Nomad
Coro — Kameron Lopreore		Militia Coro		Militia Coro		Militia Coro	Militia Coro	Militia Coro
Coro — Armando Contreras	Nomad Coro	Nomad Coro	Nomad Coro	(Off Stage Vocal)		Nomad Coro	Nomad Coro	Nomad Coro
Coro — Ron Dukes		Militia Coro		Militia Coro		Militia Coro	Militia Coro	Militia Coro

Figure 3.6 A character/scene breakdown made by assistant director, Alison Pogorelc for *Il Trovatore* at The Glimmerglass Festival.

STREET SCENE - ACT I

Opening & #1 Ain't it awful the heat		pgs. 1-23
Abraham Kaplan	Blake Ellege	Scene Time: 00:00
Emma Jones	Erin Moran	Run Time: 06:00
Greta Fiorentino	Benedetta Cordaro	
Olga Olsen	Melina Jaharis	
Shirley Kaplan	Charlotte Jackson	
Chorus	Yarham (Nurse Maid), Atkinson (Nurse Maid), Buszewski (man w/ radio), Vincent Jones (Bair), Willie (Rydel), Crowd (Hatten), Officer Murphy (Maden), Judd, Law, Mims (Graduate Girls), Mr. Buchanan (Weisman), Mrs. Buchanan (Helm), Worker (Thomas), Mrs. Hildebrant (Burbules)	
#2-Blues		**pgs. 24-27**
Henry Davis	Franklin Mosley	Scene Time: 06:00
Emma Jones	Erin Moran	Run Time: 01:35
Greta Fiorentino	Benedetta Cordaro	
Olga Olsen	Melina Jaharis	
#3 Get A Load of That		**pgs. 27-35**
Willie Maurrant	Sean Rydel	Scene Time: 07:35
Emma Jones	Erin Moran	Run Time: 02:25
Anna Maurrant	Amanda Palmeiro	
Greta Fiorentino	Benedetta Cordaro	
Olga Olsen	Melina Jaharis	
Dialogue after #3		**pg. 36**
Emma Jones	Erin Moran	Scene Time: 10:00
Anna Maurrant	Amanda Palmeiro	Run Time: 02:35

Figure 3.7   An excerpt of a character/scene breakdown for *Street Scene*. Although this is a less common way of putting together a CSB, it is just as useful. It lists all of the same information (character name, performer name, and scene and run time).

Tips from the toolkit...

Don't forget to list characters or groups of people that have any off-stage involvement such as singing or lines, which is very common in opera. Many times, these are the easiest to forget! This is information that is needed when planning for backstage monitors and additional amplification, quick changes or transitions that might overlap. An easy way to note this in the scene breakdown is with parenthesis, either as (OSS), offstage singing, or around the character name (Manrico).

MEASURE GROUND PLAN FOR TAPING

A big part of setting up the rehearsal space will be taping out the set, based on the ground plan(s).

Be sure to check in with either your production manager or technical director so you can get your hands on a copy as soon as possible. Depending on how big your set is, grabbing measurements can be a tedious job. There are a few computer programs that can help with this such as Vectorworks or AutoCad, but they are subscription based. We will discuss taping out the rehearsal room in more depth in the next chapter.

CONTACT SHEET

Another vital piece of paperwork that may get started by the production manager and then passed off to the stage manager is the contact sheet. Since many of the singers and designers are contracted so far in advance, this tends to be a working document up until the SM team's prep week. The stage manager can then decide what personal information is shared with the cast. Many times, the contact sheet that the company has put together may have additional information such as management, addresses, and personal and work phone numbers and emails. Once the stage manager has sifted through all this and taken out information that should remain confidential, it can be ready to share with the rest of the team. As for layout, again, there is no right way of displaying this information. I have found that using a table format is easier when searching across and selecting the information needed, such as a phone number or email address. The most common headers when putting together a contact sheet to share with the group are names, role/title, email, and phone number.

Other things the PSM may work on during prep week

- **Collect Emergency Contact Info:** SMs are starting to go paperless and trying to grab this info ahead of the first rehearsal. Google Forms, or a similar online survey, has been the most used software to date. Not only it is easy to import all your questions, but once responses are collected, Google puts it into an Excel spreadsheet for easy access.
- **Create a Welcome Email to Send to the Cast and Team:** The SM will send out a welcome email to the cast at least one week in advance to the first in-person meeting introducing themselves to the cast and creative team as well as some background information for the first day of rehearsal. Documents that may be included in this email are (but not limited to):
  - Overview Schedule
  - Round 1 of the Contact Sheet (ask everyone to look it over and get back to you with edits that need to be made)
  - Directions to the Space

Here is an example of a welcome email:

> *Hello everyone!*
>
> *My name is Danielle Ranno and I will be your stage manager for Gianni Schicchi.*
>
> *Our first rehearsal is this Saturday at 10:00am. You all should have received an overview schedule, as well as directions to the space from Destiny. If you need anything resent, let me know. Dailies will be sent*

the night prior to each rehearsal and will serve as the most up-to date rehearsal plan.

Email is the main source of communication when it comes to calls and or changes. If you foresee this being a problem, let me know and we can work something out.

Just to let you know, fittings will begin on Monday at 9:00am. The plan is for Court to see everyone by end of day Tuesday. These will take place at the Ballet Met costume shop. More info to follow at the end of the week.

I look forward to meeting and working with you all this weekend. If there are any questions or concerns, do not hesitate to reach out.

Safe travels!

Danielle

There is no right or wrong way or format to a welcome email. You want to make it inviting and show off a bit of your personality, while keeping it professional. Also, remember to space information/topics out. Rather than having your email look like a five-paragraph essay, space it out to give the eyes a break. This will also help the reader take in and retain information. And don't forget: Just as you would have someone/an assistant proof your reports before they are sent out, it is always a good idea to have someone do the same with your welcome email!

More often then not, stage managers and others sending emails to a large groups of people are starting to BCC or "blind carbon copy" rather than input all email addresses in the TO field. There are two great reasons for using BCC when sending out your emails; first, it removes the possibility of the accidental "reply all" that some people are prone to hit. This way, if a response is needed from someone, it will come to you or the original sender only, rather than starting a large chain with everyone on the original email. Second, it respects everyone's privacy. There may be someone on the team or in the cast of high status that may not want their email address public to the larger group. By adding everyone in the BCC field, you remove both of these risks.

Tips from the toolkit...

Before sending out your welcome email, check in with other departments to see if there is any general information they would like you to pass along to the cast. For an example, the costume shop may want the chorus to bring their own character or dress shoes, or let singers know that if they want rehearsal clothing, such as skirts or jackets, for the first few days of staging, that they should bring a stand in until fittings. The cast is less likely to miss important information if it is all in one email rather than multiples.

ASM PREP

The amount of prep the assistant stage manager(s) will have to do during prep week will depend on whether there is one or two ASMs, if there is a PA, the type of show (full opera vs a concert vs semi-staged) and what information is available to them. When all else fails, spend time learning the score and the music!

This section will break down some of the duties assigned to the props ASM and the costumes ASM. ASM paperwork is like a revolving door; it begins in prep, but will be carried through to tech and performance. What is not discussed below will come up in future chapters.

PROPS LIAISON PREP

Paperwork that will be discussed in this section will be:

- Obtaining an original prop list from the designer/director
- Prop inventory
- Rehearsal prop request

Obtaining an Original List

The first step is to obtain the original prop list from the director (and/or designer). Many times, this will come in the simplest form such as a list, and not necessarily in order of the act and scene each item is used in. Your first task as props ASM is to create a more detailed version that will be used by the SM team and shared with the props department. At some companies, the props artisan will put together a detailed inventory, but their version may not necessarily be laid out in a way that best works for the SM team.

Purpose: To have an organized list, broken down by act, scene and character where you can easily track props that are coming into the rehearsal room. Props that were not on the original list may get added during staging, so this will also serve as the most up-to-date prop list.

How to: The easiest way to organize all the information needed is in a table format. Whether it is done in Word or Excel is based on preference of the creator or the template provided.

Figure 3.8 shows the prop list for *La Cenorentola* and Figure 3.9 shows a transformed SM inventory.

Key items listed on an SM props inventory:

- Act & scene
- Quantity
- Prop name
- Column to check off if it is a rehearsal or performance prop
- Character who uses it
- Any misc. notes
- A key defining any shading, highlights, or typographical emphasis

La Cenerentola
Props List

Mismatching furniture in Magnifico house, perhaps a sitting chair (one chair standable) Wooden stool for Angelina by fire (standable)
Bellows for fire
Table (standable)
Single red rose (Tisbe)
Two shawls or blankets for girls to be "modest"
Standing mirror
Bread on plate
Coffee pot (in fire)
Coffee cups
Alidoro beggar cup
Three baskets of fabric, lace, necklaces, feathers, fans, accessories (no handles —one can be larger for fabrics)
Teddy bear (Magnifico) ??
Broom
Four rectangular pieces of cloth, "silk", red, approx 24" by 12"
Ledger/folio for Alidoro with list of names
Fancy wine goblet (Magnifico)
Wine goblets for act I finale
Finale dinner/food (one plate per principal and one glass?)
Wine bottles (coro uses to fill glasses—no liquid)
Poof
Poison vial
Pillow for Angelina crown?

Costume props:
Magnifico walking stick
Magnifico hat
Matching Angelina bracelets
2 Crowns?

Figure 3.8 Initial props list for *La Cenorentola* from the director.

As heard on headset...

I worked with a prop artisan who assigned each prop with a number, which made it easier when discussing a specific prop (sometimes there a multiple props or furniture pieces that were of different style but had the same name, such as chairs or tables) and when a note was discussed in the report, I would list both the number AND prop name; the Act II bench (#12) has a loose leg and is no longer safe to stand on. Stage management tried tightening it by hand in rehearsal as a temporary fix. Can it be looked at before tomorrow's 6:30pm rehearsal? The leg in question has been labeled with a pink Post-it. Thanks! Whenever a prop was added, it was given a new number.

—*DR*

La Cenerentola
PROPS INVENTORY

Director: Crystal Manich
Conductor: Craig Kier
Version: A - jm
Updated:06/30/18

		ACT I			
Quantity	Prop	Rehears.	Perf.	Charac.	Notes
1	Arm Chair	X?			
1	Kitchen Table	X			Standable
2	Kitchen Chairs	X			Standable
1	Bench	X			Standable
1	Fireplace				
	Coffee Pot	X			In fire
1	Bellows for Fire		X	Cenerentola	
1	Kitchen Rag	X			
1	Slice of Bread Glued to Plate			Alidoro	
1	Bread on Plate				Sliced
2	Coffee Cup	X		Cenerentola	
1	Small Wooden Stool		X	Cenerentola	Standable
1	Single Red Rose	X		Tisbe	
2	Shawls or Blankets	X		Tisbe/Clorinda	For girls to be modest
1	Hand Mirror			Tisbe	
~~1~~	~~Standing Mirror~~				
1	Walking Stick	X		Alidoro	30" "Carved from a stick" with a handle
1	Beggar Cup		X	Alidoro	
~~3~~	~~Baskets of fabric, lace, necklaces, feathers, fans, etc~~				~~No Handles~~ ~~One can be larger~~
1	Large Basket for throwing fabrics, jewels, etc			Cenerentola	Flat and Oval, Flower Basket
2	Pearl Necklaces	1			
?	Feathers				
?	Fabric	X			
	~~Teddy Bear~~			~~Magnifico~~	
1	Faceless Muslin Doll	X		Magnifico	Dressed like Magnifico
1	Broom		X	Cenerentola	
4	Rectangular Pieces of Cloth	X			Silk, red, 24"x12" Corners weighted

Italics denotes a costume acting as a prop
* denotes consumables
Bold denotes a repeating prop from a previous scene
ALL CAPS denotes a furniture piece

Figure 3.9 An excerpt of the prop inventory for *La Cenorentola* prepared by ASM Jackie Mercer.

GLIMMERGLASS ON THE GRASS 21 Production: **Zambello / Fogel**	**SONGBIRD** Rehearsal Prop Request	Page 1 of 2 *06/25/2021 dmr* Version: **A** Score: **GGF 2021**

Date: Monday, June 28   Reh. Time: 10:00 AM   Location: ABOTFP

Qty	PROP	DESCRIPTION	Sc. or No.	PRESET / CHAR.	REAL / REH.
**ACT ONE - Café des Muses**
1	Bar	10-ft. long *Will be held down with stage weights for rehearsal		Preset	REAL
1	Square Table	weight bearing		Preset	REAL
1	Round Table	weight bearing		Preset	REAL
1	Rectangle Table	weight bearing		Preset	REAL
4	Chairs	Café style, weight bearing		Preset	REAL
2	Short Bar Stools	Weight bearing		Preset	
1	Tall Bar Stool			Preset	
1	Corded microphone & stand	1920s Cord is removeable		Preset	
3-5	Round Serving Trays	various, for drinks			
1	Wooden Crate for busing				
1	Wooden crate with beer bottles			Mastriila	

Figure 3.10 Excerpt from the full props request for *SongBird*, prepared by the author for The Glimmerglass Festival.

Rehearsal Prop Request

Purpose: To request props that are needed in rehearsal and when. The full list may not be needed for the first rehearsal, and this will give the props artisan time to prioritize what it is that they need to have ready/prepared and when. Depending on what the prop is, you may even end up getting the show prop up front. If it happens to be something that needs to be special ordered or made, a stand in will be given in its place.

How to: In a table format, list the quantity, prop name and description, as well as the time, date, and location of when and where props should be dropped off. This information will be gathered from the initial prop list that the director and/or designer made.

This props request form (Figure 3.10) also doubled as the full prop list, so additional detailed information was added. Not only was it used as an initial props request, but it was also used to request for props and furniture to be transferred from one space to another since rehearsals altered between two rehearsal spaces. The stage manager would just fill out the date, time, and location of where rehearsal was taking place, highlight the items that were needed and the crew would love those items.

COSTUME LIAISON PREP

Paperwork that will be discussed in this section will be:

- Costume Request
- First Entrance Sheet

- Pocket List
- Costume Display

Costume Request

Purpose: To request pieces to use in rehearsal. You want to try to complete this as early as possible and pass it along to the shop manager to give them time to pull or produce a stand in. Some shops will have a rehearsal costume stash, whereas others will need to fit it into their rental package. Some shops may ask you to wait until the first fitting before they can send items into rehearsal. Figure 3.11 shows one example of a rehearsal costume request form.

There are multiple ways to figure out what items will be needed in rehearsal. The first way is to look at the renderings that have been provided by the designer. There are some operas where the story calls for specific costume actions to take place. For an example, in *Die Fledermaus* (The Bat), Eisenstein has a quick change from his day clothes to his party clothes in Act I during the trio with his wife Rosalinda, and maid, Adelle. Knowing this, you may ask for a coat and top hat. Or, if you are doing, *Le Nozze de Figaro* (The Marriage of Figaro), you may ask for a couple of capes for Figaro, Susannah, Count and Countess, since there is a lot of action with them in Act IV. If you know these items are not needed on the first day, try to note that in the request so the shop can prioritize what is needed. Knowing that specific items are needed right away may also help prioritize fittings.

[LOGO]   **[TITLE OF SHOW]**
Rehearsal Costume Request

Director: [Name]
Conductor: [Name]
Updated: [Date] dmr
Page 1 of 1

Character Artist	Costume Piece	Notes	Reh. Garment Received	Final Garment Received	Returned

Figure 3.11   Example of a costume request template.

Depending on the size of the company, or if the piece has a large ensemble, the costume designer or wardrobe supervisor may reach out to them requesting that they bring their own rehearsal skirts, jackets, and shoes (or asks that stage management includes these requests in their welcome email).

A few other items that are great to have in rehearsal as early as possible are:

- **Shoes:** Most singers will bring a set of rehearsal shoes, usually the standard character or dress shoe. These are great to start with but the sooner they can get their show shoes the better, especially if the staging is very physical, or if the heel of a shoe is specific.

- **Skirts/Petticoats:** Skirts are another item that some singers travel with, but again, do not assume that they want to use their own. Many shops will send the petticoat, which will be worn under their dress or show skirt to rehearsal so the singer can get used to moving around in.

- **Knee pads:** It is always a good idea to have a few spare knee pads in rehearsal, even if the staging does not originally call for it. If you are staging, for an example, *Madama Butterfly,* you know for sure that kneepads will be needed from day one. Sometimes they may just be used for staging purposes and not necessarily needed for the show.

- **Jackets:** Jackets, similar to skirts, may change the way one moves and walks. Jackets are also great as stand ins, whether for quick changes, or as prop clothes in the scene.

- **Hats:** Hats, like jackets and skirts, may also change the way a singer moves. If it is a period piece, there may even be some hat choreography. Hat tracking is also something that tends to get forgotten if it is not something that is used early on.

- **Corsets:** Corsets are not always provided until an initial fitting has taken place. If the shop does not plan to send the coreset over after the fitting, you should ask for them, especially if the singer has not worked in one before. They are great to practice with early in rehearsal since they will affect how a singer breathes, their posture, how they sing, and sometimes, even the staging.

- **Hankies:** Hankies, hankies, hankies! If you are on board to do *Il barbiere di Siviglia* (The Barber of Seville) or *Street Scene*, hankies will most likely be needed. This is another thing that can easily be forgotten when tracking, unless the actual item is in use. A hankie is another item that floats between costumes and props. Or, there may be an instance where the rehearsal hankie comes from props, but the show hankie will come from costumes. One way to help decipher which department the request should go to is to ask yourself these questions: *Is it listed on the costume piece list? Is it shown on the renderings as part of the costume?* COSTUMES. *Was it added in staging? Is it used as an item and not necessarily as a way to describe the character?* POSSIBLY PROPS.

How to: There are a few ways of putting a costume request together. If the company already has a preferred template, then all you have to do is fill in the necessary information. If not, you want to have the following information listed:

- Character and name of performer
- Costume piece
- When it used (act/scene)
- Notes regarding the garment
- List whether it is a real or rehearsal garment
- The date the item has been received/checked out

Tips from the toolkit...

Depending on the company, you may be working with a union crew in the rehearsal hall. If you do have any costume pieces in rehearsal, even if just a pair of shoes, a wardrobe crew member needs to be on-site to assist.

Keep in mind: Once you start getting rehearsal pieces in the room such as corsets and shoes, you may need to schedule extra time on either end of rehearsal so singers can get in and out of them without eating up the beginning of rehearsal or having to stay after later to get out of them.

FIRST ENTRANCE SHEET

Purpose: An easy "one sheet" with timings that reflect a character's first time on stage. If a singer is playing multiple characters, the singer would be listed each time their new character appears on stage for the first time. Wardrobe, wigs and makeup will use this to put together their calls.

How to: In order to put this sheet together, you will first need to have timed your score. First entrance sheets have been done in both table and list formats. Some first entrance sheets also list the first costume that the performer is in, but this is not always required or necessary. Each act and intermission/pausa should be listed along with its length.

Key pieces of information listed on a first entrance sheet:

- The performer name
- The character name
- Timing of their first entrance or appearance on stage

During the rehearsal process, your first entrance sheet may get updated timings. The first version will be based off of your initial timings, which were collected

PRINCIPAL ARTISTS (#)			
CHARACTER	Artist	0:00	Look #1
CHARACTER	Artist	0:00	Look #1
CHARACTER	Artist	0:00	Look #1
CHARACTER	Artist	0:00	Look #1
CHARACTER	Artist	0:00	Look #1
CHARACTER	Artist	0:00	Look #1

CHORUS (#)			
CHARACTER	Artist	0:00	Look #1
CHARACTER	Artist	0:00	Look #1
CHARACTER	Artist	0:00	Look #1

Figure 3.12 Template of a first entrance template used at The Glimmerglass Festival.

from the recording used during prep week. During staging, you will also get more exact entrances, which should not change the first entrance timing that much, unless they are appearing on stage in a prior scene to what is listed in the score, or a change in music was made (music added back in or a new cut made). If possible, try to grab timings from a run with Maestro's tempi. These will be your most exact and closest to performance timings.

A few tips for putting together a first entrance sheet:

- If a performer appears within the first 5 minutes of the opera, then I list them as a 00:00/top of show first entrance since that is when they will be called to places.

- If a first entrance falls in the middle of two timings, round it to the closest 30-seconds.

POCKET LIST

Purpose: To keep track of costumes that may need pockets, their sizes, and placement/location. This is a piece of paperwork that is not traditionally done in opera, but the times that it has been used has proven to be very helpful to designers and it is a great way to keep track of notes. Although all this information will be listed in the report, it is great to have it all on one page to then turn over to the shop at once.

How to: This will be a working document during rehearsal, and it is up to the stage manager and costume designer as to how often they want an updated version sent over. It could be every day, or every week. The format that is traditionally used and tends to be the easiest to read is a table, but as with every piece of paperwork, it can be adjusted to fit the production's needs.

CHARACTER/ACTOR	ACT	COSTUME	POCKET PLACEMENT	ITEM/SIZE
CHARACTER Name				

Figure 3.13   Template for a pocket list created by the author.

Key information listed on a pocket list:

- Performer name

- Character

- Garment or costume

- Location of pocket

- What it is for (list prop or item) and size (if you know the exact item that will be in said pocket, provide actual measurements)

- Additional notes if needed

It is important to be as detailed as possible. If they know its purpose and the size of the item, the designer may have another idea that will achieve the same thing. For an example, while working on *I Due Figaro*, a pocket was requested for the Count on the outside of his jacket so he could have easy access to his hankie. Once the request was made, the designer came back and said that period-wise, the Count would not have an outside pocket on that style of coat. Instead, she gave him a longer hankie and had him tuck it inside his sleeve.

Costume Display

Purpose: To have all renderings nicely presented in the rehearsal room.
   If time is carved out for a design presentation, the designer might offer to bring colored renderings with them and then hand them off to the SM team to display after the presentation. Other times, the designer might request that stage management print them out since they might have easier access to a colored printer.

How to: This all depends on what is available to you and/or what your rehearsal space is like. Here are a few ways to display:

- **Additional Callboard or Bulletin Board:** You want these to be in a different area than your general callboard, whether it be a different section of a large bulletin board or a separate board completely. A lot of times, the design display can be where people tend to hang out, sometimes on breaks or after a rehearsal session. You do not want attention taken away from your callboard, which houses the sign-in, and other important messages.

- **Look Book:** Simply put everything in a binder, in sheet protectors if possible to protect from rips and tears, and display the book on a communal table, or at the front of the room. Having three of these books in the room would be ideal; one for performers/staff/guest to view, one for the director's table, and one for the stage manager's table.

- **Tri-Fold Board:** This is a great alternative if a bulletin board is not available and taping on the walls in the rehearsal space is not an option. This may be an added expense if the company does not have one lying around, so be sure to check in with your production manager before moving forward with this option.

- **Taped to a Wall:** It may be easiest to just pin/tape the renderings up on a wall in the rehearsal room. Not only is this the cheapest option, but it is also easy and fast. To avoid congregation, you want to hang them in a location that everyone can have easy access to, but that will not disrupt the room if they are being viewed while other things are going on. Confirm that the tape being used will not pull up paint in case that is a concern.

VARIOUS OTHER PREP PAPERWORK

If there is a PA or production assistant on the team, many of these duties may fall to them. If not, they will get distributed amongst the ASMs.

Paperwork that will be discussed in this section:

- Sign-in sheets
- Chorus name tags
- Who's Who cheat sheet or face sheet

Sign In-Sheets

There is no right or wrong way to create a sign-in sheet. As long as the performer's name is listed and there is a place for them to initial by their name, you are set. Whether you break the names up in order of appearance in the opera, by voice type, or alphabetical order by surname is up to you. Having a separate sign-in for principals and chorus is usually the norm, although it is not required. Weekly versus daily sign-ins can be based on preference, but can also be determined by factors such as complexity of daily rehearsals or the size of the cast.

Purpose: To track when performers arrive to rehearsal.

How to: A table-like format

The date and time of the day or session should be bolded and at the top and have a line or box for each performer to initial upon their arrival.

Tips from the toolkit...

Finding ways to go green in stage management is becoming a new movement! To save on paper, I started laminating my sign-in sheets and using a dry erase marker so the same one could be used for the entire run. If laminating is not easily accessible, a sheet protector will also work. If neither of these are available options, try printing double-sided. That way, you can get double the use out of a single sheet of paper.

CHORUS NAME TAGS

Name tags are so helpful when staging! They are used for choristers, supers, and kids. Principals do not traditionally get name tags, since the staging staff will be seeing them on a regular basis and will learn their names the quickest. The chorus, however, may only be called to a few sessions that are spread out over the span of the rehearsal period. Rather than constantly checking The Who's Who and matching names to faces, having a name tag just makes it faster and easier to identify everyone.

Purpose: Help with names of a large group of people.

How to: You want the name to be big and bold so it can easily be read from a distance. Just like every other piece of paperwork, there is no right or wrong way to do this—it is based on preference and available resources. Some companies have stock of the Avery 3″ × 4″ tags with the laminated, clip-style pocket. I started using colored, 4″ × 6″ index cards (Figure 3.14). I get the color/pastel pack that comes with five colors, and assign a color to a voice type. Pink for soprano, purple for mezzos, blue for tenors, green for bass/bass-baritones, and yellow for supers.

PEGGY
Botteicher

Lead Nurse (Lt. Genevieve Marshall)

Figure 3.14 Example of a chorus name tag made to print on a 4″ × 6″ index card made by the author for a production of *South Pacific* at Opera Roanoke.

The first name is in the largest size, all caps and bold, so it is the easiest to spot. The last name, slightly smaller, not in all caps nor bold. In the bottom left corner, I list if they have already been assigned a specific character, or are costumed as a specific character, such as a soldier or peasant. To finish it off, add an ID clip, or if these are not available, tie a piece of string or ribbon to the cards so they can be worn like a necklace, and they are ready to go!

As heard on headset…

Tosca was my first large cast opera with a full chorus. My stage manager asked me to get some colored index cards and safety pins for name tags. Having no idea what the system behind it was, I got a pack of 3″ × 5″ colored index cards, a few sharpies, and safety pins. On the first day of rehearsal, I placed all of these items out on a table and told everyone to pick a card, make their own name tag then stick it to their shirt. It was not until after everyone was walking around with random colors that she confronted me that I must have misunderstood her. Thankfully, both she and the director were very understanding of my mistake, and were thankful that everyone at least had some sort of name tag, despite the fact that it was wrong.

—DR

Who's Who Cheat Sheet or Face Sheet

The Who's Who lists all the singers with their headshots. This tool is very helpful when trying to put names to faces. Some companies will list just the performers, whereas others will list everyone involved in the production broken down by department and then share the sheet with everyone.

Purpose: To put a name to a face. An easy way to study and learn the names of everyone in the cast and on the production team.

How to: The company most likely has headshots of all the performers for the program, so ask them first if you can also have access to these. Since headshots come in different orientations and sizes, it helps to crop them so all the images are uniform in size. This may take a bit of time.

1. Format your photo. In Figure 3.15, each photo was formatted to 1.2″ × 1″.
2. To help with spacing and to line everything up easily, place each photo into a table cell.
3. Add the performer and character name.
4. Take away all table borders.

Manhattan
School of Music

TITLE OF SHOW- WHO'S WHO

Kayla Uribe
Insert Role

Alex W. Seidel
Insert Role

Cindy Marino
Insert Role

Jorell Williams
Insert Role

Adrian Lester
Insert Role

Danielle Ranno
Insert Role

Gloria Cardona
Insert Role

Zoë Kim
Insert Role

Figure 3.15   Here's an example of a Who's Who page, also known as a face page. How big your cast or team is will dictate the size of each photo. This example is set to the smallest size (1.2″ × 1″) to accommodate a larger cast/group.

Tips from the toolkit…

Two other types of productions that you might work on are semi-staged and concert versions of a full opera. The paperwork that either of these productions might call for may vary, but most times, the SM team may not need to hit all of the listed paperwork that might be needed for a fully staged piece. During prep, the team will decipher exactly what is needed. Just because your prep week may not be stacked as completely as it would be for a fully staged opera does not mean that you are slacking in your work.

SCORES AND TRANSLATIONS

So how do you know what score to use? How do you get a copy? Are there different editions of the same opera score? The music staff, in conjunction with the conductor and director, will choose the score that will be used. When you receive your copy will depend on the company. Sometimes you get it upon arrival, or once your contract has been signed. I always like to request at least a digital score early so I can start to familiarize myself with it. If an on-site prep week or few days prior to the start of rehearsal is not available, asking for a score as soon as it is available will also give you time to set it up the way you like it. Do not be afraid to ask the company if they can print and send you a copy in advance.

There are a number of different publishers and editions of the same opera, so you want to be sure you are using the right one. Here are some of the most popular score publishers:

- **G. Schirmer:** An American classical music publishing company based in New York City, founded in the mid-1800s. Schirmer is one of the most popular and affordable scores. A lot of schools, conservatories, and young artists programs will select this option if it is available because of the affordability. Almost all Schirmer scores include an English translation, although they are not always the most accurate because they are trying to provide a singing translation rather than a word-for-word translation.

- **Bärenreiter:** A German publishing house based in Kassel. Since the 1950s, the company's focus has been on the New Complete Editions series for various composers, such as J.S. Bach, Händel, Mozart, Rossini, and Schubert to name a few. Known as academic scores, or collector's scores, they tend to be more expensive but are very easy and clear to read and have very accurate translations, even when they are singing translations.

- **Ricordi:** An Italian publishing company founded in Milan in the early 1800s and primarily of classical music and opera. Ricordi published some of the most well-known Italian composers of the 19th and 20th centuries, such as Rossini, Donizetti, Bellini, Verdi, and Puccini. Many Ricordi editions do have the English translation as well; unfortunately, it sometimes is listed above the Italian, which can make it difficult when the opera is being done in Italian.

Note: These are not the only score publishers out there. There are others, such as Dover, Boosey, and Hawkes (covering composers such as Benjamin Britten and Richard Strauss) and Hal Leonard (Kurt Weill), as well as Novello and Kalmus, but the list above includes the most popular and most used.

Tips from the toolkit…

Keep an eye out! Make sure the plate number is the same. This number can be found either on the top or bottom of the page. Commonly, although it can differ in some instances, it is a five-digit number. It might come up that Schirmer or Ricordi may have different editions and the plate number might be slightly off from the master that is being used. It is not the end of the world if you end up with a Ricordi with a slightly different plate number, if the differences are not that big. If you can live with page numbers being slightly off, then you will be fine.

You may be asking, why is it such a big deal that I have a matching score to the rest of the staging team? A lot of singers in your cast may have their own copy of the score either because they have sung the role before, or they prefer one publisher over the other. The people who want to match are the director, assistant director, lighting designer, and other stage managers on your team.

Here are some of the top reasons why matching scores are important:

- All your paperwork will match when it comes to page, system, measure (or PSM).
- If you need to give notes to your assistants, or even in the reports, they will line up in the score being used.
- When in tech, it will make cuing a lot easier if placements also line up.
- When giving placements of where to start from or jump to in the rehearsal room to Maestro or ASMs, they will easily be able to find the spot.

CUTS

Very rarely will a company perform an opera in its entirety. Some factors that will play into this are overall orchestra time, storytelling, and pacing. These days, more companies are entertaining the idea of a 90-minute, no intermission performance. In order to do this with the classics such as *La Bohème* or *Don Giovanni*, chunks of the music, such as repeats, or sections that do not lend to the storytelling, will get cut. Some companies are finding ways to do away with the chorus to achieve a shortened time.

A cut list will come from a member of the music staff. Either it will be emailed out to everyone, or it could be included when the company gives you a copy of the score. There are two common ways that cuts are listed, either in the form of PSM (page/system/measure), or by rehearsal numbers or letters. If your score has them, they can be found either on the top of the measure, or sometimes embedded within the measure, usually where the words are. One thing you have to pay attention to is if the cut is listed from the beginning of the listed measure or the end of the measure. Putting in cuts can be daunting at first, but if you know what the cut is trying to achieve and are comfortable with the score, the "where" should fall into place. After looking at the section as a whole, it will become clear if it was placed incorrectly. Also, if you are unsure of a placement or do not understand the cut at all, it does not hurt to contact the music librarian or a member on the conducting staff. If you have an AD on your staff, they may also be able to help you.

Il Trovatore (Giuseppe Verdi)

Ricordi piano vocal score plate #42315 is the official score for this production

Format: cut from the end of page/system/bar/beat to the beginning of page/system bar/beat

---

1. *The opera begins on page 51*
2. 52/3/2 – 56/3/1
3. 76/4/1/2 – 77/2/1/3 [*"La fuggente aura natal non isco-"* all sung on B]
4. 89/4/8 – 90/3/5 [*Beat 1 text becomes "-cor"/"lor"*]

Figure 3.16 Excerpt from the cut list for The Glimmerglass Festival's production of *Il Trovatore*.

Figures 3.17 (a and b) *Il Trovatore* with cuts from the cut list shown in Figure 3.16. *(Continued)*

Figures 3.17 *(Continued)*

Tips from the toolkit...

When marking cuts, I always like to start with a pencil. If it is a large cut, I tend to section it off with a paper clip. There have been many times where a cut, or partial cut reopened during rehearsal. If a cut has not been added back in by the final room run, then I will remove the extraneous pages.

LIBRETTOS

A libretto (Italian for "booklet") is the text used or script version of the opera. In the early days of opera, the libretto was written first (like a play) and then composers took it and wrote the music. Sometimes, the text was already pre-existing, such as the Greek myths or plays from Shakespeare. Today, there are many more scenarios for composer/librettist combinations. One scenario is that the company commissions the piece from the librettist and then pairs them up with a composer they have in mind. The librettist may be allowed to choose the composer they wanted to collaborate with or sometimes the opposite is true, the composer will choose the librettist to work with. And there are even the possibilities of the librettist and composer being the same person.

I briefly mentioned librettos earlier in this chapter, but if you can get your hands on one, whether the company sends you a copy (sometimes the director might have a translation that they prefer and share), or you find one online, read it! Especially if the piece is in a different language, this is a great way for you to familiarize yourself with the story. Some librettos are even written side by side with the original language, which can be very helpful when familiarizing yourself with what you will be seeing in the score.

In their words...

Composers have all the luck. They get to be remembered in history much more than any others in the opera field. But the truth is, audiences in opera come to see singing storytellers and the composer is there to make the singers shine in the live experience. It's a kind of servant leadership. The composer John Kander (CABARET, CHICAGO) exemplifies this. Kander scores are spectacular vehicles for the performers. In opera, I think Verdi is the best example.

—Michael Ching, Librettist and Composer

CASTELS

Nico Castel was often known as the Henry Higgins of the Metropolitan Opera, where he served as a staff diction coach for three decades. Castel was a comprimario tenor, and a well-known language and diction coach, as well as a copious translator of libretti. Castel spoke German, French, Spanish, English, Portuguese, Ladino, and Italian with native or near-native fluency. His legacy includes volumes of opera libretto translations, which consist of word-by-word English translations and phonetic symbols for each word in the original language. These are known by many as "the Nico books," and include complete librettos of operas by Mozart, Verdi, and Puccini, as well as three volumes of French opera librettos.

Although it amounts to a larger project, if you have the time and can get your hands on the Castel of the opera you are working on, do so! These are a little harder than a libretto to get hold of, but if you have access to a public or school music library, you may be able to check a copy out. Or if you are working with an AD on your production, there is a high likelihood that they have a copy to share. You'll get a more literal translation from a Castel than you might from a libretto. Castels also provide copious footnotes with additional valuable information. As a stage manager, you might be expected to verbally cue or feed a line to a singer, so the more familiar you get with the language, the more comfortable you will feel if put in that type of situation.

As heard on headset...

Although a tedious job, there have been a few instances where I have written in the Castel translation into my score under the sung text. Because stage managers are only given so much time to prep, sometimes, I was only able to do this with some scenes, or sections throughout the overall score. But it proved to be SO HELPFUL. Not only did I feel prepared for scene work in the rehearsal, but it made it so much easier when finding my spot in the score. This way of writing in translations proved the most helpful when working on a piece in a language I was not used to, or did not work on as often, such as French. Believe me, future you will be very appreciative that you took the time to do so.

—DR

PUTTING TOGETHER YOUR BOOK

Putting together your book comes down to preference and what works best for you. My book looks different if I am ASMing versus when I am PSMing. In this section, I will go through a few things that have worked for me in the past, and how these practices have evolved over the years.

THE PSM PROMPT BOOK

As a PSM or an SM of the production, I do not have to worry about moving around a lot with my book in rehearsal or in the theater. That being said, I prefer to have a one-sided score with my minis (ground plans of the set) on the left side since I am left-handed. I have a friend that uses a double-sided score when she PSMs and prints double-sided minis. She will put them between each page, which puts her minis on both the right and left side when flipping through the score. Once she gets into the second half of tech, she then removes the minis and places them in the back of her book to cut down on page turns and is able to just focus on the score.

To save on paper, I prefer to copy my minis of the back of each score page. In order to do this, it is necessary to be prepared with your minis early enough to have them ready to copy. Sometimes your scenic designer will send over a set of clean minis per act or scene and additional work will not be needed. Sometimes you may not be so lucky, so cleaning them is on you or another member of the SM team. If there is temporary furniture placements on the ground plan, you may want to remove them since they might change in rehearsal. Dimensions and other notes may also be written within the ground plan that are not needed and so should be removed. If you have Vectorworks on your computer, you can easily do this once you obtain the original (VW) file from the designer. Or, if you can have the AutoCad file (dwg) sent over, you can download a free program called DWG TrueView, which can be used in a similar fashion. This will allow you to open the dwg file and easily create minis by hiding furniture, dimensions, and any other info added from the designer that you do not need. Adobe Acrobat is also a great tool that can be used to clean up minis although, depending on how the file is prepared, some items may not be easy to manipulate or delete. Vectorworks, AutoCad, and Adobe Acrobat are all subscription-based programs, but each have a free trial to try.

Depending on the size of the opera, you may have to split the show between two books. *The Marriage of Figaro* is a large piece, coming in at 496 pages in the Schirmer score and 572 pages in the Bärenreiter score. Since the intermission falls between Acts II and III, it was easy to divide the score into two binders. When I can avoid this, I do, because transporting around two, four-inch binders is not the most comfortable. It did make my job easier in the end though, especially since I was still able to turn my pages because my binder was not filled to the brim. What may work for one score and show may not for the next, so be flexible and willing to adjust if needed.

THE ASM PROMPT BOOK

As an ASM on an opera, one of your biggest responsibilities is cuing the singers on stage. In doing this, you may be moving around a lot backstage, whether it be up and down stage or climbing up to a second level of a set. Usually, you will have a music stand, which could move with you, but many times this luxury may not be available. Knowing that I will be carrying my score around with me, I want it to be as light as possible, so I go for double-sided. As for minis, to limit the amount of paper in my book, I will add them in only if needed, whether it be for a transition, or to show ensemble or large group blocking and placements. Depending on what needs notating, I always have half and full-page minis on hand (more on this in Chapter 5). I have also printed my minis on Post-its and will just stick them in where needed, which has also been a great alternative and paper saver.

Over the years, I have tried and revisited different methods of putting my ASM book together. Sometimes this has been dictated by the size of the show and other times I was just trying a new method that I heard about and wanted to see if it worked for me as well. Here is a short list of what I have used in the past and the pros and cons of each:

- **Binder**
  - Easiest to get a hold of and inexpensive. Most of the time, the company will provide one
  - Easy to make and insert a cover and spine cover sheet
  - Easy to insert and remove things
  - Can clip a book light to the back cover so you can easily read your score backstage
  - Cannot (always) fold the cover behind, leaving you without a free hand to cue
  - Can sometimes be cumbersome when holding while moving around backstage
- **Five Star Flex**
  - A hybrid between a notebook and binder
  - Flexible rings which make it easy to add or remove papers by pulling out the rings then clicking them close
  - Can fold over
  - Lighter than a binder to carry around, both during staging and in a bag for transit
  - Not as easy to clip a light onto the back due to the flexible cover
- **Spiral Binding**
  - Easy to carry around. Only weight being carried around is the weight of the paper.
  - Can fold over
  - Easy to turn pages
  - Some companies have the punch and covers to make these in house, although most of the time this will be an added expense
  - Cannot be altered once the book is put together without taking everything apart. This includes adding in new pages or even minis
  - If pages rip, not easy to fix
  - Not always easy to clip a light onto the back cover due to the thin cover
- **Arc Binder (this is the Staples brand, but a version of it can be found in other stores)**
  - The hole punch, rings, and binder cover are all additional expenses. However, if you plan to use this system a lot, it will pay for itself and is worth it
  - Can reuse the rings and binder covers
  - Easy to carry around
  - Can fold open

- Can add a book light to the back cover
- Easy to rearrange, add, and take out pages
- Can add in dividers and page protectors
- If pages rip, may have to make a copy of page and re-punch. Cannot just add a page reinforcer like you could with binder pages

---

Tips from the toolkit...

Make copies of pieces that have repeats, or multiple verses. For example, Papageno's first aria in *The Magic Flute* has three verses to the same music. To make it easier to differentiate blocking for each verse, as well as to cut down on page turns back and forth, make two additional copies of the first half of the aria (where the repeated verses are) and highlight the verse being sung. This will also help when placing multiple cues on repeated music.

TIMING A SCORE

Purpose: Timing your score is one of the first things you will work on during prep since a lot of your paperwork will be based on initial timings. Your initial timings will prove to be an asset, during all stages of production (it will come up multiple times in the upcoming chapters). Score timings are usually done in 30-second increments, but some stage managers will opt for every 15-seconds. Because this can be a timely job, it is usually divided amongst the team, or designated to one of the two ASMs.

As heard on headset...

Don't get frustrated the first time you have to time a score. It takes some getting used to if you are not accustomed to following along and keeping your place in the music while watching the timer. This is one of the reasons why I prefer to use my iPad; because the screen is large and easy to catch if I glance up, and I can position it propped up right in front of me. The first few scores that I timed out, I had to go back and re-time sections because I got lost. If the same happens to you, do not feel like you failed or are not doing it right. One thing that does help is familiarizing yourself with the music and score as much as you can. Listen to the music multiple times. If you have the score you will be using for rehearsals or are able to find one online or at the library, listen to the music while following along. Get your eyes used to reading the music and language. The more you practice the easier it will get. You might even find it enjoyable!

—DR

Materials needed:

- Your score

- A recording. Ask the director if they have a recording they have been using. Or maybe there is a recording that is of similar tempo and/or has similar cuts. Make sure you are all using the same one.

- Headphones if you are in a public area or office

- Stopwatch, iPad or clock with stopwatch function (make sure it counts up)

- Writing utensil. I prefer to use a colored, erasable pen or pencil. This way your timing will stand out and you can erase your marking in case a mistake was made

- If there are any cuts, make sure they are all notated in your score

How to: Have one hand ready to start the timer and the other to start the recording. As shown in the example, every 30-seconds you will jot down the time where it falls in the music. One of my opera SM mentors taught me to write the timing within the measure. With a colored pen/pencil, it easily stands out, but at the same time, it is "hidden" and out of the way. A check mark is added in the outside margin of the system to make it easy to spot. Another way I have seen it done is write the timing that takes place in the system in the right margin (where I usually put my check mark), or in the empty space above the system. Again, this is all based on your own preference. Just keep in mind that it may end up covered by a Post-it or other note.

If [score] acts are being performed as one, continue your timer until you hit the intermission or pausa placement. For an example, *La Traviata* has a total of four acts, but the intermission takes place between Acts II and III. So I will time Acts I and II as one performance act and Acts III and IV as the second performance act. If you happen to run into a part that is cut in your score, simply stop the timer but keep the recording playing. Once the recording gets to the end of cut, resume your timer.

As heard on headset…

The moment I started to freak out was when I was told we were going to time the score… I did not know how to read music. I started to look up YouTube tutorials on the basics of reading music. I would spend hours after work just teaching myself how to follow the music in the score and learning what each symbol meant. I was determined to learn how to read music, make the correct paperwork, and essentially learn everything I needed to know in order to become a good assistant to my SM and director. When rehearsals began, I was still not an expert in reading music, but I felt comfortable enough to run a rehearsal because I had memorized (by ear) the music and was not afraid to ask both my SM and fellow ASM questions or help.

—Elana Deutch

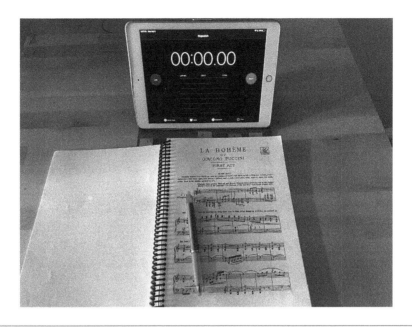

Figure 3.18 Set up of ipad (for timer), score and colored pen, in preparation for timing the score.

Figure 3.19 This score excerpt is taken from Act I of *La Boheme,* and shows one example of how to set up your score with the highlighting of staves and rehearsal letters and writing in 30-second timings into the music. To make it easier to spot, a check mark is added into the margin or at the end of the system.

Other helpful tips when setting up your score-ADs use many of these when setting up their own scores:

- If you are using a single-sided score, write the page number that would have been on the back side of a double-sided sheet (usually these are the even numbers) in the upper right-hand corner. If they are on the bottom of the page, or too small to read, write them out larger and circle them so they are easy to read and flip through.

- Highlight the beginning of your staves. This will help you differentiate where the system begins and ends, especially if they change within the page. It will also help you identify what clef you are in.

- Highlight or circle tempo changes, musical notations, or instrument name solos (sometimes in piano vocal scores changes in instruments are listed)

- If the score you are using is not the cleanest, or systems are scrunched up together, add a double slash (also known as the forward slash) to show the separation between systems.

- Assign each character a color and either highlight or underline their character name. This can be very time consuming, especially if you are working on a big piece such as *The Marriage of Figaro* or *The Magic Flute*. If you are, say, working on your first opera, this may prove helpful if you are not used to to cuing singers on stage or do not feel as confident yet taking your eyes off your score to check on places or that a transition has been complete. If you know that Figaro, who has been assigned orange, is singing, you might have an easier time finding your placement in your book.

- Highlight all rehearsal letters or numbers so you can quickly spot them. This will be very helpful in rehearsal.

- Tabbing your score can always be helpful but may be a little different than you are used to for plays or musicals. When referring to pieces in opera, the first few words that are sung are used. For an example, when referring to Figaro's first aria in *The Barber of Seville,* one would refer to it as *Largo* or *Largo al factotum* (translated into "I am the barber"). This is what you would want to write on your tab as well, so that when you hear, *Let's start from Largo al factotum,* you will know exactly where to turn.

Tips from the toolkit...

If you are working on a piece with recitative (dialogue that allows the character to move the story onward through a narrative), you usually do not have to worry about tabbing these in your score since they are coming off of an aria or scene, or going into one, they will most likely be coupled with that piece.

QUESTIONS TO ASK

About to embark on your first opera and unsure of what questions to ask during prep? Here are some of the most common:

- Is there a piano tuning schedule?

- Are there separate warm-up rooms for singers to use prior to rehearsal?

- If there are no measure numbers or rehearsal letters/numbers in the score that you were given, ask if it is possible for you to borrow a copy of the conductor's score (this would come from the music library) or a document with said info. It will be a small project having to copy them into your score, but it will be very useful to have in rehearsal

- Will there be a prop and furniture walk through with the director and props artisan? If not, what are the most important items that are needed in rehearsal from day one?

- Are there extra music stands and chairs that can be used?

- Does the set have any moving scenery pieces? Are they prominent to the scene? You may need to be creative when coming up with stand-ins

- Where will the rehearsal room/hall be located? Can you visit the space before planning on room setup and taping? Where are the bathrooms? Is there a kitchen or kitchenette that the cast and staff can use?

- Are there additional keys needed to get into spaces? Are you able to be in the office outside of office hours?

- Is there an office space for stage management to use? Is there printing? Stock supplies, such as spike tape, Post-its, steno pads, measuring tapes, First Aid?

- Will there be open WIFI at the rehearsal space or a hidden network for production?

- If it has not been decided already, what will the meal break between sessions look like? Will it be an hour or an hour and a half? Take into consideration the time of day rehearsals may be starting and ending. Are there a lot of food options in the area that can easily be picked up, or do people need to drive to pick something up?

- How's the tape supply? Will more spike and gaff tape need to be ordered for rehearsal? If so, be sure to have your requested colors, sizes, and quantities ready. (We will get into more detail regarding this in the next chapter).

These are only some of the many questions that may come up as you are preparing to go into your first week. The best kind of preparation before prep week is to familiarize yourself with the piece and know it backwards and forward. Once you arrive to start your contract, your time and energy will be spent on prepping your score and paperwork, as well as getting the room or hall set for rehearsal. In the next chapter, we will dive right into prepping for rehearsal and getting the room ready for rehearsal.

Rehearsal

And now the adventure begins! Weeks have been spent preparing and getting ready for the journey ahead. Time leading up to this moment was, for the most part, at a slower, more relaxed pace, but things will start to speed up very quickly. Unlike other rehearsal periods that could last anywhere from three weeks to a month before heading into tech, the average opera rehearsal period takes place in two to three weeks. Due to this accelerated pace, it is very important that you are very familiar with the score and music and go into rehearsal confident and ready.

In this chapter, we will review setting up the room and taping out the set for rehearsal, the responsibilities of the stage manager and assistants, and the different types of rehearsals.

SETTING UP THE REHEARSAL ROOM

TAPING OUT A SET

The first task at hand is to tape out the set based off of the ground plan. The ground plan is a bird's eye view of the set in the theater or performance space drawn to scale by the scenic designer. The scale can differ when working with different scenic designers (sometimes it is based on preference of the designer), so be sure to always ask if it is not labeled in the title block at the bottom of the drawing.

When taping out a set, you are replicating the ground plan on the floor of the rehearsal room with spike tape. Depending on the complexity of the set, this could take anywhere from a few hours to half a day's work. Because taping can be very tedious, the best way to save on time is to plot out, or measure out, all your points ahead of time. A few ways of doing this are in Vectorworks or AutoCAD, both well-known drafting programs, or the old fashioned way, with a scale ruler. Although the Vectorworks route could be faster, you would have to either own a license or have access to a computer that does. There is a measuring tool that can be used, and you can either place the measurements right on the ground plan or make a separate list for yourself to read from.

DOI: 10.4324/9781003047391-5

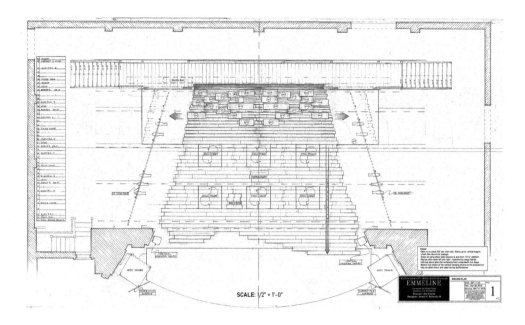

SCALE: 1/2" = 1'-0"

Figure 4.1   Ground plan for Boston University Opera Institute's production of *Emmeline* by scenic designer Jimmy Rotondo.

If access to Vectorworks is not available, ask the production manager or technical director for printouts of the scaled drawings (these will most likely be printed from a plotter, so they will be quite large) so you can plot out the points by hand. This cannot always be done right away, so be sure to ask for these with plenty of time to measure before taping.

Take a look at the *Emmerline* ground plan (Figure 4.1) and make note of the information you might need for taping. You'll notice by looking at the bottom of the drafting, as well as in the title block (the badge at the bottom corner of the drafting listing the designers, the show, and the plate number) that the scale is set to ½″, which means that is the side of the scale ruler you will use to measure out points. This should be the first piece of information you look for, and if you do not see it, ask your technical director or production manager. If you end up measuring the set in the wrong scale, it may end up being bigger or smaller than intended.

SUPPLIES NEEDED FOR TAPING

- **Architectural Scale Rule:** Check the plates for the scale that they are printed in. (Note: if you get plates from an international design team, be aware of the units and scales. The United States uses imperial units while many other countries use metric.)

- **At Least Two Measuring Tapes:** You will want them to be at least 50–100' long and be able to lay flat. This will be your "y" axis, which will lay vertically from downstage to upstage. Your second tape measure, which will be used for as your "x" axis (which will measure horizontally from your y-axis) should be at least 50' and retractable.

- **Gaff Tape:** This will be used to tape out the edge of stage and off-stage wings. Gaff is also sometimes used to tape out line sets or flying scenery with a straight line across the stage.

- **Spike Tape:** Never underestimate how much tape will be needed and always have a couple rolls of each color that will be used. The number of rolls and colors needed will depend on the size of the set and how much scenery there is to tape out. You will also use spike to rip off small pieces to mark measurements, which we call dots.

- **Sharpies:** Have a few black and silver pens on hand. Having a black sharpie with a chisel tip will also comes in handy when having to mark heights of scenery or labeling large pieces because it is easy to read.

Tips from the toolkit...

Need to tape a revolve or rotating set? Ask for a large piece of muslin or similar fabric. Measure it out and trim it to the size of the revolve and then tape right on it! Not only will it save the SM team time from having to tape out every location, but it will give you a head start on timing out the revolves within the scene!

QUESTIONS TO ASK BEFORE TAPING

The PSM will have to evaluate the size of the rehearsal space when determining the best spot and orientation for taping out. If a discussion has not been had already, check in with the director to get their preferences on the overall room setup and taping. Never assume that one thing is more important than another without speaking to them first. Nine times out of ten, they make taping a little bit easier for the SM team by cutting certain things.

- If the room is not as deep or as wide as the performance space, what should be minimized or altered? Should the stage have less depth, if you can have the width in one orientation over the other? Which is more important to the overall storytelling and what will translate easiest to the stage?

- Are there some scenery pieces that can have stand-ins rather than being taped out?

- If the set has multiple levels, would the director want the top level to be further upstage so both levels can be accessed at the same time?

Once you get into the space, you will want to survey the room. Here are some additional thoughts and questions to ask yourself:

- Locate (via measuring) the center of the room. Will it work with your current taping plan, or will you have to place the set slightly off center in order to get everything to fit?

- Locate the main door. Is it possible to set up the room so the door everyone will be entering from is in the back of the space, or behind the production table? This will be the least distracting if the director and conductor do not have to catch a glimpse of everyone entering the room while they are working.
- Are there other obstacles in the room that cannot be removed and need to be worked around, such as mirrors, structural columns, or beams?
- Is there space on either side of the room for the performers to make entrances and exits?
- Where will scenery pieces and large props live?
- Where will off- stage seating be? Is there a waiting room or green room where everyone will wait or leave their things? What about seating for guests or designers to drop by rehearsal?
- Where will the conductor be placed? Are they able to be centered in the room? Is there also space for the piano to be off to either side of the conductor?

CRASH COURSE ON TAPING

- Identify either the plaster line (the imaginary line running left to right on the upstage side of the proscenium) or edge of stage. Run your tape measure across the length of the stage/performance area. Once you have this down, you will use it to find center. Mark center with "T" in spike or gaff tape.
- Identify your center line (the imaginary line running from downstage to upstage in the center of the theater or performance space. Sometimes the set designer will already have this drawn on the ground plan). Run your tape measure to the furthest upstage measurement.
- Each point has two measurements and they are listed as (x,y).
- When listing measurements, I number each one and list them on the ground plan. This makes is easier to communicate with your team what point you are working on and when it is time to connect.
- The easiest and fastest way to tape out a set is with three people: one calling out the points, one working on the "y" axis and one working on the "x" axis. Once the measurement is located, a dot (small piece of spike tape) will be placed with the corresponding number from the ground plan written on it.
- Once all the points for a completed piece of scenery have been laid, connect the dots by number.
- If there are any doors or windows that open and may do so within action, be sure to tape those out and place music stands or something where the performer could perform the action.

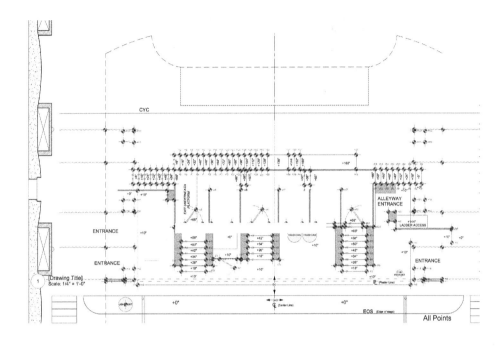

Figure 4.2 Ground plan for Brevard Music Center's production of *Street Scene* by scenic designer Bethanie Wampol Watson.

(B) Stoop #1 (DSR)

U#	Purpose	YCoord	VW X Coordinate	User 1
B1		5'-10"	-13'-4"	Note 1
B2		5'-10"	-9'-10"	Note 1
B3		6'-8"	-13'-4"	Note 1
B4		6'-8"	-9'-10"	Note 1
B5		7'-6"	-13'-4"	Note 1
B6		7'-6"	-9'-10"	Note 1
B7		8'-4"	-13'-4"	Note 1
B8		8'-4"	-9'-10"	Note 1
B9		9'-2"	-13'-4"	Note 1
B10		9'-2"	-9'-10"	Note 1
B11		10'	-13'-4"	Note 1
B12		12'	-13'-5"	Note 1
B13		10'	-9'-10"	Note 1
B14		12'	-9'-10"	Note 1
B15		6'-8"	-14'-4"	Note 1
B16		6'-8"	-8'-10"	Note 1
B17		12'	-8'-10"	Note 1

Figure 4.3 An excerpt of taping points for Brevard Music Center's production *Street Scene* that were done using Lightwright by lighting designer Tláloc López-Watermann.

Figure 4.4 Here is a completed taped out set of BMC's *Street Scene* taken from the catwalk. It was sharing the space with *Figaro* rehearsals, at the time the photo was taken, which is the reason for any half circles in purple spike tape that you see overlapping the stoops and houses.

Figure 4.5 Model of Brevard Music Center's production of *Street Scene* by scenic designer Bethanie Wampol Watson.

Tips from the toolkit…

Need to tape out a circle or half a circle? Grab a piece of string (tie line is preferred due to its stiffness) and cut it to the measurement of the radius of the circle. After putting down a spike for the center of the circle, place one end of the string on it. With one person holding one end at the center, the second person can place spikes to mark out the circle with the opposite end. Once the preferred marks are made, you can either leave the outline, or make it whole by connecting all the marks.

As heard on headset…

My first experience taping out a set was at my first summer stock. One of the biggest takeaways I learned from it was that it's just tape. It's all just a representation of the set, so don't stress if it's not exactly perfect. The singers will find it helpful, but it will never be as helpful as the real set. I think that when you go to tape out a set, you should always clarify with your TD what scale you'd like your ground plan to be at. In addition, even though you plot out your points ahead of time, always bring your ground plan and scale rule to the tape out, because 9 times out of 10, at least one of your points won't make sense and you'll want to go back to the ground plan for reference.

—Kayla Uribe, Freelance Stage Manager

Taping is always an interesting adventure. It can be tedious but is also a great time to bond with the team! I'm a person who loves puzzles and that is basically what taping is. You must find the points that make up the set and then you get to recreate it to a life-sized image using only dots (small pieces of spike tape) and spike tape. It's pretty amazing if you only have to do it once. One show I did had a massive set. We began to tape it out only to realize an hour in that the tape wouldn't stick to the floor. We tried everything to get it to stick; cleaning the floors again, weighing the tape down and even trying completely new rolls of tape. The floors ended up having to be replaced and we had to hold out a few days before we could tape out in that space. I learned after that debacle to always test the floors as soon as possible because taping the same set thrice is not a fun time.

—Jackie Mercer, Freelance Stage Manager

ADDING THE FINISHING TOUCHES

The location of the front of the room will revolve around the location of the conductor. The conductor stand and chair is always located at, or closest to, center [of stage] as possible. In a traditional space, the Maestro would be center in the pit. Now, if you are working in a non-traditional space, you should check in with your conductor as to where they want to be placed in the room. Do they want to start in the traditional spot down center and then move to their "performance spot," or do they want to be in their performance spot from the beginning, so the singers get used to looking in said directions? Once the location for the conductor has been set, next comes the location of the piano. Traditionally, the piano will be placed on the side of the baton. If you have not worked with the conductor before, send them a quick diagram (Figure 4.6) and ask them for their approval. Not only will they appreciate you asking them, but it will save you from having to move a piano on the first day of rehearsal.

Next comes the production table. Depending on where the piano is set up, the table can most likely be placed on the opposite side. Traditionally, from left to right you would have the SM, AD, and director. The director would ideally be placed at the end of the table closet to the conductor (Figure 4.7). If there is an assistant conductor, they will set themselves up behind, or close to the conductor, or even by the pianist. Next are the ASMs. Ideally, one would be setup with a music stand stage right, and one stage left. They would each have a prop table close by where props and rehearsal costume pieces are stored during rehearsal. With their music stands or just score in hand, they will move up and down the sides of the stage wherever entrances are made.

Figure 4.6 Music rehearsal setup for *The Barber of Seville* at Opera Columbus. Diagram produced by the author.

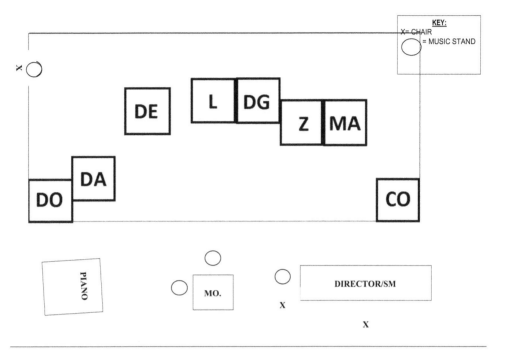

Figure 4.7 Rehearsal room setup for *Don Giovanni*, at Opera Columbus. All the singers were in their own individual vinyl towers, which we actually had in the rehearsal room from day 1. Diagram produced by the author.

HOSPITALITY TABLE

Slowly, we are seeing less and less hospitality tables, or companies are limiting them to hot water for tea and coffee. If a hospitality table does end up in the room, try to be strategic as to where it is placed. Like the water cooler, people tend to gather and chat when getting water or coffee. That being said, try placing it in the back of the room or in a corner that is as out of sight and ear shot of those working as possible. If snacks are being provided, or if someone brought things in to share, be sure to check allergies and food restrictions within the company. If your rehearsal does have a hospitality table, the task of keeping it up—making coffee, heating water, replenishing and keeping it clean—will fall under the PA or ASMs duties.

TYPES OF REHEARSAL

In opera, there are four different types of "rehearsals," all which you may end up encountering during your rehearsal period.

MUSIC REHEARSAL

Whereas in theater the first rehearsal tends to be table work or a table read, in opera the first day is dedicated to music. Music stands will be set up accordingly in front the conductor. This rehearsal is more or less the conductor's rehearsal. Depending on how the day is laid out, Maestro will either work through the piece with notes (stop and start) in one session and then do a full sing through during the second session, or try to fit both in one block. Although the stage management team is not directly needed for this session, they are great to have in the room to keep track of breaks, any lateness, or to answer questions Maestro may have. It also does not hurt to listen in to get a feel of the music and watch the visual cues that the singers may get or ask for from Maestro. These may be helpful when it comes to teching the show.

In their own words...

I adore collaborating with directors who know the music and know how to use it to create drama. That is always the most fun for me, because it can totally transform how I hear the music.

—Kamna Gupta, Conductor

Tips from the toolkit...

Seating for music rehearsals, just as for a table read, are more specific than random. Many singers will sit in the general area they think they should, depending on voice type and character. To avoid any confusion and to cut back on the musical chairs, tape place settings (either with singer or character names) on the front of the music stand. Singers sometimes tend to shift or move around depending on who is singing together in a certain duet or trio, but setting a starting location can be very useful when pairing names to faces. Having a cheat sheet for your conductor, such as a seating chart or a face page (headshot, performer name, and character name) will also be much appreciated by your conductor!

STAGING REHEARSAL

Staging rehearsals in opera for the most part, run the same way as they do in any theater-type rehearsal. This is the time the director is given to stage the show. Now, just because these are staging rehearsals does not mean that music rehearsal is over. It is not unusual for the conductor and/or director to request that they run through musically everything that will be worked on and staged during the session. This helps with repetition, as well as giving everyone the opportunity to fine-tune the small [musical] details. It does not hurt to ask early on if this is how the directing and music staff want to run staging rehearsals—music review around the piano then staging. If so, keep this in mind when scheduling each session, knowing that anywhere from 10 to 30 minutes may need to be put aside for music.

During staging rehearsals, singers may not always sing full out, but rather mark so they are not putting too much strain on their voice since sections and scenes may be rehearsed a number of times. When marking, a singer will either sing an octave lower, or sing in a half-voice to reduce their vocal load. Some things may be discovered during staging rehearsals that you were not able to plan for ahead of time such as where off-stage monitors might be needed, or if certain blocking needs to be altered so the singer can see the conductor. These are all good things to make note of and always ask about if they do not come up organically. The sooner you can pass this information on to the production manager, the more likely it is for it to happen and be ready for the beginning of tech.

In their own words...

The best collaborations I've had with SMs involved a mutual respect for each person's skills and responsibilities, and a recognition of and high regard for the ways in which we have to interact. I try to keep pace with the rehearsal but occasionally I am taking a note and don't hear where we're starting, and the same could be true if I'm paying close attention and the SM is dealing with another issue, so our ability to communicate quickly is essential. Together, the SM team and the pianist keep the rehearsal on track and save the director from being frustrated by not wasting any time. For this reason, it's helpful to know whether or not they can read music and/or recognize words in the language of the opera, because then I will know how to help them find a place or interpret the way they see and hear a score. I prefer when an SM tells me when to start playing, but it can be different for each person so it's important to determine that right away - then there's never a question as to who makes that call. I love it when an SM keeps track of the time and calls regular breaks. Directors get very involved in their process and will often forget to take a break, so it is essential for the stage manager to set up that structure from the first day. Each director is different, so obviously you need to create something that works for both of you, but as a pianist I am always really thankful for their leadership in that way.

—Eileen Downey, Rehearsal Pianist on the collaboration with Stage Managers

RECIT REHEARSAL

Recit or recitative (or recitativo in Italian) rehearsals may only be called if the opera you are working on has recits. Recitative can best be described as the narrative or dialogue parts of an opera, sung in the rhythm of ordinary speech with many words on the same notes. Rather than being unscored by a full orchestra, recit is usually accompanied by chords, and most commonly played by a harpsicord or piano forte. Sometimes recit can prove to be harder than singing a full aria and the conductor may ask to have a separate rehearsal just to review all the recit in the opera. Many times, recit rehearsals are scheduled ahead of time and sometimes they will need to be squeezed into the schedule. Similar to music rehearsals, although stage management might not be needed physically, it is always nice to be in the room to have an ear on the conversation between the singers and conductor. Not only can recit be some of the hardest music to sing, but it can also be very easy to get lost in your score if you are not paying attention. It usually goes by quickly, and there is no underscoring of music to look for to find your place again, so the more you hear it, and in the speed and style that the singer will be performing in, the more helpful it will be. Plus, you never know what may aid in future cuing!

Opera facts!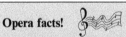

Recit is the closest opera and straight plays have come to intersecting, as the singer has near total control over the pacing and phrasing of the text! When a recit includes the orchestra, it becomes recit accompagnato, or accompanied recitative. With the addition of the orchestra, the singer has less freedom with the pacing, and coordination between singer, conductor, and orchestra becomes much more important. Unlike secco recitative (dry recitation), each recit accompagnato has a specific tempo and regular meter (also known as number of beats per measure).

Tips from the toolkit…

If the opera you are working on has recits and you do not see a dedicated recit rehearsal on the overview schedule, check with your production manager and conductor to see if they want to set time aside (if needed) on the schedule before it gets published. Often times, a conductor may request there be a recit warmup prior to the performance. These are normally scheduled 2–2 ½ hours before downbeat, depending on other calls. If a recit rehearsal is requested prior to the performances, be sure that wardrobe, hair, and makeup are aware because they may adjust calls on their end so everyone who is needed is available.

SITZPROBE

A sitzprobe (German for "seated rehearsal") is the first rehearsal where the singers will sing with the orchestra. This is one of the last rehearsals prior to moving into tech week. A sitzprobe either takes place in another hall or with the orchestra already in the pit and singers sitting on stage with music stands and their scores. As per tradition, singers usually dress up (more business casual than rehearsal casual) for music rehearsals. It is common that singers remain seated and stand up when they are about to sing. This rehearsal is run by the conductor and orchestra manager. There will be stopping and starting to work with the orchestra and singers. Sometimes, Maestro may not start at the beginning of the opera, but wherever they last left off in the orchestra read. These rehearsals are not usually supported by tech or backstage staff and only include those directly needed for the orchestra rehearsal.

WHO'S WHO IN THE ROOM

AND THERE'S A HIERARCHY?

There is an unspoken hierarchy that has been passed down through centuries of opera. Although it has mellowed out a bit in recent times, there are certain rehearsals that belong to the conductor, the staging director and the stage manager—basically, who can call a "hold" and stop a rehearsal. Although we are in the 21st century, there are some things that have stuck around. In the end, the team works together to put forward the best product possible. In order to do that, at times the captain of the ship will change.

Conductor: Also known as Maestro, which literally translates to "master" in Italian. Maestro is the courtesy title of the conductor. Although the title can be used for both male and female conductors, Maestra is also commonly used.

Rehearsals Maestro "Runs": Music rehearsals, sitzprobe, wandelprobe, first orchestra dress.

Director: The director is involved strictly with the staging and have very little to do with the music. That being said, the director can comment on the music and how it works dramatically with the staging.

Rehearsals the Director "Runs": Staging rehearsals, spacing/piano tech, final dress rehearsal (with conductor and stage manager).

Calling Stage Manager: The role of the stage manager alters a bit if there is an assistant director involved. Rather than keeping a detailed book, the stage manager keeps key blocking notations such as entrances, exits, transitions, and placements on stage (think what info is needed in tech or for lighting). The calling stage manager is also known as the PSM, or production stage manager.

Rehearsals the Stage Manager "Runs": Staging rehearsals, tech rehearsals, performances.

Assistant Director: In opera, the assistant director plays the role a stage manager might in theater. They are responsible for keeping the full blocking book, which will then stay with the company, or travel with the director if it is the production will be remounted in the future. In addition to taking the blocking and notes for the director, they put together cheat sheets for ensembles, make breakdowns, and construct the bow list.

Rehearsals the AD "Runs": Cover rehearsals (also known as put-ins) and sometimes large ensemble or children scenes.

Assistant Stage Manager(s): It is preferred to have two assistants, especially when ensemble and or supers are involved, but there are times where a company is only able to provide one ASM, or one full-time ASM and one part-time ASM. If that is the case, some of the ASM duties may spill over to the PSM. Sometimes, the ASM may assist the AD in cover rehearsals. The ASMs are involved with everything that the PSM is present for.

Production Assistants: PAs are not as common in the opera world as they are in the theater world. When the extra hands are available though, they float to where additional support for the production is needed, whether that be helping with scene shifts, standing in for an ASM or walking a role on stage during rehearsal. They do, however have some type of stage management background. PAs are also involved with everything that the PSM and ASMs are present for.

Other music staff in attendance:

Rehearsal Pianist: The rehearsal pianist plays all of your rehearsals, and sometimes will coach singers. They will play during the piano tech and, if there is not an assistant conductor, will conduct off-stage choruses. A rehearsal pianist, many times, will work in residence as part of the music staff with the company. If the opera has recit, many times, they are the ones playing the harpsichord or piano forte in the pit.

In their own words...

Describe your role as a rehearsal pianist:
My role as a rehearsal pianist is to be the closest sound to what the singers will hear from the stage once the orchestra is under them. It requires not only to know and understand the score very well, but also to be familiar with the full score and sometimes edit or add to what is printed in the piano reduction of the full score.

—Aurelian Eulert, Head of Music Staff at Opera Deleware

Assistant Conductor: No need to call them "assistant Maestro," they are simply called by their name. Most of the time, the assistant conductor has worked with the conductor or is their traveling assistant. The assistant conductor may conduct the early music rehearsals, as well as the early parts of staging if the conductor is in the middle of another concert or opera elsewhere. If there are any musical notes that come up in rehearsal, the assistant conductor will bring them to the conductor for final say. Once the conductor arrives in rehearsal, the assistant will stay on to take notes, or work/coach privately with a singer if needed. During tech, they take orchestra notes for the conductor by sitting right outside the pit. They may roam around the house (theater/auditorium) and listen for balance of the orchestra and singers on stage.

Chorus Master: The rehearsal pianist will sometimes double as the chorus master. The chorus master rehearses the chorus in advance of rehearsal so by the time staging begins, they are off book and familiar with their parts.

In their own words...

Describe your role as a chorus master.

In the simplest terms, my job as chorus master is to make sure that the singers learn and memorized their chorus music for the productions each season. It was my responsibility to ensure that everyone is well-prepared for the additional events and collaborations in which they were involved, and that all the pieces came together successfully.

—*Eileen Downey*

Composer and Librettist: You will most likely only have the composer and librettist in the room if you are workshopping a piece or working on a world premiere. Similar to working on a new play or musical, they are in the room to collaborate with the director, conductor, and performers. They may also make adjustments or changes after hearing the piece on its feet. Or, if a singer has a request about a note that needs to be sung or word changes, the composer and librettist can help make the change as long as it does not take away from the overall story.

IN THE ROOM

GETTING THE DAY STARTED

When preparing for the day, you want to give yourself and the rest of the stage management team enough time to prepare the space and get ready for rehearsal before the rest of the team and cast start to show up. Showing up early will give the SM team time to pull all scenery, props, and any stand-in pieces, set up for the rehearsal, and prep any offstage items that will be needed for the scene without having to rush. Nine times out of ten, once everyone starts to show up, your attention will then shift to getting them ready. You may be answering questions, making sure those called show up on time, and getting them into rehearsal costumes. Once the director, AD, and conductor have arrived, do a check-in with them to make sure the plan for the session has not changed.

RESPONSIBILITIES OF THE STAGE MANAGER IN THE ROOM

- Keep track of entrances, exits and overall action on stage
- Take more detailed blocking if NOT working with an AD
- Call hold to stop staging or singing
- Call breaks
- Keep the room on schedule

Blocking

When an AD is present, they will take more detailed blocking in what will become the archived book of the show. As for the stage manager, when trying to figure out what type of blocking they should be taking, ask yourself:

1. *What information is important for lighting?* Placements on stage, and when/where people move.
2. *What information is needed when putting together deck paperwork?* Where furniture starts on stage. Where it moves to.
3. *What information is needed for possible costumes or other quick changes?* Where do people enter and exit. Also, keeping track and taking timings for quick changes.

Essentially, the stage manager should take down any notes that would, at some point be needed when putting together paperwork and for calling the show. As for detailed blocking, unless you are doing cover or put-in rehearsals, you do not *have* to take down notes like "Cassio picks up the mug with his right hand." Rather, noting that at a specific moment Cassio picks up the mug is sufficient. The AD on your production will stay on top of these specifics.

Calling Hold

There have been many times in the rehearsal room where the director asks to stop, and no one is able to hear them because they are going up against a piano and a full operatic voice(s). Or the director might be up on their feet walking through the scene with a singer and they ask to stop, but the conductor is unable to hear them over the piano. In these types of situations, it is up to the stage manager to grab everyone's attention to stop. To do this, either put your hand up with a "stop" gesture (use the hand closest to the pianist and conductor) and in a

Figure 4.8 (a–d)   An example of an AD's blocking book for *La Bohème*. Notice how she numbers each piece of blocking and then places it in the score, similar to how blocking would be taken for a musi-cal or play. Courtesy of Cara Consilvo. *(Continued)*

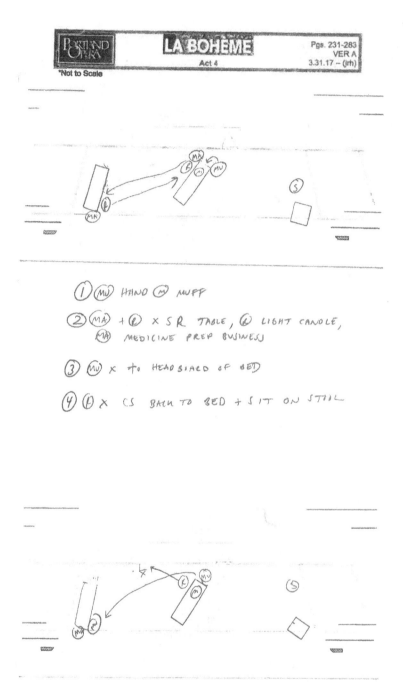

Figure 4.8 (a–d)   (Continued)

279

CP 115494

Figure 4.8 (a–d)   *(Continued)*

loud and clear SM voice call "hold please." It is sometimes helpful for the stage manager to stand up as well. That way, there is movement that the conductor and/or pianist will catch out of the corner of their eye. The conductor will then put up a similar hand gesture for the pianist that will stop the music entirely as well as indicate to the singers to stop singing.

Once the necessary notes are given, it might be up to the stage manager to get the room started again. If the director is not looking at their score, they may just give a placement, or describe a piece of staging that they want to see again (*let's go back to Zita handing off the will*). The conductor may not always know exactly where in the music that happens, so it is up to the stage manager to give a placement to the conductor (this could be with rehearsal letters or numbers, or with a vocal line). After checking in with the room and the assistant stage managers, the stage manager will make eye contact with the conductor and simply say, "thank you Maestro," which will indicate it's time to begin.

Tips from the toolkit...

There may be different scores being used in the room. For an example, the pianist, director, AD, and stage management may be working out of the piano vocal score, whereas the conductor is working out of the orchestra score. If that is the case, you may have to give both the PSM and rehearsal letter/number when picking up in the middle of a piece. You may also need to let the singers know as well since they may not necessarily have a score in front of them. This can easily be announced as such: "We will pick up at rehearsal 4 (can also be referred to as big number 4), 73/2/1, 2 bars before Ernesto's *Cer-che-ro.*" Although, you are saying the same thing three different ways, it will ensure that everyone in the room will be starting in the same place.

BREAKS

Rehearsal sessions typically run three-hours long so one, twenty-minute break will be taken halfway through, roughly an hour and ten minutes to an hour and a half in. Depending on the overall temperature of the room, the director might decide to break that up into two ten-minute breaks. You have a little more room to play with when working on a non-AGMA (American Guild of Musical Artists—the union that many opera singers, choristers, stage managers, and directors are a part of) contract, such as with a regional or smaller opera company, and can adjust the breaks easily. If you are working under an AGMA contract, be sure to read over the company's agreement because they can be very strict and failure to follow these rules might not end well for the stage manager.

Tools from the toolkit…

There truly is an unspoken art form to calling breaks! After a few days with the team, you will start to pick up on how people work in the rehearsal space. If someone wants to go back and run a section of the scene that is 15-minutes long and you see that there are 10-minutes left until the break, try suggesting that you break early and then run the scene. Or if you see that it is time for a break but notice that the director or conductor have about a minute left of notes, or is in the middle of a thought, let them finish and then call it. Take the temperature of the room and the rehearsal at hand, and always be open with the director or AD with time. Everyone will soon fall into a rhythm, and it will be a lot easier to call. You may even be lucky and get a director who is just on top of when breaks should happen!

KEEP THE ROOM ON SCHEDULE

Keeping everyone on schedule is sometimes easier said than done. One thing you should remember is that although a schedule was set, occasionally it takes more time than everyone anticipated to stage a specific scene or to work and run music. Maybe the scene is a bit difficult, whether it be musically, the subject or staging-wise. Maybe the singer is having a slow start. If you happen to be running behind in a session, look at what was scheduled for the rest of the day as well as, the following few days and come up with a few different options as to how the extra time can be spent while still staying on the projected overview schedule. Then have a quick chat with your director or AD and present the options you came up with. Anticipation is everything and being able to sense the direction and speed in which the room is moving towards will only strengthen you as an opera SM.

RESPONSIBILITIES OF THE ASSISTANT STAGE MANAGEMENT IN THE ROOM

- Cue singers on stage
- Take down blocking: entrances, exits, and placements of choristers/supers
- Setting/resetting if a scene is being repeated, or if the director is moving on
- Stand-in or walk roles if singers are not available
- Keep track of attendance
- Keep track of furniture and prop placements on stage and spike if and when needed

WHY DO I HAVE TO CUE SINGERS ON STAGE?

In "traditional" opera, and still in many European houses, a singer could be brought in to sing Iago in Berlin and then Don Giovanni in Sydney a week later. The singer may not necessarily be present in any or all of the rehearsal sessions prior to moving onto stage, and may only get one or two staging sessions with the director or AD, so it is the responsibility of stage management to guide them onto and off stage.

HOW DO I CUE A SINGER ON STAGE?

The key is to make eye contact with the singer you are cuing. Put your arm straight up as a standby. Personally, I like to either mouth or whisper the words "stand by" so that they hear me as I connect with them. Sometimes, they are waiting to go right on stage and be in front of the ASM or only see them from the corner of their eye. When it is time for them to "GO" drop your arm down. The point is to be low-key, as to not take the singer out of their zone before going on stage, but also clear so there is no confusion as to what you are telling them to do.

Figures 4.9 and 4.10 are examples of how to cue a singer on stage, demonstrated ASM by Sarah Stark.

Figure 4.9   An ASM will first give the singer a stand by, by putting their arm up.

Figure 4.10   When it is time to go, the ASM will either drop their arm or point at the singer to GO.

HOW DO I KNOW WHEN/WHERE TO PLACE MY STAND BY AND WHEN TO GIVE THE "GO"?

You want to place your standbys a few measures prior to when the action happens (whether this is a singer entering or cuing a transition). This may change depending on the tempo of the piece, how long it takes to travel onto stage, or when they may begin to sing. Cues may also get altered once you move into the performance space from where they were in the rehearsal room. Do not feel bad if at the last minute during tech the director or conductor asks for an entrance to be moved drastically. There are some things that cannot always be anticipated. Use your judgement when placing standbys. If the singer feels that the standby is too long or too short, they will likely say something.

Tips from the toolkit...

Sometimes it is pretty dark backstage, so how are singers supposed to see you? A tip that I took from an assistant conductor who was conducting an off-stage chorus was to use a glow stick! He was using it as a baton

> *so everyone could see without needing much light. After that, I started using one when cuing large groups, or multiple groups from different entrances (I would have two, and sometimes in different colors). The glow sticks would allow me to position myself so everyone could see my hand up and would go as soon as they saw the glow stick drop. Rather than having to purchase a new glow stick for each performance, I have turned to a reusable/battery-powered glow stick, which can be found either with camping supplies, or flashlights.*
>
> *—DR*

HOW DO I LIST STAND BYS AND "GOS" IN MY SCORE? WHAT ABOUT EXITS?

It is just as important to list your exits as well as your entrances in your score and what said singer or group enters and exits with so you can keep track of props and costume pieces. An ASM might need to assist a singer or group off stage due to darkness, or they may be walking off into light being shone in their face. Or, there may be a lot of props and scenery in the same wing that they are exiting in, and you need to assist them getting off while not bumping into anything. How an ASM decides to list them in their score is completely up to them. Some people use Post-it notes, others use Post-it flags. Some write the entrances and exits right into their score and circle or highlight them with different colors.

Figure 4.11 shows one example using a 1.5 × 2 size Post-it. This shows an entrance and exit that takes place during the first scene of *I due Figaro*. You will see that the ACTION (either the entrance or exit) is abbreviated and listed in the upper left corner. The WHERE is also abbreviated and listed in the upper right corner. And the WHAT is listed in the middle. This includes who, and any props or costumes that they enter with. What is nice about listing

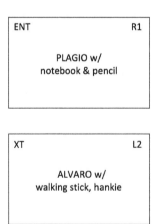

Figure 4.11   Example of how to write out an entrance on a Post-it.

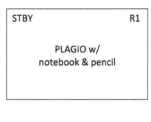

Figure 4.12 Example of how to write out a standby on a Post-it.

any props or costume pieces (such as a hat or hankie) that they should be entering or exiting with is that it reminds the ASM to do a quick check and if they do not see these items, they can either have someone fetch them (have the SM page wardrobe/props/hair and makeup over the PA system), or they can remind the singer that they are forgetting necessary props or costume pieces for their upcoming scene.

You can also use this way of listing your stand bys (Figure 4.12) and just have a simple arrow or other type of marking in your score for the GO. Although it is not necessary to have standbys listed in your score for the opposite side of the stage, it is, however, a good idea to note them. What if something were to happen and you need to fill in, or you have to track something over to the other side and need a quick reference as to when it was used next? Just as the PSM has everything listed in their book, it is also a good idea that the ASMs have both tracks listed in theirs.

Tips from the toolkit…

To help differentiate between what entrances and exits pertain to my specific side of the stage, I like to use pastel and florescent Post-Its. I use the pastels for the opposite side of the stage and the fluorescents for mine. That way, the ones that I need stand out, whereas the others are there, yet "in the background."

—DR

ASM BLOCKING

On top of entrances and exits, ASMs will want to keep placement diagrams of choristers, supers, and/or large scenes. This is where name tags come in handy!

Similar to how you would take blocking down by character name, with the choristers, you can take down their initials on a full-page ground plan/mini. Have a clipboard and many copies of each mini available. As the director places them on stage, jot down their placements. Do not be afraid to move around, whether it is along the sides, or to the front of the room, in order to notate this information. If you are careful to not get in the way of the actual staging, no one will say anything. To save on time, each ASM can take down their half of the stage and then combine their notes at the end of rehearsal. If the director is moving on before you can grab everyone's placements, snap a quick picture, and then transfer the information to the mini post-rehearsal, or check in with the AD or PSM to see if they have the info you are missing.

RESETTING DURING REHEARSAL

Whether you are the PSM or the ASM, the ability to multitask is the key to success. You will always want to keep an ear open as to what is always going on everywhere in the room and try to anticipate when things are going to happen, such as resetting the current scene, running a full section, or moving ahead. You will have a better feel of the overall flow of the room, as well as how the director works after a few days of being in room with them. If you know that the director likes to review after giving notes, try resetting while they are finishing their notes. That way, everything will be ready to go as soon as the performers, director, and conductor are ready. Or, if it sounds like the room maybe moving on to the next scene, start to gather the pieces needed and be ready to jump on stage to change or move furniture and props. Nothing makes a director happier than not having to stop the overall flow of rehearsal!

Tips from the toolkit...

Think outside the box!
Sometimes it is discovered in the moment that a character has or needs a certain prop. If this is the case, think outside of the box to see if something could be made as a stand- in for the time being. Many times, there is something in the SM kit or another prop that isn't being used that can be manipulated to become a new item. In Act II of *Don Pasquale*, Norina is pulling petals off of a flower as she contemplates her love for Ernesto. The original staging just called for her to longingly stare at the flower rather then pull the petals off, so only one fake flower was provided by props. My assistant was quick to her feet and was able to make a temporary flower out of Post-its (Figure 4.13) and a plastic coffee stirrer! Not only was Norina able to pull them off during her aria, it could easily be reassembled if we wanted to run the scene again!

Figure 4.13   Impromptu flower made in rehearsal by ASM Jackie Mercer.

STAND-IN OR WALKING A ROLE

If the director is staging a scene with principals only but there are others involved in the scene, the ASM(s), Pas, and sometimes the AD may be asked to stand in as the other bodies on stage so the director can get a clear stage picture. Maybe a scene that is being rehearsed has supers who interact with the singer. Or a singer was delayed in their arrival. Regardless, of delays or schedule conflicts, the director will stage the scene as long as they have the principal players in order to stay on schedule. Not only does standing in keep you active in the room and occasionally get you out of your seat, but it is also a great way to learn the opera! Don't worry, you will not be expected to sing the role, or do all of the detailed staging. But having a body standing in place or moving around within the scene will not only help the staging team better visualize full picture, but it will also help the principals in that scene have someone to play off of. Although walking a role in rehearsal may not be the highest thing on an ASMs list, it will pay off come tech time when they have to light walk or assist with light walkers. What better way to learn a show than to be a part of it!

> **As heard on headset…**
>
> *I was assisting on the world premiere of Songbird, a new adaptation of Offenbach's La Pérochole at The Glimmerglass Festival. The opera took place over the span of one day in a bar during Mardi Gras in New Orleans. It was a fairly prop heavy show and my task as the props ASM was to figure out an organized way to preset all props behind the bar as well as, track the types and number of drinks that were used throughout the show so the props department could make them. Two days into staging, we found out that our Mastrilla, the bartender, was having travel issues and would end up missing most of the first week. Since she was onstage the entire time and interacted with everyone, it was clear that we needed a stand-in behind the bar, so I ended up doing it. Not only did it help me figure out how to best pre-set and where behind the bar, but it also helped with drink tracking since I was the one making and serving them!*
>
> *—DR*

IF THERE IS ONLY ONE ASM

Sometimes, you may run into a situation where you have only one ASM. If this is the case, the PSM (at least for rehearsals) will stand in and pick up any loose ends. This may include cuing singers from the front of the room or lending a hand when changing out furniture and props, all while keeping on top of the PSM duties of taking blocking, rehearsal notes, and keeping track of where in the score everyone is. This is yet another example of why knowing the score and the music like the back of your hand prior to staging is so important. Once the SM team has an idea of how the room flows, they can collectively decide the best way to divide and conquer.

In the next chapter, we will take a deeper dive into all the paperwork that the team should be working on to prepare for tech, as well as touch a bit more on the responsibilities of the assistant director and the paperwork that they assist in creating.

Rehearsal Paperwork

In this chapter, we take a closer look into rehearsal paperwork, and what the team should be working on in preparation for tech. As mentioned before, not everything you see in this chapter is required for each show since the type of show will dictate the type of paperwork you will prepare. Paperwork might also have to be altered if you are performing in a less traditional space, or at a site-specific venue. You may ask, why is stage management in charge of generating so much paperwork? In many theater tracks, some departments will spearhead a lot of their own paperwork; in opera, however, the SMs and AD are the ones who do most of the legwork. It all comes down to time! In many regional companies, four to five weeks is the average time from start to finish. Due to this limited amount of tech time, it is the stage management team who will ultimately know the show the best and will be able to produce the most useful paperwork.

STAGE MANAGEMENT PAPERWORK

DAILY SCHEDULE AND ITS COMPONENTS

Opera daily schedules (dailies) are not that much different than your average theater rehearsal schedule. They list the goals for the day, the performer's call time(s), fittings, and any other related calls. A singer's voice takes time to warm up, even just for rehearsal, so the earliest a session may start is 10:00 or 11:00 am. Typically, there are two, three-hour sessions in a day with the meal break spanning an hour to an hour and a half in length. If the show has a chorus, then a third session is added in the evening after the dinner break, which principals may or may not be called to attend.

    Some companies, most often summer festivals and a number of large organizations, will have a designated scheduler, so the only responsibility of the stage manager is to give them the next day's schedule. Once all the information is gathered from all the departments, the scheduler will distribute the master daily schedule. Although having a scheduler around to piece together the daily is great, it is not the norm at many companies; most often, it is the stage manager

DOI: 10.4324/9781003047391-6

who will create and distribute it. Below are a few examples (Figures 5.1-5.3) of different styles of dailies. If the company already has a template that they use, all you have to do is update the general information (such as the title of show, date, location) and add in the necessary calls. Remember, the goal is to produce the simplest and easiest-to-read schedule rather than something pretty and decorative. If time is needed to decipher it, your schedule is too complicated.

Tips from the toolkit…

With some contracts, soloists or principals are permitted to work only six hours each day, which can be complicated when scheduling sessions that involve both principals and chorus, who normally have day jobs and are only available nights and weekends. If this is the case, be sure to have a strategic plan to present to the director. If you have an AD on your team, they can help with this scheduling puzzle.

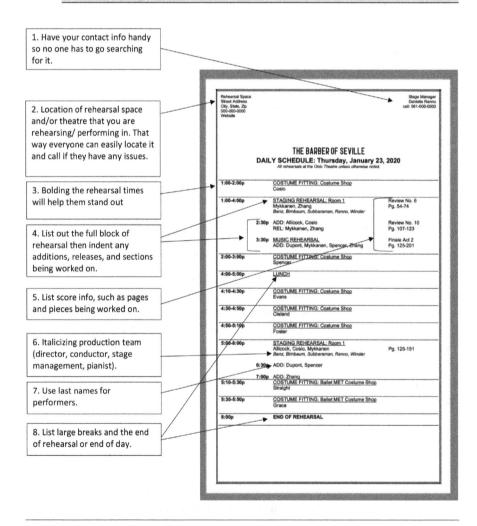

Figure 5.1   Example A: A daily schedule for *The Barber of Seville* created by the author.

List the Stage Manager's Contact Info: Of course, it will be easy to find the stage manager's info in their email signature, but when a performer needs to contact you to let you know they are lost, having issues getting into the building, parking, or going to be late, a quick phone call is always the easiest and quickest way to solve an issue. Although not shown here, it does not hurt to add the ASM's contact info in case the SM is unavailable or cannot get to their phone due to rehearsal.

Provide Location of Rehearsal Space and Theater: You can never go wrong with repetition. Adding the address to the rehearsal space and theater on your schedule will make it easier for performers to find the location. Welcome emails, which usually have such information listed, tend to get buried or lost in a sea of emails, whereas a daily schedule tends to be easier to access and closer at hand. This is also great to have if a guest or donor happens to be dropping by.

Bold Rehearsal Times: Important things that you are trying to communicate on a daily need to stand out. **Bolding** and <u>underlining</u> things will help with that. These things will help draw the eye toward important details.

List out Your Full Block, then Indent the Details: Think of this schedule like an outline. Identify the topic, such as STAGING REHEARSAL, then add in your points that support the topic, such as what the details of the staging rehearsal are. Will additional singers or performers be called within the full block? Will people be released when moving on to another section? This will also help make your blocked sessions easy to break down, while still listing all the necessary detail.

List Score Info, Such as Pages and Pieces Being Worked on: I find that listing this information off to the side rather than within the center column makes the schedule less muddy to read. Not only does this help with the overall symmetry and design, but it also lends a hand with breaking up information, so it is easy to process. It gives the overall schedule more of a "reading a book" feel. Start with your WHEN (time), then move to the center with your WHO (who is expected in the rehearsal), and WHAT (what will be worked on), and continue to the right with the DETAIL of the WHAT.

List the Production Team on Your Schedule: Although the production team knows when and where they need to be, it is always nice to list them on the daily as a courtesy. It also gives the rest of the cast and team an idea what is being worked on. If music staff is not listed for the first hour and only the director and AD are, then the singer knows that they may just be focusing on staging before introducing music and singing.

How to List Performers: Traditionally, names were listed in the formal with *Mr.* or *Ms.* before the last name. We are slowly getting away from the formal, and simply just using last names. This also avoids any assumptions on personal pronoun preferences. Some companies do have a preference as to how singers and staff members are referred to, so be sure to check.

List Large Breaks and End of Rehearsal/End of Day: There is nothing
more satisfying then seeing when a break or end of day is coming up!
Listing these breaks in rehearsal will also help other team members and
performers know when a space might be available, or when they could get
in contact with say, the director or conductor.

Figure 5.2 is an example of another format for a daily schedule. Overall, it
carries the same information, but is laid out differently. Here are a few key
differences:

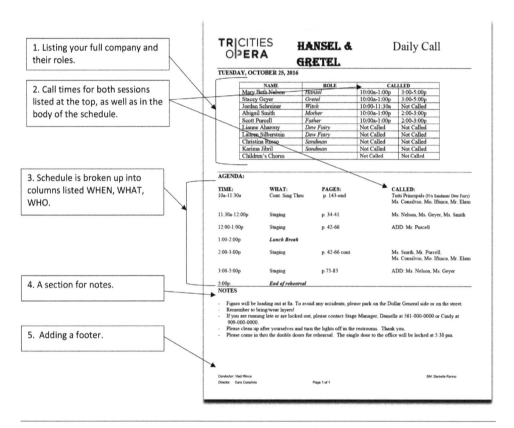

Figure 5.2   Example B: A daily schedule for *Hansel & Gretel* created by the author.

List the Full Company at the Top: There are a few things that are very
helpful about this. First, it gives the company and team a full cast
list with roles. This is nice to reference, especially in the early days of
rehearsal. You will notice in the extreme right a column titled "called."
This is also a nice reference for performers to see when they are going to
be called during each session. Overall, think of the top half of this daily
as the overall summery of the day, with the bottom half giving the full
details of the day.

Agenda: Whereas the first example was laid out in an outline, this example is
laid out in columns, broken up in WHEN, WHAT, and WHO. Since this

is the most important part of the schedule, you want it to be clear and easy to read. You will notice the symmetrical aspect of the agenda, which again, is easy on the eye.

Notes: It is always nice to have notes added onto your dailies if there is room. A lot of times, we put our daily notes to the company in the body of the daily schedule email. Again, repetition can never hurt. What if someone just skims through the email and jumps right to the agenda to see what they are called for, then they run into potentially missing important information.

Adding a Footer: One thing that can be useful in footers are page numbers. Rarely, the schedule spills onto two pages. But if it helps to spread information out so everything is not jammed together on one page, or to avoid a page break in the middle the schedule or notes section, use the second page. Adding in page numbers will remind everyone reading the schedule (especially if they are not used to getting multiple pages) that there may be additional information on the following page. The footer can also be a good spot to add in SM/ASM contact info.

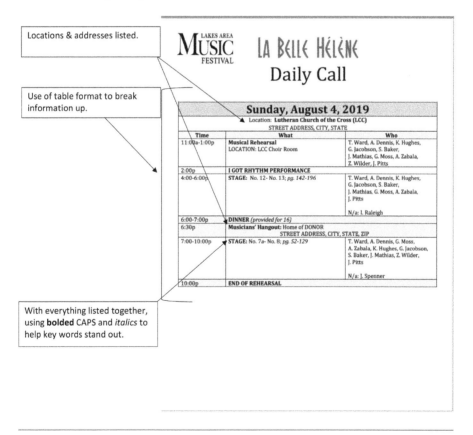

Figure 5.3 Example C: A daily schedule for *La Belle Hélène* created by the author.

Out of the three examples provided, Figure 5.3 is probably the simplest, but it holds just the same amount of information. Here are a few things to point out:

List Locations When They Change: In some situations, you may find that rehearsals happen in different rooms, or even buildings. Similar to the other examples, the location of the rehearsal space is present somewhere on the rehearsal schedule. You will notice some of the location acronyms in parentheses; these are also listed to match with the overview schedule. If you are going to use shorthand or acronyms for locations, be sure to list or share a key with the company so they do not run into any trouble reading and understanding the schedule.

Use a Table Format with Visible Borders and Lines: This layout was chosen for this production because it was the easiest and cleanest way to display multiple events going on during the day. There are events displayed that were not always pertaining to staging rehearsal but did involve some of the singers.

SCHEDULE TIPS

Daily schedules are always something you want to get out ASAP, but many times this must wait until the end of rehearsal.

* Draft up the next day's schedule prior to the current day's rehearsal with what was projected to be worked on from the overview.

* Try to check in with your director and AD (and conductor if anything is music specific), mid-day or during a break.

* Do a final check-in with everyone at the end of rehearsal. Updating throughout the day should make any final edits quick and easy before it gets sent off.

* Check in with the production manager regarding who should be on your distribution list. Sometimes the company likes to include additional people who are not typically on your everyday list, such as board members, volunteers, and other guests.

* Always have someone on the team, whether it be the AD or ASM, proof it before it goes out!

REHEARSAL REPORTS

As mentioned before, some companies may have standard templates whereas others may be open to the stage manager using their own. Regardless of what the template may look like, the information that is put in it will be the same. If a company does not have a preference, make sure to ask them if there is any additional information they would like added, for an example, a Building & Facilities or Front of House section.

Although the rehearsal report will come from the PSM, it is very much a "group project." The full team should come together to give their notes and observations so all the necessary information can be compiled and sent to the production and design teams. Although most notes will filter through the PSM throughout the day, on occasions, the ASMs might have some additional notes, especially when it comes to how props and costume pieces are used or what is needed for specific staging or singer comfort, that the PSM didn't catch. Maybe a singer mentioned that the addition of a pocket for their letter would be helpful, or that the cane slides and needs some traction added to the bottom. Many of these types of notes will come up in the moment, or as they are waiting offstage to go on, and it most likely will be said to the ASM closest to them.

If possible, it is always a good idea to try to catch the directing staff before they leave for the day to quickly run down the notes from the day. This way, there will not be any surprises when they read the report that night. Also, it's a great way to weed through notes that were taken throughout rehearsal, as well as, get additional clarification on things. For example, maybe a note was taken about a prop, but is no longer applicable because the issue was solved with alternate staging. Or a note was given quickly while resetting for a scene, but you are not clear on what exactly was being asked. This should not take more than 10-minutes, and your director will appreciate the check-in.

Tips from the toolkit...

Some SM teams are starting to use Slack, a communication platform available for most smart phones and desktops with the app. Although this should never replace face-to-face communication, SM teams are using this as a SM text hub. Since you can create multiple channels, there can be a "Notes for Reports" channel, or a "General SM" channel, or even an "Off Topic" channel. What is great about using Slack over email is that conversations do not get lost or missed as easily in chains. If you have a specific question or comment for someone on the team, all you need to do is tag them directly and they will get a notification.

Here are some "report starters" per section to get those juices started. To ensure certain notes stand out, use key words such as ADD, CUT, and FYI. As with the daily schedule, be sure to have an ASM proof the report before it is sent out. Figures 5.4 and 5.5 are two rehearsal report examples.

Tips from the toolkit...

It's a nice touch to acknowledge when new things are brought into the room. A simple thank you shows appreciation and recognition for the work that everyone is putting in. It also just feels good to get a little shout out from time to time!

General Notes

General notes can sometimes be the hardest section to write, but I find it to be the most informative and helpful. It does not need to be very long, just a few sentences summarizing the day.

Why is this important? You want those who are not in the room to be and feel included. This is also the one section where you can get a little more personal with your audience. Instead of reporting questions and facts, which tend to be more straight forward, in this section, talk *to* your audience.

- Always remember who your audience is. Is the report going to board members on the distribution list? Younger audiences? Limit inside jokes and watch your language. Avoid the work like if it is not used to describe something. Always use punctuation. Avoid "text message language."
- How was rehearsal? What was covered? Did you get further ahead or fall behind from what was projected to be completed before end of day?
- Any short or fun anecdotes?
- Were there any accidents? Injuries? Be careful with this one. If it is too personal, do not put it in a report. Mention that there was an incident and that details will be emailed separately to those who need to know. Avoid too many details if not needed. Was an accident report filed? Was the accident due to a scenic element/prop/costume/staging?
- Was there a run through? What was the run time?
- Have there been schedule changes or updates?
- Are there any upcoming special events or PR events?
- Were there any special guests at rehearsal?
- Will an upcoming rehearsal be closed? This may be due to content or material that needs to first be worked with only those directly involved. Give everyone notice.

Properties

- Was anything added that was not originally on the prop inventory?
- Has something been cut?
- Is there dancing/walking/standing on any furniture or set piece that was not previously discussed?
- Does anything get thrown? Roughly handled?
- Is a specific size/thickness of a prop needed? Always add in dimensions. Include this under scenery if it applies.
- If a prop is being added, include as much detail as possible. How does it get used? Was a rehearsal prop or stand in used? What was it? Is a specific color needed/necessary? Include under scenery if necessary.

- Does a costume get used as a prop? Include under costumes if it applies.

- Will a prop/furniture piece need to be preset in a specific area? Visual aids are always helpful for specifics, so if a picture can be added, do so.

- Are chairs getting stood on? Thrown? This is important especially if the set/props/furniture are rented. Include under scenery as well.

- Mention if something specific was labeled (a cup that gets drunk from or thrown, or a chair that serves a special purpose or is stood on). DON'T USE SPIKE TAPE. Use Post-its or paper only. Spike tends to leave residue or pull paint.

- Will there be any eating or drinking? Are there any allergies? Include this under costumes as well.

- Are there any consumables? This involves food, but also anything that gets destroyed. Paper/letters? Breakaway props?

- Does something need to be worked on? If a prop is not being used for some time, let the props department know. If they need to take it, let them know where it is being left and when it is needed back in rehearsal.

- If rehearsal props or dead props can be struck, let props know. Start a pile or bin, separate from the rehearsal/show props so the wrong items are not being struck.

- If props have been numbered (via prop master request,) always include the number when referring to it in the report.

- Always acknowledge new props/furniture. Don't forget to say thank you!

Scenic

- Was a new discovery made with the current set?

- Are any or additional handles needed?

- Will there be crawling on the floor? Include this under costumes.

- Is there dancing/walking/standing on any furniture or set that was not previously discussed?

- Do doors or windows slam?

- Do doors need catches?

- Do doors or windows need to stay open on their own?

- Does an actor need to get somewhere quickly? Do they need to run up a flight of stairs? Will there be extensive running or jumping on platforms? Are more railings needed somewhere for safety? Will any of this involve costumes?

- Does an actor with a large skirt need to get through a small opening or run up and down stairs which was not previously discussed? Include under costumes if necessary.

- How do things move? Will sliders or specific casters be needed?
- Has a singer been staged to interact with a piece of scenery that was not originally discussed?
- Will singers be taking part in scene changes?
- If you (the SM), director or singer have any questions on how scenery pieces moves or operates, you can either list them in the report or send a separate email to the technical director, including the designer and production manager.

Lighting

Lighting is one of those sections where you may need to think outside the box when it comes to what may or may not be applicable. Many times, notes that may come up for scenic may also need to be brought to the LD's attention.

- Are there practical lighting fixtures (referred to as practicals)? Lamps? Overhead lights? Will they need to be operated on stage? Do they need to fade? How do they need to operate? Has this already been discussed or is it new?
- Are there any specific cues that the director mentioned? The timing of a cue? Should it be a bump or fade? Should it time out to music? Often times, these specifics are not discussed heavily during rehearsal, but if it does come up, it helps to give a heads up to the designer.
- Have specials and positions been mentioned?
- Will a prop be electrified? Include this under props if necessary.
- Time of day notes from director?
- Will there be any quick changes on stage?
- Have there been any color changes, regarding props/scenic/costumes?
- Will anyone be traveling into the audience/off stage? Bring this to the house manager's attention as well.
- Is light needed somewhere else besides on stage?
- Are any cue lights needed? Where? On the set? Off stage? Rail? Include usage. If you are in a traditional theater with an orchestra pit, you will definitely want one down there to cue the orchestra tune. Include under scenic and production management as well.
- Are there candles? Torches? Live fire? How long will there be live flame? Include under props/costumes/scenic if needed, as well as production management. The production department may want to weigh in due to facility health and safety rules.
- Are there special effects? Strobe/dry ice/haze? Smoking? Does it need to come from a specific area/side of the stage? Include under scenic as well as costumes if it applies.

- Will a singer be standing on something? This may affect how they are lit. Will the LD need this information because it was not previously discussed?

Costumes, Hair and Makeup (HMU)

Often times, hair and makeup will have its own section from costumes on the report. This will limit notes from getting lost or unseen if they are meant to go to two different departments. If the designer is the same for both costumes and hair and makeup, ask them if they have a preference. Even though the designer may be the same, the crews and supervisors may not.

- Is there dancing/walking/standing on any furniture or scenic piece that was not previously discussed?
- Are knee pads needed or being used? Include who is wearing them and when, as well as the action in case it affects the costume.
- Are hankies needed? Are they dressing or will they be used? Will they get thrown? Swung? Do they need to be a specific size? Do they need to be washed? Are they touching someone's face? Never use a hankie or costume piece that touches someone's skin on multiple people. Always label them in rehearsal and mention this in the report. This may need to be under props as well.
- Will the choreography affect the costume? Think of skirts/tumbling/climbing or even being thrown around.
- Are there quick changes? Where will they happen? How much time is needed? Do costumes need to be rigged? Will a dresser be needed? Will zippers or velcro be needed? Does someone need to undress on stage? Will a singer be helping another singer get dressed? Is a quick-change booth needed backstage? Depending on the house crew (if they are union or not), the request of a quick change booth might fall under props or scenic. Include production management as well, and they can also help facilitate where this info should go.
- Think of shoes: heel size, how quickly do they need to come on and off? Are grips needed on the bottom for dancing?
- Will a necklace or any type of jewelry need to be placed on a singer on stage? What kind of clasp is needed? Does it need to be quick rigged, or will there be time to put it on? This may fall under props as well.
- Did a rehearsal piece rip or need to be washed? If it is being dropped off in the shop, include this and specific details on where it will be left.
- Is anyone going to be barefoot? Will off stage slippers be needed? Include this under scenic if it applies.
- Do costume pieces need to be preset? On stage? Within another prop? Include this under props if it applies.

- Will costume pieces be thrown/pulled/tugged?
- Are singers staged to swap costume pieces, such as capes, hats, or jackets? If this is something common to the piece, then costumes most likely already knows about it. But, if this is a new discovery from rehearsal, they should be made aware.
- Are additional pockets needed? Include placement, size, and what they are needed for. If a prop goes in a pocket, add dimensions. Include this under props as well.
- Will glasses be used, or have they been added? Do they serve a special purpose? Include this under props as well.
- Will dancing or any other choreography affect hair style? Include this for quick changes.
- Will hair come down on stage? Do props get placed in hair? Will there be hats? Do they come off?
- Always acknowledge rehearsal pieces/shoes etc. Don't forget to say thank you!

Music

- Are there any additional cuts?
- Will there be offstage singing? Include this under sound (if there is a sound department) and/or production management.
- Are there any moments where Maestro should hold before moving on in the music? If so, how will it be communicated as to how and when they can move on? Will cue lights be involved? Include under lighting/electrics if necessary.
- Are there any requests for additional music or recit rehearsals, or one-on-one coachings?

Production Management and Facilities

- Are you in a rented space? Think of bathrooms and other like facilities. Has everything been stocked?
- Does stage management take care of hospitality or does company or production management? How is the coffee/water stock?
- Is First Aid stocked? Does anything need to be restocked?
- Does or will the schedule need to be adjusted in any way?
- Are there any specific needs for tech?
- Were there any incidents? Accidents? Was a report filled out and submitted?
- Are off stage monitors and Maestro cams needed? If so, will they be stationary, or will they need to move around? Include under Sound if applicable.

REHEARSAL REPORT #7

Production: Barber of Seville	**Date:** January 27, 2020

Director: Mary Birnbaum
Conductor: Mo. Kathy Kelly
Stage Management: Danielle Ranno, Melissa Belman, Chloè Rawlins

Location: Ohio Theatre	**Call Time:** 12:00p & 4:00p

Personnel (late, absent, injuries etc.): N/a

GENERAL NOTES:
We continued to tweak the Act 2 Finale during the first session with principals. We had a blast working with the full chorus this evening. Everyone is very excited and pumped to be in the room! It truly was a great way to end a Monday night!

SCENIC:
1. FYI: The diplomas hanging in Bartolo's office will need to easily be removable and reattached. Some of the police officers will take them down to examine during the Act 2 Finale.
2. The dolphin inflatables are A LOT smaller than expected. Two, full size dolphin inflatables are needed.
3. Another full size pool inflatable is needed. The gator is smaller than expected and can only fit two people. The additional one would be for Berta.

PROPERTIES:
1. ADD: Dry cleaning: 1-2 pieces that belong to Rosina. The laundry list will be attached and taken off on stage.
2. The yellow pads that were brought in today are great for rehearsal, but mini steno pads (3"x5") will be needed for performances so they can fit in officer's pockets.
3. Could a pair of handcuffs be available for Wednesday's rehearsal (4p). FYI: They will need to easily come off on stage.
4. Please see **Scenic Notes #2-3**

Thank you for the new props that were brought in today!

COSTUME/HMU:
1. Is there/could there be a piece that Ms. Spencer (Berta) takes off as the rest of the principals reveal their pool outfits?
2. Please see **Props Note #1.**

LIGHTING:
No notes at this time. Thanks!

MUSIC:
No notes at this time. Thanks!

PRODUCTION MANAGEMENT & STAGE MANAGEMENT:
Thanks for blowing up the pool inflatables Greg!

SCHEDULE:

Today's Schedule: Monday, January 27	Next Rehearsal: Tuesday, January 28
12:00-1:30p: Review Act 2 Finale 1:30-1:45p: Break 1:45-3:00p: Cont. Act 2 Finale 3:00-4:00p: Lunch 4:00-5:30p: Stage chorus into Finale 5:30-5:40p: Break 5:40-7:00p: ADD principals, cont. staging Act 2 Finale 7:00p: End of rehearsal	12:00-3:00p: Staging: pg. 201-231 3:00-4:00p: Lunch 4:00-7:00p: Staging: pg. 232-257 7:00p: End of rehearsal

-END OF REHEARSAL REPORT-

Thanks!
Stage Management

1 of 1

Figure 5.4   *The Barber of Seville* rehearsal report provided by the author.

GLIMMERGLASS ON THE GRASS '21	No hardcopies.
IL TROVATORE Verdi/Cammarano **Rehearsal Report #2** Alex W. Seidel From: <u>Tuesday, July 20, 2021</u>	**Email (75):** Ayala, Bardo, Bean, Becker, Bell, Bleecker, Bryant, Butcher, Carroll, Castro, Catovic, Christian, Colaneri, Davison, DeLucia, Devlin, Flanagan, Fogel, Freedman, Gabriel, Gill, Glinski, Gupta, Harper, Hinman, Jordan, Kahut, Kohen, Kozak, Landers, Lesavoy, Lindquist, Loving, Luna, Ludwig, Lyons, Matou, McMaster, Morain, Morrill, Norbury, O'Leary, Orkiszewski, Partenheimer, Perriello, Pogorelc, Ranno, Richardson, Roberts, Rodd, Rotundo, Rourke, Rundell, Schettler, Schifano, Seidel, Sellars, Schaefer, Shippee, Spear, Stark, Stolnack, Sycle, Tabler, Taylor, Toro, Walsh, West, Wierzel, Williams, Zambello, *musiclibrary@glimmerglass.org, glimmerglassAVtrailer@gmail.com, handt@glimmerglass.org, hairmakeup@glimmerglass.org*

GENERAL
1. This morning we staged Act II, Sc. 1 from p. 51-89. In the afternoon we had our sing through of the piece followed by some notes with Maestro.

SCHEDULING
1. We will be having weapons training with the full cast on Friday from 10-11am in the Pavilion. We will also be having an onstage rehearsal from 11am-2pm on the Opera Lawn that day.
2. We released Armando Contreras, Ron Dukes, Mary-Hollis Hundley, and Lisa Rogali at 12:15pm from the morning session. Spencer Hamlin and Stephanie Sanchez remained to observe as covers.
3. We released Armando Contreras, Ron Dukes, Spencer Hamlin, Mary-Hollis Hundley, Kameron Lopreore, Peter Morgan, Lisa Rogali and Stephanie Sanchez at 4pm.

HOUSING & TRANSPORTATION / YAP TRANSPORTATION
1. None.

PRODUCTION MANAGEMENT / SAFETY
1. None.

SCENERY / STAGE OPERATIONS
1. None.

PROPS
1. Please ADD a large hunting knife and sheath for Manrico. Confirming that he also has pistol.
2. Could you please type the letter out for Manrico to read in the scene? Attached to the email is the text.
3. It has been requested that Nomads have handguns and knives (no wooden rifles).

COSTUMES / WARDROBE
1. Please ADD kneepads for Azucena (Raehann Bryce-Davis) and Fate (Amanda Castro).
2. Please see Props Note #1 & 3.

WIGS / MAKEUP
1. None.

ELECTRICS
1. None.

AUDIO - VIDEO
1. See Music/Titles note #3.

MUSIC / TITLES
1. We are ADDING a cut from 65/2/3/2 to 65/L/L.
2. We are CUTTING the Messenger's lines on p. 84-85.
3. Kathy Kozak will be providing a pitch to Ferrando (Peter Morgan) prior to his entrance offstage on p. 2.
4. Kathy Kozak will be conducting backstage for the Nomad's entrance on p. 56.
5. Manrico will sing the text to his first verse in the Miserere at Reh. J and will sing the second verse text starting at Reh. K.

Page 1 of 1

Figure 5.5 *Il Trovatore* rehearsal report. Courtesy of Alex W. Seidel.

Although the above departments are the more commonly known, there may be additional departments added specifically for your show such as projections, sound, and special effects.

The distribution list will grow between rehearsal and tech since the theater staff and crew heads will be added. If this information was not gathered at the beginning of the rehearsal process from the production manager, be sure to get it before moving into tech.

As heard on headset...

A note was given that a long table was going to be entering and exiting from the furthest upstage left wing with singers on either side to push it on. Although this note was listed under scenic, it was also listed under lighting as "please see scenic note #1." Why would lighting care to know about a large furniture piece entrance? The entrance happened to be the same wing as a light boom. In the end, we discovered that the table could still make it out of the wing with only having to move the boom as close to the upstage wing as possible. With it being brought to everyone's attention early, the lighting designer was able to communicate this to the lighting team prior to load in.

—Danielle Ranno while working on
I due Figaro at The Manhattan School of Music

ASSISTANT DIRECTOR PAPERWORK

Remember, if the show you are working on does not have an AD, some of this paperwork may fall to the PSM.

Cast Transitions: Recently, it has become more common for directors to choreograph internal scene shifts. Sometimes this eliminates an additional intermission for a small move or crew members going out on stage. Anything that is too large or not safe for singers to operate or move, of course, would be done by a crew member, either in their blacks, or in a simple costume. Between the director, AD, and stage manager, cast transitions will either get crafted ahead of time (meaning prior to rehearsal) or on the spot while everyone is present. Depending on the complexity, often times, it is easier to do with the actual people to move around and try out different options with.

> **Purpose:** To provide the cast/chorus with a run sheet of transitions they are involved in.

> **How to:** Try to make this transition sheet as simple and straight forward as possible. If you are able to include diagrams, that's a plus! Transition sheets can be done in either a table or list form.

Key pieces of information listed:

- Who is involved?
- Where are they entering/exiting from?
- What are they doing? Are they striking a prop or piece of furniture, or are they setting up for the following scene?
- Any additional details. Are they going to be placing the item on spike marks? Are they holding a prop or piece of furniture a certain way so it gets set in the right direction? Is there an order to the shift?

SWEENEY TODD
Transitions

ACT I

Prologue
Tatiana & Colleen take lid off and auto XT L2-**stage hands catch**

Transition #1 from 'No Place Like London→ Pie Shop RED SPIKES
    <u>CUE:</u> Sweeney XT L1, Transition Music
- Hayden & Jack bring coffin lid and place on coffin
- Zach bring on table. Put on yellow X ML (#4)
- Leslie NT L2 bring on stools (Short stool SL/ Med stool ML of table)
- Rachel & Sarah bring on X2 black chairs. Place on SR yellow spikes (Pie shop)
- Hayden & Jack bring coffin to chairs SR/ Rachel reposition MR chair under coffin
- Erin place mug & plate DCL corner of coffin (plate on outside)

Transition #2 from Pie shop→ Green Finch RED SPIKES
    <u>CUE:</u> *…. Rosy skin of righteousness*
- Altos XT R1 and auto enter w/ ladder R2 (Christie & Krystal set)
- Hayden & Jack strike coffin L3
- Zach strike X2 stools R1
- Cedar & Roger strike table L2
- Rachel & Sarah strike black chairs R1
- Zach re-enter with Bird cage

Transition #3 from Green Finch/Johanna→ Elixir WHITE SPIKES
- Adam strike ladder R1
<u>CUE: BLACKOUT</u>
- Sarah & Rachel NT R3 w/ X2 black chairs. Place on either side of the doors UC
- Hayden & Jack NT L2 with coffin

Transition #4 from Elixir → Barber Shop RED SPIKES
- Dustin & Ian strike black chairs w/ XT R3
    <u>CUE:</u> Sweeney: *… closest shave you will ever know*
- (on re-entrance) Hayden & Jack move coffin to UC spikes (*labeled Wait*)

Figure 5.6 *Sweeney Todd* cast transitions.

Chorus/Supernumerary (Super) Cheat Sheet: As you will learn, opera rehearsal schedules are quick. Rehearsal with chorus and supers sometimes are limited. Sometimes members of the chorus will be staged to help with scene shifts but will not necessarily be in rehearsal during the initial staging of the transitions. To help keep everyone up to date and so no one falls behind, the stage management team will

PORTLAND OPERA	LA BOHÈME	
Version: 4	SUPER RUN NOTES	Page 1 of 7 / 4/26/17 CMC / Director: Kathleen Smith Belcher / Score: Ricordi CP 115494

SUPER BREAKDOWN BY ACT (NO SUPERS IN ACT I OR IV)

SUPER	ACT 2	ACT 3
Matt Birkeland	Waiter	Crossover
Kendall Carr	Band/Drum Major	
Laura Christensen		Buona Donna
Paul DeLano	Waiter	Crossover
Steve Hotaling	Band	Priest
Brent Hudgins	Waiter	Crossover
Jan Kem	Waiter	Crossover
Larry Moiola	Waiter	Crossover
Weston Roth	Waiter	Crossover
Jim Sherman	Maitre D'	Crossover

ACT II

PLACEMENT	WHO	NT/xt	PROPS	NOTES
87/1/1	**1 Super** Jim Sherman	Preset on platform at the top of the stairs		Head waiter overseeing his team
87/1/1	**2 Supers** Paul DeLano Brent Hudgins	Preset on Platform standing behind SR table		Standby waiting for tables to get up so you can clear and re-set them. The SL table will pay and get up first. As soon as they do, clear the table of props and re-set with place settings and menus.
On Curtain opening	**1 Super** Jan Kem	NT US from inside café	Check	X to SL platform table and present the check to the restaurant guests, stand US of table until they pay
87/3/6 or following Kern's NT	**1 Super** Matt Birkland	NT US from inside cafe	Plate of Chicken	X to SR platform table asking if anyone ordered chicken, (they didn't), then try the SL platform table, (they also didn't), consult with your boss head waiter who is standing on platform and you decide that someone put in the wrong table and table must be inside. X inside the restaurant and hand off plate of chicken. Wait backstage until next cue.
Visual on Birkeland's return backstage (approx. 89/1/3)	**1 Super** Weston Roth	NT US from inside cafe	Tray of glasses	As Birkeland returns, NT Platform. X wobbly with tray behind SR platform table, then SL Platform. Almost drop the tray, X inside the café and lose tray. Wait on back platform until next cue.

Figure 5.7   Super Run Notes for Act II of *La Bohème* by AD Cara Consilvo.

put together cheat sheets for them to reference. Along the same lines of crew paperwork, you want this to be clear, concise, and easy to understand. You want it to be informative, but not too wordy.

Purpose: A quick reference for choristers and supers to reference for staging. This also works as a great run sheet they can have with them or post backstage for a quick reference.

How to: Again, you want to make this cheat sheet simple and as straight forward as possible. A table is a great way to separate all the information listed.

THE ANATOMY OF A CHEAT SHEET

When: List when an action or piece of staging should happen. Will they be cued by an ASM? Are they on stage and are looking for a visual cue, or are they listening for a musical cue or lyric? Listing the page or the P/S/M (page/system/measure) is also very helpful so performer can refer to the score if needed.

What: Similar to putting together a run sheet, you want this to be straight forward and to the point. Avoid long winded sentences and explanations if possible. Listing actions in all CAPS and **bolding** names will also help things pop and make it easier to read.

Props/Costumes: Listing any props entered or exited with and/or costume pieces. This is also a great column for any other quick notes or reminders.

Diagrams: It is not always possible to include diagrams on the cheat sheet but can be very helpful if the chorus or supers have done the staging only a handful of times before moving to the stage.

Depending on the show's needs, sometimes the cast transitions and the chorus/super cheat sheet will be combined into one piece of paperwork. The last thing you want to do is confuse your chorus by giving them multiple run sheets and asking them to piece together all the information.

ASSISTANT STAGE MANAGEMENT PAPERWORK

It is always nice to get a head start on your tech paperwork, but many times, you cannot truly work on it until the end of the rehearsal process, or at least until the full opera has been staged. Although it is not required to have your running paperwork close to completion this early in the process, it will help you during tech when having to make changes or updates. You will also find it handy to work off of when doing runs or while slowly piecing together the opera in the rehearsal room.

As heard on headset...

*The best advice I can give is to start running paperwork early in the
rehearsal process, so instead of burning the candle at both ends rushing
to finish paperwork in the days before tech, you can take time to meal
prep and get enough sleep. My number one priority is going into tech
prepared and rested. You can always prepare paperwork in advance, but
you can't stockpile sleep hours. From day 1 of rehearsal, I keep hand-
written lists of top-of-show and top-of-scene presets (Figure 5.8 a-c).
I print and insert a preset sheet for every scene so I know exactly where
props start and where they end up between scenes. If I keep track of
everything as we go, creating running paperwork for the prop crew is
just a matter of typing up what I have recorded. I always have a draft
of my running paperwork ready for the final room run so I can use that
run to answer any questions I have: quick change timings, exit locations
for prop catches, ideal monitor placement for offstage singing, etc. At
some companies, crew heads are able to watch the final room run, and
having paperwork ready to hand to them is especially helpful - and
sometimes expected.*

—Sarah Stark, Freelance Stage Manager

KEEPING UP WITH PROPS INVENTORY

The props inventory is an ongoing living document that will forever be evolving
throughout the rehearsal process. When sending out a rehearsal report with a lot
of new or updated prop notes, it is always helpful to attach an updated inventory
that reflects the same type of notes; that way, the props artisan can just reference
the most recent inventory. Figure 5.9a and b is an example of a props inventory
from *Candide*.

As discussed in Chapter 3, the ASM put together this props inventory
based off of the props list received by the director. As items were brought into
rehearsal, they were checked off either in the "Reh." (rehearsal) or the "Perf."
(performance) column. Props that are checked off in the rehearsal column are
items that the props department brought in for rehearsal only, meaning they
are just stand-ins until the actual item is made or comes in. Whereas props
that are checked off in the performance column is the actual show prop or
furniture piece. You will also notice that certain props have been crossed out,
which signifies that they have been cut. Some props are also highlighted in
different colors. When there are new or added notes about a prop, it is great to
find a way to make them stand out for the props artisan. What this ASM has
done to help with that is highlight them in a different color, which is defined in
the key in the footer. Continuously updating this will make archiving, which we
will discuss more about in Chapter 8, a lot easier as well.

PRESET FOR TOP OF SHOW

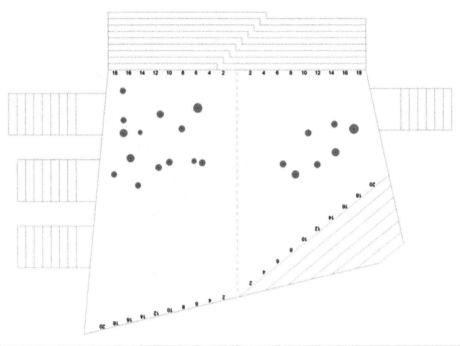

Figure 5.8 (a–c)   Preset sheets from *SongBird*, created by ASM Sarah Stark, to help keep track of all top of show and top of scene presets. Set design by Peter J. Davidson. *(Continued)*

PRESET FOR TOP OF SHOW CONT'D

OFFSTAGE RIGHT	OFFSTAGE LEFT
☐	☐
☐	☐
☐	☐
☐	☐
☐	☐
☐	☐
☐	☐
☐	☐
☐	☐
☐	☐

NOTES

Figure 5.8 *(Continued)*

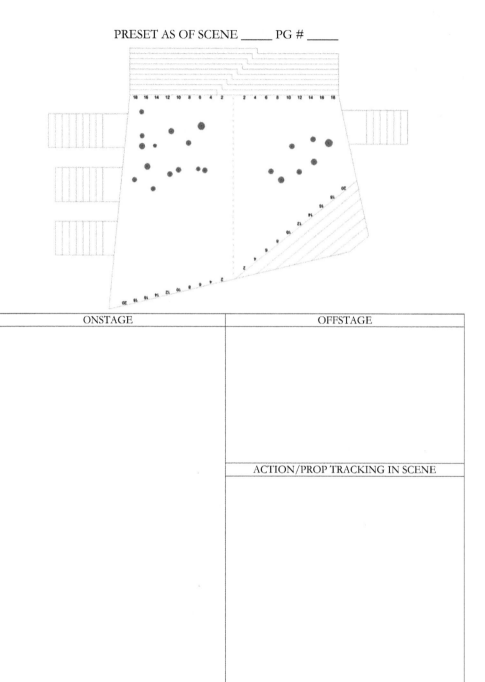

Figure 5.8 *(Continued)*

Candide

PROPS INVENTORY

Director: Dean Anthony
Conductor: Michael Sakir

Quant.	Prop	Reh.	Perf.	Character	Notes
ACT I					
4	Small Planks		X		
8	Large Planks		X		
8	Crates		X		
4	Feather Dusters		X		
4	Bed Sheets		X		
2	Mops		X		
2	Buckets		X		
2	Ropes				Scenic
1	Large Manuscript Book		X		
1	Inkwell		X		
1	Quill Pen		X		Needs to be trimmed
1	Globe		X	Voltaire's Hole	Set dressing
1	Candle		X		Set dressing
1	Megaphone		X		
1	Hourglass		X		Set dressing
4	Stools		X		Need to be painted
1	Falcon			Candide	
1	Glove		X	Candide	
1	White Rose		X	Cunegonde	
1	Mirror		X	Maximillian	
4	Books		X	Candide, Cunegonde, Paquette, Maximillian	Clean & matching
1	Pointer Stick		X	Voltaire	Painted Black
~~1~~	~~Handkerchief~~	~~X~~		~~Cunegonde~~	
1	Riding Crop		X	Baron	
1	Fan	X		Baroness	
1	Hobo Stick		X	Candide	Needs to be reinforced & painted / Gets Thrown on Stage
2	Side Satchels		X	Jeremy, Old Lady	
1	Brown Bag		X	Cody	
2	Roasted Chicken Legs		X	Man 2	
1	Wine Bottle		X	Man 2	No label, with a cork
1	White Flag		X	Man 2	
1	Body Bag		X	Man 1	Dirtied

1   As of 07/19/18 EDD

Needs Work	Missing
Costume as prop	

Figure 5.9 (a and b)   Props inventory from *Candide* created by ASM Elana Deutch. *(Continued)*

Candide

Director: Dean Anthony
Conductor: Michael Sakir

PROPS INVENTORY

Quant.	Prop	Reahrs.	Perf.	Character	Notes
9	Swords		X	Chorus Men	
1	Fancy Sword		X	Jew	
A LOT	Wad of bills		X	Jew	
1	~~Star of David Necklace~~				~~Wearing Them?~~
1	~~Dimond Cross Necklace~~	X			~~Wearing Them?~~
1	Gold Box		X		
1	Jewels	X		Cunegonde	Necklaces, Broch, Rings, and rubies
1	Neck Whistle		X	Jeremy	Need new chain
1	Flog		X	Jeremy	
1	Flog Stand				
1	~~Blindfold~~				
1	Gold Vase		X	Grand Inquisitor	Needs to be bejeweled
1	Gold cup		X	Jew	Needs to be bejeweled
1	~~Dominos~~				
	~~Wooden Cane~~			~~Old Lady~~	
1	Bottle of Oils		X	Old Lady	
1	Rag		X	Old Lady	
2	Rope Handcuffs		X	Candide and Voltaire	Hemp rope
1	Noose	X		David	
23	Fruit/Vegetables		X	Chorus	Round shaped
~~2~~	~~Riffles~~		~~X~~	~~David and Sam R.~~	
1	Dead Body		X?		Dressed like Pangloss
2	Pistols		X		
1	Letter of credentials	X		Candide	
4	Masks		X	Acting Troupe	
1	*Hat*		*X*	*Cody and Candide*	

Furniture					
Quant.	**Furniture**	**Reahrs.**	**Perf.**	**Character**	**Notes**
1	Chaise		X		Reupholstered
1	Chair		X	Governor	
1	Thrown		X	Grand Inquisitor	

2   As of 07/19/18 EDD

Needs Work	Missing
Costume as prop	

Figure 5.9 *(Continued)*

PROPS/DECK RUN SHEET

Depending on the show needs and crew breakdown, this could be two separate pieces of paperwork (deck running and props running). Crew breakdowns can vary between union and contract and size of the house. If you are working on a scenic heavy show, many times the PSM will make or sometime assist with making the deck running paperwork.

REHEARSAL ROOM RUN SHEET

The great thing about putting together a rehearsal room run sheet is that it will, in time, turn into your performance run sheet. It will save you from doing a lot of work from scratch if you begin to work on it slowly throughout the rehearsal period. On the rehearsal room run sheet, many of the duties will be split up between the stage management team, and many of the scenic pieces and props may be stand ins. But once you move into tech, said duties will be reassigned to the crew assigned to your show. Figure 5.10 shows an example of a room run crew sheet for a production of *Roméo et Juliette* at Brevard Music Center. As you can see, the formatting and overall layout is very similar to what the performance run sheet is going to look like. If you happen to have crew running the transitions during rehearsal or in a run, you do not want them to have to learn how to decipher and follow along something new once you move to the stage. The information can change, but the overall look and how it is read, should not.

Roméo et Juliette
Room Run Crew Sheet

TIME	WHO	WHERE	WHAT
PRESHOW			
	Penelope, Claire, Patrick, Hannah, Micki, Meghan		Sweep stage
			Dry mop
			Check all spikes
			ASSIST with backstage props **Refer to props appendix
			SET for Street Scene for fight call
	Penelope & Claire		**PRESET** Prelude curtains
	Penelope, Claire, Patrick, Hannah, Micki, Meghan		POST fight call: PRESET for Prelude
			Check in with ASMs for additional duties
TRANSITION: PROLOGUE→CAPULET'S BALL			
SM CUE	Hannah & Patrick	DSL	**STRIKE** curtain in TOWER C. Place x2 pillows on bench. Exit DL
	Claire & Penelope	DSR	**STRIKE** curtain in TOWER A. Place x2 pillows on bench. Exit DR
CAPULET'S BALL			
SM CUE 18/1/3	Hannah	DSR Door	Cross up SR stairs with tray of X4 goblets. Offer to Tybalt (Achilles). EXIT R1 Mezz w/ tray & X3 goblets
SM CUE 26/1/2	Penelope & Claire	DSL	**REMOVE** BENCH 2 from TOWER C, **PLACE** on turquoise spikes. EXIT DSL
	Hannah & Patrick	DSR	**REMOVE** BENCH 1 from TOWER A, **PLACE** on turquoise spikes. EXIT DSL
SM CUE 32/4/1	Hannah	USR Door	Cross DR with tray & x2 wine bottles. Mercutio (Joe Sandler) will grab a bottle as you cross upstage of BENCH 1. EXIT DSR
	Penelope & Patrick	DSL	**MOVE** TOWER C to red spikes as Montagues are moving TOWER B and BENCH 2. EXIT DSL

Figure 5.10 This is an excerpt of a run sheet that was made for the crew that attended the final room run of *Roméo et Juliette* created by PSM Danielle Ranno and ASM Meghan Crawford.

COSTUME PIECE LIST AND RUN SHEET

The costume run sheet will probably be the one piece of paperwork that will have the most holes in it until you are able to receive a piece list from either the designer or their assistant. The piece list is a detailed list of what each singer/character is wearing throughout the opera. An early version of it may be available, but a more up-to-date version will most likely be available after everyone has had their fittings since a lot of items change, get cut, or added during this time. Until you receive it, just try to put down as much information as possible, such as entrances, exits, and timings for quick changes. From the renderings, you will at least have a base idea that they are going from in Look A to Look B, not the details of what those looks will entail. Piecing together the costume run sheet in rehearsals will also help map out if or where costumes need to be preset, quick changes that were not discussed prior, and if additional assistant or quick change booths are needed close to stage.

Figure 5.11 is an example of a piece list which was created by the assistant costume designer. As the SM or ASM, the information that you will find the most helpful is the "piece" and "description" columns. This information will be very helpful in rehearsal when asked either by the singer (if they have not had their fitting yet) or the director what their character may be wearing in a specific scene, or if a piece is removable or not.

		Trovatore						
		Costume Piece List						
Performer:		Mary-Hollis Hundley	NOTES:					
Character:	Nomad Woman #2 /Nun 2							
Act/scene	**Piece**	**Description**	**Build**	**Buy**	**Pull**	**Rent**	**Source**	**Item Name/ code #**
ACT I SC 2	stockings	white; knee-high		x			Amazon	Link
Nun 2	soft cup bra	tan colored, soft cup, underwire		x			Shop (Glimmerglass)	
	slip	Tan colored mid length		x			Shop (Glimmerglass)	
	dress	grey habit		x			CM Almy	Link
	collar/dickie	mock turtleneck dickie	x				Shop (Glimmerglass)	
	scapular	nun scapular, powder blue	x				Shop (Glimmerglass)	
	belt	brown leather belt			x		Shop (Glimmerglass)	
	waist rosary	brown wooden with large cross,			x		Shop (Glimmerglass)	
	shoes	black, round toe, slip-on		x			Amazon	Link
	veil	Extra-long white veil, attached to nun day-d	x				Shop (Glimmerglass)	
ACT II SC 1	soft cup bra	Repeat						
Nomad W #2	slip	Repeat						
	shirt	White boho shirt w/large scale	x				Goodwill	
	skirt	Patchwork print maxi skirt;	x				Amazon	Link
	shoes	Brown slip-on loafters	x				Salvation Army	
	scarf	Green headscarf; traditional polish	x				Etsy	Link
	Jacket	Light brown track jacket w/side stripe	x				Etsy	Link
	earrings	Silver hoop drop earring	x				Amazon	
	necklace	Multi-strand beaded necklace		x			Shop (Glimmerglass)	
	ring	Silver ring black diamond shape	x				Amazon	
	ring	Silver ring 4 triangles (RIGHT RING	x				Amazon	
	ring	Silver pinkie ring (RIGHT)	x				Amazon	
	Bag	TBD						
	knife belt	brown leather						Props
	sheath	brown leather						Props
	knife							Props

Date   1 of   Author

Figure 5.11   A piece list created by Assistant Costume Designer Heather Freedman for *Il Trovatore*.

WHO, WHAT, WHERE

The Who, What, Where (WWW) is what I like to call "the mother of all paperwork." Essentially, you will take all the paperwork that you have made throughout the production (such as props run sheet and tracking, first entrance sheet, costume run sheet, and deck run sheet) and marry them all together into one tracking sheet. The best way to tackle this to have both assistants working on this at the same time, with each heading up everything that takes place on their side of the stage. The AD and PSM will also contribute to this, adding in scene shifts or large transitions. The WWW will be discussed in more detail in Chapter 6. It is great for archiving the show, into which we will go further in depth in Chapter 8, but it can also be used to run sheet for the ASMs.

Having spent time on all this paperwork throughout rehearsal is only going to make prepping for your designer run (also known as the final room run) and tech week easier! Not only will it leave some time for sleep (and you'll need it), but also lend more time to updating, perfecting, and altering if the crew asks for it. In the next chapter, we will take a closer look at the designer run and all it entails, as well as, the start of tech week and the different types of rehearsals that will take place throughout this process.

Tech

One thing you may not notice when going through this chapter is how quickly tech for opera happens. Now, schedules do tend to change from company to company, but it is nowhere near your average *lengthier* theater tech schedule. Many theater stage managers are used to having a minimum of two weeks for tech alone and then a few previews before opening. In opera, we could tech, open and close a show within that same amount of time! The timetable that will be described mostly in this chapter will be an average, regional company's tech schedule.

You may ask, why is stage management in charge of generating so much paperwork? With many theater tracks, the wardrobe and props department will take charge in spearheading a lot of their paperwork. Due to limited amount of tech time (shown in Figure 6.1), it is the stage management crew who ultimately will know the show the best and will be able to produce the most useful (and complete) paperwork. Throughout this chapter, you will also see the comparison of working with a union crew (known as IATSE) or on a union contract vs not. You can read a more in depth breakdown of working with IATSE in the appendix.

DESIGNER RUN

The designer run, also known as the final room run, is (typically) the last rehearsal in the room before loading into the theater. Setting up the room for the designer run can sometimes be the biggest puzzle! In many ways, you may have to go back to square one and re-evaluate the room, similar to when the SM team was prepping to tape out the set. Except this time, you must survey the full room, rather than just the stage space. Placement is everything, especially for a successful designer run. You want to be sure that with all these new personalities in the room, the rehearsal can proceed with the minimum amount of distractions. It may even be the first time the whole show has had a full run, and possibly the last time the show runs before the final dress rehearsal!

DOI: 10.4324/9781003047391-7

LONG BEACH OPERA

2013 **THE FALL OF THE HOUSE OF USHER**

LBO MASTER SCHEDULE

version 5 as of 12/09/12 SUBJECT TO CHANGE

JANUARY 2013						
Su	M	Tu	W	Th	F	Sa
	1	2	3	4	5	
6	7	8	9	10	11	12
13	14	15	16	17	18	19
20	21	22	23	24	25	26
27	28	29	30	31		

FEBRUARY 2013						
Su	M	Tu	W	Th	F	Sa
					1	**2**
3	4	5	6	7	8	9
10	11	12	13	14	15	16
17	18	19	20	21	22	23
24	25	26	27	28		

TUESDAY, JANUARY 22	**10:00am-midnight**	**Warner Grand**	**LOAD IN /SPACING REHEARSAL**
		10:00am-1:00pm	light focus, set notes
		1:00pm-1:30pm	break
		1:30pm-5:30pm	light focus, set notes
		5:30pm-6:00pm	break
		6:00pm-6:30pm	set up for rehearsal
		6:30pm-10:30pm (4)	**SPACING REHEARSAL w full cast**
		10:30pm-11:30pm	notes
		11:30pm-12:00am	clean up, vacate building

WEDNESDAY, JANUARY 23	**10:00am-midnight**	**Warner Grand**	**PIANO TECH/ORCH TECH**
		10:00am-1:00pm	finish notes
		1:00pm-1:30pm	break, costumes arrive
		1:30pm-2:00pm	cast arrives into costume
		2:00pm-5:00pm	**PIANO TECH (principals only)**
		5:00pm-5:30pm	notes, cast out of costume
		5:30pm-6:30pm	break
		6:30pm-7:00pm	cast into costume, orchestra arrive
		7:00pm-10:00pm	ORCHESTRA TECH (full cast)
		10:00pm-11:30pm	notes
		11:30pm-12:00am	clean up, vacate building

THURSDAY, JANUARY 24	**10:00am-midnight**	**Warner Grand**	**PIANO DRESS/ORCH DRESS**
		10:00am-1:00pm	finish notes
		1:00pm-1:30pm	break, costumes arrive
		1:30pm-2:00pm	cast arrives into costume
		2:00pm-5:00pm	**PIANO DRESS (full cast)**
		5:00pm-5:30pm	notes, cast out of costume
		5:30pm-6:30pm	break
		6:30pm-7:00pm	cast into costume, orchestra arrive
		7:00pm-10:00pm	ORCHESTRA DRESS (full cast)
		10:00pm-11:30pm	notes
		11:30pm-12:00am	clean up, vacate building

FRIDAY, JANUARY 25	**10:00am-10:00pm**	**Warner Grand**	**FINAL DRESS**
		10:00am-12:00pm	finish notes
		12:00pm-12:30pm	prep for top of show
		12:30pm-1:00pm	break
		1:00pm	house opens
		1:30pm-4:30pm	FINAL DRESS (student matinee)
		4:30pm-10:00pm	break TBA

** There is a Farmer's Market from 10am-2pm in front of Warner. Please plan your travel accordingly. **

Figure 6.1   The above is an example of an average opera tech week. This was taken from an overview schedule from Long Beach Opera's production of *The Fall of the House of Usher*. Courtesy of stage manager Cindy Hennon Marino.

Think about seating. Is there enough table space for all the designers, or will some of them have to be seated in chairs off to the side? If you do have to divide them up, how would you do so? Who will the director be talking with the most during the run? If you do have to move some of the designers and crew into seats, think about location. They need to be able to see everything that takes place on stage, so you want to place them somewhere with as little sight line blockage as possible. Also, they too may converse with their teams throughout the run, so try not to place them directly behind the director or conductor. The cast has most likely seen the show, so if they need to be placed further back or off to either side to make room for designers, go for it.

Tips from the toolkit…

If there are going to be a lot of people in attendance for the room run, it might help to print up "Reserved" signs or name tags for assign seats. This way, you can orchestrate where everyone sits, ensure that departments stay together, and limit the amount of traffic coming in as people are trying to find seats together. With assigned seating, you can also just leave paperwork for designers on their seats. You want to keep in mind that there is nothing impeding a direct line between the conductor and pianist.

Timing will be tight. Not only will you have almost twice the amount of people to wrangle, but you must aim to finish in the (typical) three hours allotted. If it looks like everyone is in the room a few minutes early, or at least the majority, feel free to get the ball rolling with intros and any other announcements that may need to be made prior to the start of the run.

Potential announcements for the beginning of the designer run:

- Does everyone in the room know each other? Does the full cast know all the designers? If not, do quick introductions.
- Do you need to explain any of the tape marks on the ground?
- Explanation of any stand-in scenic or props?
- Will you be calling out certain things during the run, such as a rotation of the turn table, sound or lighting cues, or when scenic pieces are flying in and out?
- If there are more than two acts, will the break fall where the intermission will be, or will it be broken up differently for time?

As heard on headset…

I did a production of Street Scene that had around 50 people on stage. We had the full cast including an ensemble, extras/supers, a handful of kids, and even a dog! There was no way that I was going to fit the full company (including some parents) and designers in the room without it being completely crowded and over capacity. To solve my problem, I did some out of the box thinking. Being in a black box, there was a small catwalk on either side of the stage. I asked the production manager if one side could be cleared out so some designers and guests could sit up there. It ended up being the best seat in the room since it was elevated and guests could see the full stage and crews could discuss/talk with each without distracting to anyone on the ground.

—DR

PAPERWORK

It is always nice to have some version of paperwork for your designers and crew at the final room run. Don't feel bad if there are holes or question marks all over your paperwork. It is all part of the process. Plus there are some things that may not be figured out until you are in the theater. Also, your designers may be able to answer some of your questions or fill in any blanks after they see a full run. Remember, the type paperwork may vary from show to show and its personal needs.

Tips from the toolkit...

When giving out paperwork, try to only give one set per person. For example, avoid giving a copy of the Who What Where, props running, and an updated props inventory to the scenic designer or head of props. Not only can this be slightly overwhelming, but they are also less likely to look at any of it at all, if not glance at it. Think about what would be the *most* useful to them in that moment.

WHO GETS WHAT

In this section, we will go over some suggestions of paperwork to have prepared by the final room run and who would get what. Always have a few copies on hand in case a designer or crew head asks for something additional.

Who, What, Where (WWW)

Who Gets It: Lighting designer and assistant lighting designer.

Why: The WWW is the mother of all paperwork. LDs find it helpful because it lists everything that happens in the show all in one document. Key things that they may be looking for are when and where entrances and exits are happening. It also gives them an idea of scene shifts, where and when they happen and how long (timing) they may be. If there is an assistant lighting designer on the show, they will use the WWW to put together spot paperwork for the spot operators.

Who Else May Get It: The scenic designer may ask for a copy because it shows the full overview of the show and how it runs.

GLIMMERGLASS ON THE GRASS 21	IL TROVATORE	Page 1 of 11
Production: **Zambello/ Fogel**	WWW (Who, What, Where)	08/08/2021 dmr, ku Version: **FINAL** Score: **GGF 2021**

TIME	PLACEMENT	NT/ex	WHO	WHERE	PROPS	WARDROBE
	**PART ONE (80:50)**						

PRESET:						
DECK:	ONSTAGE PRESET: See Deck & Props Running Sheet. OFFSTAGE PRESET: See Deck & Props Running Sheet.					
PROPS:	ONSTAGE PRESET: See Deck & Props Running Sheet. OFFSTAGE PRESET: See Deck & Props Running Sheet.					
ELECTRICS:	See Deck & Props Running Sheet.					
AUDIO / VIDEO:	See AV Running Sheet.					
WARDROBE / WIGS & MAKEUP:	See Wardrobe + WMU Running Sheet.					

	**ACT II-1**
Pg. 51 Nomads						
00:00	51/1/1	NT	**AZUCENA** R. Bryce-Davis	USC	Baby blanket double	Look #1
00:05	51/2/1	NT	**FATE** A. Castro	USC	Knife	Look #1 (Nomad)
00:20	52/1/1/4	NT	**7 NOMADS** L. Rogali	USC	Duffle & backpack Ash blanket Knife	Look #1 (Nomad)
			S. Hamlin		Duffle bag Chair Handgun	Look #1 (Nomad)
			A. Contreras		Blanket Folding stool Handgun	Look #1 (Nomad)
			M. Hundley		Wooden chair Plaid bag Large purse Knife	Look #1 (Nomad)
			R. Dukes		Plaid bag	Look #1 (Nomad)

KEY: **Bold = First Entrance**, *Italics = Exit*　　DECK　　RAIL　　PROPS　　ELEX　　AV　　WARD/WMU

Figure 6.2 (a and b)　The above is an excerpt of the WWW from *Il Trovatore*, created by both ASMs, Kayla Uribe and Danielle Ranno. The use of color coordinating/highlighting, bolding vs italicizing text is strategically used throughout the document. *(Continued)*

GLIMMERGLASS
ON THE GRASS 21
Production: Zambello/ Fogel

IL TROVATORE
WWW (Who, What, Where)

TIME	PLACEMENT	NT/ex	WHO	WHERE	PROPS	WARDROBE
			S. Sanchez		Hand gun Chair Duffle bag Backpack Knife	Look #1 (Nomad)
			K. Lopreore		Knapsack (w/ tent) Hand gun	Look #1 (Nomad)
00:45	56/3/1		ONSTAGE ACTION: 2 Nomad Men rig up tent in USR trees (K. Loprepre, R. Dukes)			
Pg. 63 Manrico and Azucena						
1:25	58/1/3/2	NT	**MANRICO** G. Kunde	USR	**Hunting knife** Hand gun	Look #1 Messenger bag
5:55	66/1/3	ex	*4 NOMADS* *R. Dukes*	*USR*	*Plaid bag* *Hand gun*	*Look #1 (Nomad)*
			K. Lopreore		*Knapsack* *Hand gun*	*Look #1 (Nomad)*
			S. Hamlin		*Duffle bag* *Wooden chair* *Hand gun*	*Look #1 (Nomad)*
			A. Contreras		*Hand gun*	*Look #1 (Nomad)*
			<u>PROPS CATCH – SR Fence:</u> 4 Hand guns from NOMAD MEN (S. Hamlin, R. Dukes, K. Lopreore, A. Contreras)			
			<u>COSTUME CHANGE: 13:00 (PAVILION)</u> NOMAD (S. Hamlin) CHANGE to Militia (Look #2) NOMAD (A. Contreras) CHANGE to Militia (Look #2) NOMAD (R. Dukes) CHANGE to Militia (Look #2) NOMAD K. Lopreore) CHANGE to Militia (Look #2)			
11:45	76/1/1		ONSTAGE ACTION: 3 Nomad Women STRIKE tent (L. Rogali, M. Hundley, S. Sanchez)			
12:00	76/2/4	ex	*3 NOMADS* *L. Rogali*	*R3*	*Duffle bag* *Backpack* *Knife*	*Look #1 (Nomad)*
			M. Hundley		*Plaid bag (w/ baby blanket double)* *Large purse* *Tent* *Knife*	*Look #1 (Nomad)*

KEY: **Bold = First Entrance**, *Italics = Exit*   DECK   RAIL   PROPS   ELEX   AV   WARD/WMU

Figure 6.2 (a and b)   *(Continued)*

Props Running

Who Gets It: Head of props and props crew.

Why: If you are lucky to have a member or head of the props team who is also running the show backstage present at the run, it could be very helpful for them to see what they may be doing during the show, how and in what order. The room run gives them the chance to see how the ASMs make it work in the room and then adjustments can be once the show moves to the stage.

GLIMMERGLASS ON THE GRASS 21
Production: Zambello/Fogel

SONGBIRD
Deck & Props Running Sheet

Page 9 of 11
08/14/2021 dmr
Version: **FINAL**
Score: **GGF 2021**

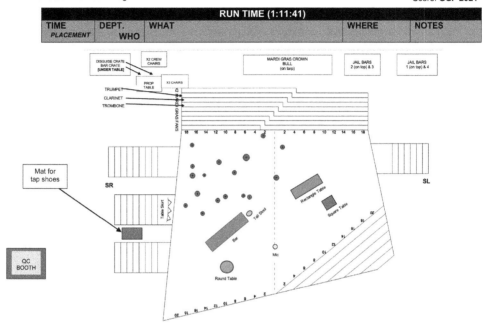

PLACES	PROPS Sam	ASSIST Mob (A. Keeney) into gun harness.	Fence	

TIME PLACEMENT	DEPT. WHO	WHAT	WHERE	NOTES

RUN TIME (1:11:41)

PLACES	PROPS Sam	ASSIST Mob (A. Keeney) into gun harness.	Fence	
No. 1 Overture (00:00-2:15)				
No. 2 Introduction (2:15-4:10)				
No. 3 Café des Muses (4:10-7:20)				
No. 4 Seguidilla Duet & dialogue (7:20-10:45)				
No. 5 Incognito & dialogue (10:45-15:40)				
No. 6 The Letter (15:40-19:00)				
18:35 *54/3/3*	PROPS **Manny**	**CATCH** pre-made champagne coupe from Songbird (I. Leonard).	QC BOOTH	Danielle will cue
Dialogue & No. 7 Finale A (19:00-22:00)				
21:30 *65/2/1*	PROPS Manny	**HANDOFF** champagne coupe with water to Songbird (I. Leonard)	XT side of QC BOOTH	
No. 7 Act I Finale B (22:00-27:20)				
No. 7 Act I Finale C (27:20-29:15)				
No. 7 Act I Finale D (29:15-32:00)				
29:15 *87/2/1*	PROPS Manny, Shannon	Cross to USC as cast is exiting stage to PREP for Mardi Gras. **Shannon will be USC for the rest of the show	Fence→USC	Danielle will cue 4:30 till next cue

BOLD: New Information   *Italics: costume piece*

Figure 6.3 An excerpt from the props running paperwork from Glimmerglass' production of *Songbird*. You will notice that the run order is listed, even though there are not any running notes taking place during those numbers. Since your crew will not know the show as well as you, having musical numbers and times, or some other type of marker of placement, will assist your crew with following along.

Deck Running

*As mentioned before, this might be combined with the props running.

Who Gets It: Scenic designer and deck chief.

Why: The deck running will give the scenic designer an idea of how the scene shifts are being tackled and completed. Knowing how pieces move and work, the deck chief might be able to suggest an easier way or a second option as to how something might work or move based on what the action on stage is. This will also give them an opportunity to mark up or assign who from their crew may be on certain shifts then present it back to the ASM to update for the first day of tech.

Tips from the toolkit...

For a production of *I due Figaro* at Manhattan School of Music, I put together what I call a "tech master" for the final room run since all of the shifts on stage were done by cast members. This gave the designers an idea of what was changing per scene rather than the detail of how it was happening. A tech master is not something that would necessarily be used as a run sheet, but could be used as an outline for the overall show.

 Manhattan
School of Music

I due Figaro
Tech Master: Final Room Run

Director: Dona Voughn
Conductor: Stefano Saranzi
Stage Manager: Danielle Ranno

Scn./Time	DECK / RAIL	PROPS	SOUND / LX	WARDROBE
ACT 1				
			SR Maestro Monitor in R1￼SL Maestro Monitor USL	
ACT 1 PRESET				
	SCENIC:￼Double Doors￼Large Orange Trees up SR & SL￼￼RAIL:￼LX, Legs & Border IN￼Main Rag (1) IN￼Show portal (2) IN￼MS Portal (17), Clack Scrim (30),￼Back Drop (33) IN	PRESET in SL3 wings:￼ Long Table￼ Garland￼ Table cloth￼ 5' Ladder￼ Pig spit￼ Cook's station￼￼PRESET in SR wings:￼ 8' Ladder￼ Bench (for long table)￼￼PRESET US of Double Doors:￼X2 Fancy Chairs		

Figure 6.4 This was taken from the first page of the Tech Master for *I due Figaro*. Although it is still laid out like a run sheet, each column is broken down by department.

Costume/Wardrobe Running

Who Gets It: Costume designer, costume crew, hair and makeup.

Why: This will be the closest that the costumes and hair and makeup crews will have to understanding *how*, *when,* and *where* any quick changes or costume changes may take place. They may have a better idea of how long it will take for a specific change to happen, but you will know best where and exactly how long it will have to take place. After seeing the full run and the way in which certain changes have to happen, they may go back and simplify or alter a costume.

Tips from the toolkit...

If your crew heads are unable to attend the final room run, try to set up a meeting with them to check in and review running paperwork prior to the first tech. Sometimes they may help assign duties based off of responsibilities of the crew, or may help you fill any holes or answer questions that you may have.

OPERA COLUMBUS	**THE BARBER OF SEVILLE** WARDROBE RUNSHEET-DRAFT	Director: Mary Birnbaum Costume Designer: Amanda Seymour Stage Manager: Danielle Ranno

ACT I PRESETS		
Stage Right	**Onstage**	**Stage Left**
N/a	Rosina Act 1 Look-In bedroom? Rosina Pool Look-In bedroom?	N/a

WHO (Staff)	EXT TIME PLACE	CHARACTER Artist	COSTUME CHANGE		LOCATION	WIG CHANGE	LOCATION	TIME FOR CHANGE	ENT. TIME PLACE
			FROM	**TO**					
			ACT 1 RUNNING NOTES (75:00)						
	AUTO XT SL	**BERTA** E. Spencer	**REMOVE**: Apron		CATCH off SL ?	N/a	N/a	N/a	N/a
	11:40 SR	J. Straight	Boyband	Police	Dressing Room	N/a	N/a	50:00	1:05:00 SR
	11:40 SR	L. Foster	Boyband	Police	Dressing Room	N/a	N/a	50:00	1:05:00 SR
	11:40 SR	I. Coe	Boyband	Nosiy Neighbor	Dressing Room	N/a	N/a	50:00	1:05:00 SL
	11:40 SR	J. Cleland	Boyband	Police	Dressing Room	N/a	N/a	50:00	1:05:00 SR
	31:21 SL	**COUNT** M. Mykannen	Lindoro	Soldier (Underdress swin suit)	Dressing Room	N/a	N/a	15:00	56:00 SR

Version: A
Updated: February 06, 2020
dmr

Figure 6.5 The first draft of the wardrobe running for *The Barber of Seville*. Placements and information that is questionable or unknown are highlighted or followed by a question mark. This lets the wardrobe team know that these are answers needed or still to be determined.

AFTER THE FINAL ROOM RUN

In many schedules (unless working in rep), the final room run is the only thing scheduled for the day with singers and stage management. If the SM team has not already, this would be the time to measure out all spikes and pack up the rehearsal room so everything can be moved over to the theater. A spike mark map will be used to note and keep track of all the show spikes. Depending on the style of map the SM prefers, this can be just a list of spike locations OR both a list and a diagram which will show rough location and angle of each spike.

SPIKE MARK MAP

Purpose: To note all your spikes from the rehearsal room. You will use this when setting spikes onstage. Although some of these might move or adjust from their location in the rehearsal room, it is still a good idea to grab all spike measurements. The director may still want to use the marks from rehearsal to get a starting location of furniture and props in relation to each other before moving or adjusting them to help fill the larger stage.

How To: Your spike mark map does not need to be anything fancy; it is truly a document that only stage management will use. You will measure out spikes the same way you taped out the set, with the use of two tape measures, setting one down on the center line ("y" axis) and the other to measure out left and right ("x" axis). If possible, having three people to measure out (two to measure and one inputting the information to the chart) will also make move fast and smoothly, similar to when taping out the set prior to rehearsal.

Here are a few other things to keep in mind when measuring out your spikes and noting them into your chart.

- Whether you are measuring a corner spike (shaped like an "L") or an "X" spike, you want to take your measurement from the corner of the "L" (where the two pieces of tape meet) or the center of the "X". Always notate what type of spike it is on you spike map to avoid any confusion when placing them in the theater.

- If you are not using the same furthest downstage point as you did when taping out (for an example, you plotted your taping points from the proscenium and now are measuring from the edge of the stage), be sure to note that! If not, your points will be off by a few feet in the theater from what they were in the rehearsal room.

- In many instances, you can round up to the closest ¼″ or ½″ to make laying down spikes faster and easier.

- If the object or piece of scenery has multiple spikes, you will want to note that, either when naming the item or in the notes section. This way, you can get the angle and direction correct.

- Unless a piece of scenery has changed significantly, no need to remeasure everything. Your technical director will have all those measurements and will be the one heading up the crew when loading it into the theater. Stage management only needs to worry about furniture pieces and smaller items that move.

Brevard Music Center 2019
*Measured from edge of stage
* Start w/ 1' @ 0

Romeo et Juliette
Rehearsal Room Spikes

ITEM	LOCATION	SPIKE	UP	ACROSS	NOTES
Prologue Tower A DS	SR	Navy	15'1"	11'3"	
Prologue Tower A US	SR	Navy	18'9"	7'8 1/2"	
Prologue Tower B SR	SR	Navy	22'3"	2'8 3/4"	
Prologue Tower B SL	SL	Navy	22'3"	3'2 3/4"	
Prologue Tower C US	SL	Navy	18'4"	8'4"	
Prologue Tower C DS	SL	Navy	14'9 1/2"	11'10 1/2"	
Opening Tower A DS	SR	White	6'3"	16'6 1/4"	
Opening Tower A US	SR	White	11'	14'4 3/4"	
Opening Tower C US	SL	White	10' 8 1/2"	14'8 1/4"	
Opening Tower C DS	SL	White	6'1 1/2"	16' 8 1/2"	
Dance Tower A SR	SR	White	11'10"	2'8"	
Dance Tower A SL	SL	White	11'10"	2'4 3/4"	
Dance Bench 1 DS	SR	Turquoise	6'	8'6 1/2"	
Dance Bench 1 US	SR	Turquoise	9'5 1/4"	5'4"	
Dance Bench 2 US	SL	Turquoise	8'5"	6'4 3/4"	
Dance Bench 2 DS	SL	Turquoise	4' 5 3/4"	9'3 1/2"	
Mab Tower B SR	SR	Red	15'8 1/2"	2 1/2"	
Mab Tower B SL	SL	Red	15'8 1/2"	5'10 1/2"	
Mab Tower C US	SL	Red	14'5 3/4"	10' 1/4"	
Mab Tower C DS	SL	Red	10' 7 1/2"	13' 3 3/4"	
Mab Bench 1 DS	SR	Red	3'11"	9'6 1/2"	
Mab Bench 1 US	SR	Red	8'9"	7'4 3/4"	
Mab Bench 2 SR	SL	Red	8'9"	6 3/4"	
Mab Bench 2 SL	SL	Red	8'10 1/2"	5'8"	
Dance Tower B SR	SR	Pink	18'8"	3'1"	
Dance Tower B SL	SL	Pink	18'8"	2'11 1/4"	
Garden Tower A/C US	SL	Red	19'7"	7'2"	
Garden Tower A/C DS	SL	Red	16'	10'8 1/4"	
Garden Bench 1 US	SR	Red	18'4"	5'11 1/2"	
Garden Bench 1 DS	SR	Red	14'11 1/2"	9'3 1/2"	

Figure 6.6 Spike mark map of rehearsal room spikes for *Roméo et Juliette.* You will notice the note in the top, left corner stating that these measurements were taken from the edge of the stage and with 1' at the 0 mark or at center.

LOADING INTO THE THEATER

More often than not, loading into the theater (meaning everything from the rehearsal hall, such as props, furniture, and SM supplies) will take place on the day off, which means that many times, stage management does not get a full day off. To help with the transition from the rehearsal space to the theater, sending over a tech request (Figure 6.7), or checklist of how you envision the space to be set up for each tech session can be very helpful. This should be sent over prior to moving into the theater, preferably at least a week in advance (your production manager may have a specific due date in mind), so everyone has a chance to look it over before set-up. You never want to assume that things will be setup the way you want it to be unless you ask. Each show has different needs, so it is great to specify exactly what is needed for a smooth tech. Every department is busy leading up to tech week, and unless they are told exactly how something needs to be set up or where it should be placed, they are just going to do what they know.

Street Scene
Tech Request

Requested by Danielle Ranno, SM
Email: Dranno@brevardmusic.org

TO BE COMPLETED BY July 24 at 5p
Phone: XXX-XXX-XXXX

GENERAL
- Tech table(s) in house in standard position; 2 for stage manager/ designers, 1 for Dean (set in row behind)
- Additional clamps to clip curtains backstage

LIGHTING
- All as specified by design.
- Q Lites: 1 at Conductor's podium (Visible by concertmaster, conductor), 1 in center house
- Q Light control at SM Console (in house Mon & Tues, booth on Wed)
- Backstage running lights where necessary (crossover, props tables SR/SL)
- Conductor down light for all onstage rehearsals

SCENERY
- All as specified by design.
- Set AND Offstage areas swept

ORCH
- Piano in standard Piano Tech position
- Conductor stool (being used in MPH) with 2 music stands, flatten and pushed together. (Feel free to take the two in MPH. They are adjusted to Mo. preferred height)
- Music stands w/ lights in pit
- Music stand w/ stand light for chorus master (Eileen) in the back of the house
-Clock visible by conductor

PROPS
- Two Prop tables: 1 SR and 1 SL (both from MPH-already taped out)
- Two Prop closets in outside hallway

SOUND
- God Mic at tech table for director & stage manager
- Conductor monitor camera focused on Conductor at tech table
- FOH monitor focused
- Mic on upright piano in standard Piano tech position w/ amplification to stage for onstage rehearsals
- Headsets: Hookup for SM @ tech table (Com channels: **Channel A**: Lighting, **Channel B**: ASMs/Sound)
     ASM positions SL/SR (2 wireless)
     Light board op @ board
     Lighting designer @ tech table
- (2) Walkies and ear pieces for Katherine (kid wrangler) and stage manager
- Backstage paging ability at tech table
-Cable for Qlab computer @ tech table
- Program feed and paging system ON and functional.
-Backstage video monitors SR/SL for off stage singing/ conducting. Both should be on roll carts.
-Wireless mic SL for Dean (Performances only)

Figure 6.7 Tech request for *Street Scene*. This is usually no longer than one page and completed by the stage manager in advance to moving into the theater for tech.

Tips from the toolkit…

It is always nice to show your face around the theater. If there is someone that you do not know, introduce yourself to them! Know that the crew will be very busy and will most likely not have time to stop and chat, but making yourself present and available for any questions, will not only show how dedicated you are, but that you respect and appreciate the crew's work and what they are doing.

OTHER ITEMS TO ACCOMPLISH DURING LOAD-IN

- **Set up the SM Headquarters:** This could be a production office, a classroom, or even an extra dressing room. Stage management will want a space where everyone can house their personal belongings or where private meetings can be held. This space can also be where valuables are stored during the run, or as a removed space to "get away" for a few minutes. This will also be where you setup the SM road box or supplies that were brought over from the rehearsal hall.

- **Set up the Callboard:** One of the first things to locate once you are in the space is the callboard. Hopefully this is in a central location that is either closest to the stage door or on the way to the dressing rooms. If the theater does not have a traditional callboard area, ask if you can take up a section on the wall that is in an easily located or central spot.

- **Set up Directional Signs (Figures 6.8 & 6.9):** Directional signs are always nice to have up before the company arrives because you may not be available to meet everyone upon their arrival or give everyone a tour of backstage as soon as they arrive. Putting a sign with and logo on the stage door, or whatever the main entrance for the cast and staff members will give them a landmark to look for. Large arrows giving the cast a general idea of how to get to the dressing rooms, either side of the stage, warmup and green room and front of house, can also be very helpful. When putting any type of signage up backstage that's not on the callboard, check in with the head of props if you are in a union house, or your production manager regarding the type of tape to use. More likely than not, you will be asked to stay away from using gaff or scotch tape on the walls or doors because it will rip up the paint. Rather, use painter's tape or a similar adhesive.

- **Put up Dressing Room Assignments (Figure 6.10):** The dressing room assignments is a collaborative project between stage management and wardrobe. They may have some suggestions as to where to place people based on calls or dressers. When assigning rooms, don't forget to also make a space for wigs and makeup, wardrobe, and Maestro, and sometimes stage management if an office space is not. Traditionally, Maestro's dressing room is always closest to the stage and/or the pit entrance. If the space is available, Maestro and the two lead principals typically get their own dressing room, then secondary characters will share a room, two to three each, and the chorus will have a male and female room. If the space is a non-traditional theater, dressing room assignments may need to get creative. Post a copy of dressing room assignments on the callboard once they are available for singers and Maestro to use. And don't forget to share a copy with wardrobe, hair and makeup!

- **Setting Spikes on Stage and Adjusting Furniture:** If load in time allows it, try to set up a time where the team can get in and put down spikes and look at furniture placements with the director and AD on stage. This will save you time when it comes to spacing, as well as help your lighting

LAKES AREA

MUSIC

FESTIVAL

WELCOME
CAST & CREW OF
LA BELLE HÉLÈNE

ENTER HERE

Figure 6.8   Stage door sign for the cast and crew of *La Belle Héléne*.

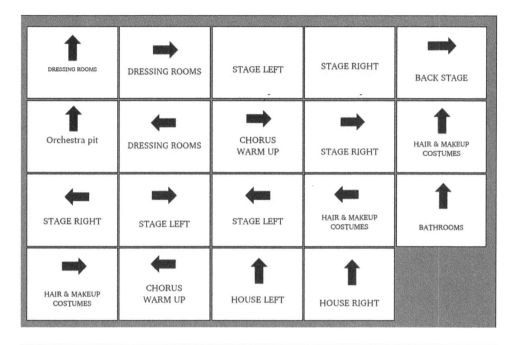

Figure 6.9   Directional signs which were posted around backstage to direct the cast where to go. You can either keep them general (and reuse them) or use the show font for a little extra fun backstage.

designer when focusing. Finding this time might be tricky if you are working in a union house, so connect with your production manager to find the best time. Sometimes, stage managers are able to work around other meal breaks and work when the stage is free. If it is a union house, stage management may not be allowed to work onstage unless a crew member is on the clock (meaning not on a break). If that is the case, you may be working around other onstage work, or during lighting.

Tips from the toolkit…

To save spikes means to cover them with vinyl, clear tape called Marley or dancer's tape. Unless lighting and scenic are working on stage with genies and other large equipment that would pull up your tape, try to wait to save your spikes until their placements have been finalized by the director. If the floors needs to be painted after spikes have already been placed, cover them with painter's tape and pinch a tab at the top so they can easily be pulled up once the floor has dried.

Gianni Schicchi

Dressing Room Assignments

Lower Level

Orchestra room
Mo. Kathy Kelly

4th Floor (Wardrobe to the left of elevator)

ROOM 1
Hair & Makeup

ROOM 2
Ms. Lee Gholston
Ms. Merryman
Ms. Spencer
Ms. Tackett
Ms. Willis

ROOM 3
Mr. Banion
Ms. Bunsold
Mr. Clark
Mr. Eder
Mr. Humbert

ROOM 4
Mr. Kerr
Mr. McKeever
Me. Nevergall
Mr. Schlabach
Mr. Swain

As of 09/22/19

Figure 6.10   Dressing room assignments for *Gianni Schicchi*. This sheet was emailed to the cast and wardrobe as well as posted on the callboard. Individual signs were also posted on each dressing room door.

SET UP/ORGANIZE BACKSTAGE WITH FURNITURE AND PROPS

If you happen to be at the theater when props and furniture are being loaded in, see if you can assist with where things go. The crew unloading things from the truck to the theater do not necessarily know what side of the stage things belong or start on and will just put things down wherever there is space. If you help direct where things should live, you could save everyone from moving furniture and props around multiple times. More likely, everything will get unloaded when you are either not available or around. If this is the case, ask the props head (or your production manager) when the best time would be to connect and start moving things into their preset areas. This would also be a great time to set up and tape out prop tables (or assist if you are working with a union crew) so everything is ready for the first tech. If you are not working with a union crew, you might be allowed to start moving things around yourself to save on time while they work on other projects. If time permits and you have not talked through run paperwork, ask your deck chief or crew head when would be a good time to do so.

As heard on headset...

One of my greatest failures and moments of growth happened when working my first professional gig as an ASM at an opera summer festival. I had never really assisted before, and especially not on an opera. It was my first day of tech with the running crew and I had not assigned any tasks ahead of time thinking that I would do it as we went, which turned out to be a big mistake. Needless to say, things did not go as smoothly as I hoped. Scene changes which were supposed to happen quickly behind a scrim during a 2:00 pausa took much longer than they should have and were sloppy. I started getting more and more flustered and began making more mistakes. By the end of the rehearsal, I was gutted and had not been a good leader for my team. Although it felt like the end of the world in that moment, it made me a better stage manager. For the next show I worked that summer, I made sure every moment was assigned and I knew how everything backstage would work before we had our final room run.

—Jackie Mercer, Freelance Stage Manager

Tips from the toolkit...

If you are working in a union house, you are not allowed to touch or move anything yourself onstage. This can be a big adjustment if you are used to working with companies that do not perform with union crew and you can pick up and adjust say, a chair's position onstage a few inches. Instead, a union props crew member will have to be onstage with you and they will move the furniture piece or prop to the new position that you or the director gives them. In some houses, the staff are flexible and will allow you to be more hands on with some duties that are typically union only, whereas in other houses, the crew can be very strict. It is better to go in to a new house assuming that they run a tight ship and then be told that you can be a bit more lax than assuming the reverse and then be given a strong talking to.

ADDITIONAL TEAM MEMBERS

As you move into the theater, and begin to work more with the orchestra, there are two additional team members that you may be in contact or work with.

Librarian

The librarian is responsible for the day-to-day operations of the music library. They work closely with the music director, musicians, staff, conductors and guest artists. The only time you may see the librarian in the theater is during music rehearsals or at the beginning (pre-set) and end of rehearsals or performances. The interaction between the librarian and stage management team will be very little, but it is always great to know when new team members are around.

Some of their duties include:

• Arranging the purchase of rentals/materials needed for the orchestra.

• Responsible for all aspects of music preparation, which includes editing, proofing and distribution.

• Work with conductors and soloists to prepare music according to their specific requirements.

• For rehearsals/concerts/performances- arrive early to execute any changes in stage set-up. They also ensure that all musicians have the correct music and if not, will provide alternative materials. At the end of each service (rehearsal period), they will collect and store all music parts.

• At the end of each rehearsal, they will follow up with the conductor and string principals regarding any changes or mistakes that need to be corrected in parts.

Orchestra Manager

The orchestra manager is the liaison between the orchestra and the production/stage management. Together with the conductor or music director, the orchestra manager will set rehearsal and performance schedules, and oversee venue preparation. During all rehearsals leading up to performances, the orchestra manager is the one keeping time throughout the service (per the contract) when it comes to breaks and start and end times of rehearsals. During performances, they keep track of all musicians and make sure they arrive on time. The orchestra manager will report that all musicians have arrived and are in the pit for the start of the opera and may also help assist with notifying the concert master when to tune. Depending on where the pit entrance is located, they may also send the conductor out via the ASM. Or the ASM will cue the conductor directly to enter the pit, and the orchestra manager will notify the PSM that they are in and ready to begin via a hand or headset, or through the ASM. Although you will be able to see them via the Maestro monitor, it is always great to get a verbal OK before beginning.

REHEARSAL DURING TECH WEEK

The first rehearsal in the theater to final dress rehearsal can be anywhere from four to five total rehearsals! One big difference between opera tech and theater tech is that on opera, we do not tech with the singers. Meaning, all the lighting looks for the show are set with stage management, the director, assistant director, and light walkers. Light walkers can be someone not related to the project at all such as over hirers, or even members of the chorus. Light walkers do not need to have any previous experience, they just need to follow directions as to where to cross to, where to stand or sit. Depending on the contract (whether it is a union contract or a non-union piece), the ASMs, and even the AD may stand in. All runs/rehearsals with the cast will be moved to the evenings to give all tech departments the day to be in the theater for work. Do you recall in Chapter 5 when I mentioned how different rehearsals were "run" by either the director, conductor, or stage manager? This will change up throughout the tech week. Although the stage manager is the one who ultimately runs all of the rehearsals, each session will have a different focus, working each piece of the puzzle before putting it together.

ORCHESTRA READ

An Orchestra Read is typically the first rehearsal the conductor has with the orchestra. Depending on the company's contract, this can be one session or multiple sessions. This rehearsal will be the first time the orchestra and the conductor will have worked with the score, so there may be a lot of stopping and starting. This will also be the time the conductor and orchestra will go over any cuts in the score (the librarian will have put in all cuts in advance) and add any cuts or changes that might have come up during rehearsal if they have not been transferred in already. Stage management is usually never called to reads—many times they overlap with staging rehearsal, or even the early stages of tech—so do not feel like you are required to attend.

SITZPROBE

Translated from German as a "seated rehearsal," the sitzprobe is the rehearsal where the singers sing with the orchestra, with the focus on the integration of the two groups. It is often the first rehearsal where the orchestra and singers rehearse together. Often, this rehearsal will take place in a hall with the pit set up as it would in the theater and the singers would be set up at chairs and [music] stands in front of Maestro. Ideally, this would take place in the actual pit and singers would be up on stage, but the schedule does not always allow that.

Traditionally, singers will come in business casual attire rather than the normal rehearsal apparel or street clothing. This is to show respect for the orchestra and Maestro. Although stage management is not required to be in attendance, it is always welcomed as long as it does not overlap with something else the SMs are required to be at. The nice thing is that SMs do not need to worry about "running" the rehearsal. The orchestra manager will take care of all breaks and making sure all members of the orchestra are accounted for. If anyone from the SM team is present, it would be helpful to assist singers with breaks, and make sure they are back on time. Once the orchestra break is over, the Maestro will start as soon as the tune is complete, regardless of whether or not the singers are ready to go. Remember, everyone is on orchestra time!

Tools from the toolkit…

If the sitzprobe does not overlap with another tech call that stage management is involved in, the team should try to attend, especially if this is their first opera. Stage management can quietly sit in the back, update and work on paperwork, or just follow along in the score. For some, this may be the first time they are hearing the show with a full orchestra, and although it should not sound that much different than in the rehearsal room with the piano, it will sound a lot fuller, and for some beginners, be easier to follow along since they will have other instruments to listen for.

Opera facts!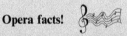

Orchestra breaks change with each contact, which is an agreement between the company and the orchestra or union. Commonly, orchestras take a 20-minute break within every 60 to 90 minutes of rehearsal. Sometimes this can be broken up into two, 10-minute breaks. Whether to take the one, 20-minute break vs the two, 10-minute breaks will be up to the Maestro and how they feel would be the best use of time based on the work that needs to get done. All in all, stage management is not involved with any of these negotiations, and it is the orchestra manager who is the keeper of their time during most orchestra focused rehearsals.

SPACING OR PIANO TECH

This will be the first rehearsal on the set. Prior to actual rehearsal, either the stage manager or technical director will give everyone a safety tour of on and off stage. How the director decides to use the time after is up to them. Instead of running the full piece, they may choose to adjust spacing, or they may want to skip around and hit large scenes or transitions. If the opera has recitative, it will likely be skipped unless it leads right into a piece that is being worked. Since this rehearsal is not focused on the music or singing, many times the conductor may not be present. Instead, music will be ran by the assistant conductor or the pianist.

Who Runs this Rehearsal? The director will run this rehearsal along with the AD and stage manager.

What Is the PSM Doing? The PSM is keeping everyone, both on headset and over the God mic, on track, especially if there is a lot of jumping around.

What Are the ASMs Doing? The ASMs are running backstage, helping to gather singers, and cuing singers and transitions onto stage.

What's the AD Doing? Keeping the director on schedule via the train schedule. They may also be the one communicating with the cast over the God mic, or running up on stage to make adjustments as the director looks at the full picture from the house. If there are enough headsets, it can be very helpful to give one to the AD. With a lot of stopping and starting, having direct communication between the AD and PSM will help move things along.

To help keep everyone on schedule, the stage manager, sometimes with the assistance of the AD, will put together a train schedule. A train schedule is not to be confused with the tech schedule, which gives the overview of the entire day, and sometimes lists work calls that are happening around rehearsals. A train schedule gives an overview and projected breakdown of how each individual rehearsal will run. Similar to a daily, a new one will be produced for each day/rehearsal.

Purpose: To list out the goals for the rehearsal. Each section will be broken down in "actual time," meaning how long the number/scene/section is and "rehearsal/tech time," meaning how much time you are setting aside to work on that section. This is to help the director and rest of the team stay on schedule and complete everything discussed in the time allotted. Remember, tech time, especially with the cast, is limited!

How to: In a table or list format, you want to breakdown the full three to four hours into blocks. You will list what will be worked on, how long that section is (this you will grab from the 30-second timings in your score), and then how long is needed to tech or work it. As for the other information listed, it may differ depending on the needs of the show. If it is a tech heavy show, or if you are hitting those moments because of tech concerns, then list what those concerns are. If you are working transitions with the cast and lighting will alter how said shift is done, add in a column for light cues if you have them already. Adding in the pages and/or a placement in the score will also be helpful for anyone following in the score.

Tips from the toolkit…

The first spacing rehearsal will be one of the biggest to keep coordinated. Not only will you have to relay to the room where you are or moving to, but you must keep everyone on schedule. This may be something to tag team between you and the AD. One can announce over the God mic what will be worked on next and give a page and placement, where the other one is keeping track of time. Always remember to relay on headset what you are working on or what is coming up. Just because it was announced over the PA system does not necessarily mean everyone heard it.

Here are two examples (Figure 6.11 & 6.12) of train schedules. Both hold the same information just slightly laid out differently. The *Roméo et Juliette* train schedule has a separate column for page numbers, which makes it slightly easier to quickly reference and breaks down time as "run time" and "rehearsal time." Whereas the *Il Trovatore* train schedule includes page numbers in the "what"

Glimmerglass on the Grass 21
Production: Zambello/Fogel

IL TROVATORE
Tech Train Schedule

Page 1 of 1
7/24/21 aws
Version: a
Score: Ricordi

Sunday, July 25, 2021

Time	TT	RT	What	Who	Tech Concerns
4:00-4:10	10	5	Act II, Sc. 1 p. 51-65 (Anvil Chorus-Stride La Vampa)	Bryce-Davis, Kunde, Ensemble	Entrance of Nomads
4:10-4:30	20	15	Act II, Sc. 1 p. 66-91 (Azucena Aria-Azucena/Manrico Duet)	Bryce-Davis, Kunde, Ensemble	Exit of Ensemble, Changes to Milita/Nuns
4:30-4:40	10	8	Act I, Sc. 1 p. 1-20 (Ferrando)	Morgan, Men's Ensemble	Entrance & Exit of Militia, Change to Nomads
4:40-4:50	10	8	Act I, Sc. 2 p. 21-33 (Leonora's Aria)	Moore, Women's Ensemble	Entrance & Exit of Nuns
4:50-5:00	10	7	Act I, Sc. 3 p. 92-107 (Count's Aria)	Mayes, Morgan, Men's Ensemble	Placement of Offstage Singing
5:00-5:10	10	4	Act II, Sc. 4 p. 115-136 (Act II Finale)	Tutti	
5:10-5:20	10	6	Act III, Sc. 5 p. 167-177 (Manrico/Leonora Duet)	Kunde, Moore, Hamlin, Contreras, Women's Ensemble	Exit of Nuns from Back
5:20-5:25	5	1	Act III, Sc. 5 p. 180-183 (All'armi! All'armi!)	Kunde, Moore, Mayes, Morgan, Hamlin, Contreras, Bryce-Davis, Men's Ensemble	
5:25-5:40	15		BREAK		
5:40-5:55	15	7	Act IV, Sc. 1 p. 184-198 (Miserere)	Moore, Kunde, Morgan, Bryce-Davis, Men's Ensemble	Placement of Offstage Singing
5:55-6:10	15	5	Act IV, Sc. 2 p. 206-223 (Leonora/Count Duet)	Moore, Mayes, Morgan	
6:10-6:30	20	7	Act IV, Sc. 3 p. 224-233 (Azucena/Manrico Duet)	Bryce-Davis, Kunde, Ensemble	Placement of Chair Row.
6:30-6:45	15	4	Act IV, Sc. 2 p. 234-244	Bryce-Davis, Kunde, Moore, Mayes, Morgan, Castro, Ensemble	
6:45-7:00	15	5	Act IV, Sc. 2 p. 244-252	Tutti	Gun Shot
7:00-7:15	15	0	Bonus Time		
7:15-7:30	15	0	Cast out of Costumes		
7:30			**END OF REHEARSAL**		

TT: Tech Time   RT: Rehearsal Time

Figure 6.11 Example of a train schedule for Glimmerglass' production of *Il Trovatore*.

Roméo et Juliette

Train Schedule- Piano tech

Director: Dottie Danner
Conductor: Kelly Kuo
As of 08/11/16
SCORE: Schirmer 13203

Time	Pg.	Run Time	Rehearsal Time	What	Who
Act 1					
2:00-2:15p	1-2	1:00	15:00	Prologue fight	CREW: Hannah, Patrick, Claire, Penelope
2:15-2:45p	4-32	8:00	30:00	No.1 Prologue thru top on Mab (transition)	Tutti Company
2:45-3:05p	64-77	5:00	20:00	No.5 Act 1 Finale	Tutti Company. N/a Friar, Duke
3:05-3:15p				**10 MINUTE BREAK**	
3:15-3:30p	78-79	1:00	15:00	Top of No.6 Transition into Garden	Chorus in transition
3:30-3:45p	84-102	12:30	20:00	No. 7 (Balcony)- end of No. 8; Scene & Chorus	Gertrude, Men's ensemble, Romeo, Juliet, Stephano
3:45-4:00p	117-124	11:00	15:00	End of No. 9 (Transition)- Top of No. 10 Friar's Cell (Juliet, Gertrude, Romeo entrence into cell)	Chorus in transition, Gertrude, Friar, Gertrude, Romeo, Juliet
4:00-4:10p				**10 MINUTE BREAK FOR INTERMISSION CHANGE**	
ACT 2					
4:10-4:30p	--	--	20:00	Fight Call	Romeo, Mercucio, Gregorio, Stephano, Tybalt, Benvolio, Ethan
4:30-5:00p	141-180	26:00	30:00	No 12 Street Scene thru Top of No. 14 Transition into bedroom	Tutti Company. N/a Friar
5:00-5:15p	181-200	11:00	15:00	No. 14 (Romeo & Juliet bed duet)	Romeo, Juliet
5:15-5:20p	224-247	5:00	10:00	End of 18; (Transition into Chapel)- No. 22 (Transition into Crypt)	Tutti Company. N/a Duke
5:20-5:35p	257-265	10:00	15:00	No. 22 Romeo/Juliet Death	Romeo, Juliet, Friar, Capulets, Robert, Alea

**25:00 BUFFER TIME LEFT OVER

Figure 6.12   Second example of a train schedule for *Roméo et Juliette*.

column and breaks time down as "TT" or tech time and "RT" or rehearsal time. Tech time is the time the PSM is allotting for the scene, whereas the rehearsal time is the rough timing of the scene when done in time. If you are going to break things down with acronyms, make sure you add a key so your audience can easily decipher them.

Tips from the toolkit...

If the costume shop provided shoes and rehearsal costumes such as skirts or robes, request that those items be used for the first walk through or spacing on stage so singers can get used to the set with these pieces on. This is especially important if the set has levels or stairs that are used throughout.

PIANO TECH WITH COSTUMES

Still with piano, this is the first rehearsal with costumes, hair and makeup. Whereas the spacing rehearsal was used to figure out spatial usage of the stage and transitions, this rehearsal will most likely be the first run through on stage, focusing on costumes, quick changes, and overall pacing; this is probably the first time the company has ran the full piece since the room run. Although it is preferred not to stop, you have a little more wiggle room since you are not working with the orchestra yet. Depending on the company and schedule, you could have just one piano tech/dress or a few of them.

Who Runs this Rehearsal? The director will run this rehearsal, along with the stage manager.

What Is the PSM Doing? The PSM is calling any cues that are available. Sometimes the lighting designer may not have every cue written yet, but the cue number exists, and they will ask the PSM to call it even if it does not do anything just so they can be following along and be working in the correct cue. Piano dress is also the first time where the PSM will be making calls over the PA system for places, shifts, and quick changes.

What Are the ASMs Doing? The ASMs are running backstage as close to a performance as possible. If a singer does not show up for their places call after they have been paged, the ASM will alert the PSM and ask them to re-page. Because this is the first full run, the ASMs and crew will be working off of running paperwork. Any notes or changes that need to happen will be made to paperwork prior to the next run with full crew.

What Is the AD Doing? The AD is following the director if they are wandering through the theater, taking notes and looking at spacing and sight lines. If something on stage needs a small adjustment, they may run up on stage and do so. Similar piano tech/spacing, having the AD on headset (if available) can be very helpful if there is a starting and stopping, and can assist with keeping the rest of the team on the same page with the director.

WANDELPROBE

Translated from German as the "wandering rehearsal," the wandelprobe (wandel) is where the orchestra and singers come together for the first time in the performance space. The main focus of this rehearsal is balance of the orchestra and singers, but also to make sure that both can hear each other from different locations on stage. A wandel is generally done with loose/minor blocking and traditionally without scenery, props or costumes, although rehearsal costumes and shoes may be requested, as well as some hand props if the singer wants to use them. The assistant conductor or a member of the music staff will move around the house to listen for balance. If adjustments need to be made, Maestro will stop and address them.

Who Runs this Rehearsal: The conductor.

What Is the PSM Doing? They could be working with the lighting designer as they continue to write cues and build looks. They may have to page singers if they are not hanging out in the house or backstage

(Maestro will not be happy if they get to a section and a singer is missing in action). If the PSM is not working through the wandel, they should take the time to really listen to the music, follow along in the score, and watch Maestro on the monitor for cues. Since this rehearsal may not run continuously through or in order of the score, the PSM is not generally paging or making calls over the PA system, so making it to places is either on the singers themselves, or with the help of an ASM.

What Are the ASMs Doing? Both ASMs will be backstage for the wandel but depending on how the rehearsal will run will dictate how involved they are. There may be the occasional cuing of singers on stage and making sure that transitions and shifts happen when they should. Many times, ASMs will help wrangle singers to stage since some of them may hang out in their dressing rooms, while others hang out in the house to listen and watch when not onstage.

What Is the AD Doing? Depending on how the rehearsal is being used (either as a version of a run or strictly as a wandel), the AD is taking notes for the director during the run, walking around and checking sight lines, typing up past notes for the singers, or working on paperwork in preparation for another rehearsal.

Check-ins with Maestro before the wandel:

- Check with Maestro to see if they are ok with lighting happening during the wandel. Sometimes they prefer work lights to be on and find the changing of lighting during this rehearsal distracting. Others do not have a preference as long as the stand lights and Maestro light are parked, meaning those specific lights will not move or change, for the rehearsal.

- If Maestro was unable to complete the show during the sitzprobe, they may want to pick up where they left off and double the use of the wandel as a second sitzprobe. It is great to have this info before the start of rehearsal so the cast can be alerted. Also, if it has been decided that scenery or partial stage setups are being used, the crew can have everything setup in the correct orientation.

- Ask Maestro where they plan to take the break (the orchestra manager might also have this info). To save on time, they may decide to skip over the pausa after Act 1 or plan to take the break somewhere else in the score rather than where the intermission falls. Regardless, the orchestra can play up to 90-minutes before a 20-minute break is needed. Depending on how much work vs how much music there is, and what will save on time, Maestro may decide to break up the 20-minute break into two 10-minute breaks. This is good information to then distribute amongst the team and cast.

If everyone is in agreeance and crew is available, many times, the creative team will use the wandelprobe as another opportunity to run the show. Regardless of whether or not everyone voted to use the wandel as a run, the main focus is still Maestro's needs with the orchestra and singers. If there are transitions and they are going to be performed during the wandel, traditionally, singers will step downstage, or off to the side and continue singing. Once the set is safe, the singers will then take their place back on the set.

In their own words...

Speaking to a conductor just after they have conducted a cut-off is like trying to have a singer speak immediately after having sung a loud high note. It takes just a second or two to recover enough oxygen in the brain to think and speak coherently!

—*Kelly Kuo, Conductor*

ORCHESTRA DRESS

The orchestra dress is the first rehearsal that will run as close to the actual performance, where props, transitions, costumes, hair and makeup and full orchestra all come together for the first time.

Who Runs this Rehearsal? Ultimately the stage manager, but the conductor can stop or call a "hold" if it is absolutely needed.

What Is the PSM Doing? Running and calling the show as close to a performance as possible. The LD may still be tweaking and working on cues, but hopefully you have all cue placements in your book. If you have a cue coming up but hear the LD adjusting something with the board op over headset, still call the cue, and the LD will direct the board op to take it once they are finished working. Since you are running on orchestra time, it is important to start as close to on time as possible to avoid going into overtime.

What Are the ASMs Doing? Running the backstage in show conditions. Continue to take notes on run sheets so updates can be made. Always check in with crew heads at the end of rehearsal to grab their notes.

What Is the AD Doing? Taking notes for the director. Following them if they are moving around the theater or checking sight lines. If a small adjustment or note needs to be given, they may run backstage to talk to the singer or ASM, but they are not getting up on stage like they were during the spacing rehearsal.

FINAL DRESS REHEARSAL

The final dress rehearsal is the last run before opening. This rehearsal, many times, is the closest a company will get to a preview. Although it may not be advertised as a performance to the public, many times schools, donors, or volunteers of the company will attend. If this is the case, the director might ask that audience members sit in a specific area of the house so the creative team can still work and discuss throughout the show. The PSM will move to their calling position either backstage or in the booth. Most of the house will get struck of tech tables in preparation for opening, but designers may request to have a table out for any last minute tweaks. Even though this is the final dress rehearsal and audience may be in attendance, remember that this is still a rehearsal. You may make a mistake and call a cue too early or a beat too late. As long as the mishap does not cause danger to anyone in the company or make performing conditions unsafe, do not beat yourself up about it. That is the beauty of live theater, every performance is different in one way or another. The preference from the designers and Maestro is to try to forge through as much as possible, but if a hold is absolutely necessary, do not be afraid to call it. Someone from team, whether it be the artistic director or the production manager, will also make a speech prior to curtain letting the audience know that this is still a working rehearsal and that there could be a hold, Maestro could decide to stop and start a section over, or there may be some occasional marking [with singers].

Schedule wise, this is not much planned after the run. This session does not exceed the three-four hours block. The director or AD may meet singers backstage as they are on their way out to give any notes, or they may decide to just type them up and email them out later. As for tech, there may be a final production meeting in the house to go over last minute notes or tweaks. Depending on the crew schedule, the lighting designer may do a few last minute fixes and the rest of the tech tables will get struck and the house will get fully restored in preparation for opening.

THE CALLING STATION

Since the calling SM (in most instances) will not move to the calling station until the final dress rehearsal, it is important to set aside time to setup the station the way that works best for you. Does something need to be swapped to the opposite side? Where and how do you like to have your book set up? Are you able to see everything needed to call? Front of stage? Maestro? Is there a call box used to communicate with different channels on headset, or is everyone on one channel via a headset pack? Is the pack or Clear Com box located in a spot that is quick and easy to get to? What about the height of your chair? Would a stool be easier because of the height of the table? Are there any additions to your station that would be helpful? It is important that you are comfortable and can do your job with ease. There are times that certain things need to be set up in a specific way because of cabling or even table space, but if you ask nicely, the house staff or crew will try to accommodate you as much as possible. Every theater's calling space, whether it be in a booth or backstage, is different. Some have spacious areas, and some have only a music stand available. You should be willing to adapt, but always be vocal about the things that you *absolutely* need in order to call a successful show.

Key items at a stage manager's calling station:

- Maestro audio and visual monitor.
- View of front of stage. Infra-red if possible so scene changes in blackouts or low light can be seen. If you are calling from the back of the house in a booth, you may not always have this.
- Call box (this will have all your headset channels) and headset. Everyone may just be on one channel, in which case, you will not have a full call box.

- Way to page the dressing rooms or PA system.
- Light to see the prompt book. This could be an extra music stand light, a desk light, or a simple book light. A trick to take down the brightness is to ask for a piece of blue gel.
- Cue light switcher or box.
- Cue list monitor from the lighting console—this is not always available, but is always a plus! Having the cue list allows you to watch as cues are being called and triggered.

Other things to look for/think about when getting settled into your calling station:

- Is the cable for your headset pack long enough so you can move around, or stand if needed?
- If you are calling from a booth that is enclosed, does the light used to read your score cast a shadow on the window in front of you, obstructing your view of the front of the stage?
- If you are backstage, how can you limit the amount of people congregating around or trying to speak with you during the show?
- Are you able to adjust the volume on your Maestro audio monitor yourself or does sound have control of levels?

Below are three different views of PSM calling stations. Figures 6.13 and 6.14 were taken of SM calling stations backstage, whereas Figure 6.14, illustrates a more traditional calling station in a booth Figure 6.13 shows a calling station for

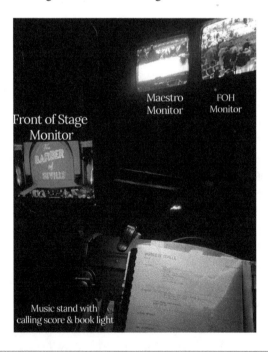

Figure 6.13   Calling station for *The Barber of Seville* at the Southern Theatre with Opera Columbus.

Figure 6.14 Calling station for *South Pacific* at Virginia Tech with Opera Roanoke.

The Barber of Seville at the Southern Theatre in Columbus, OH. Because of the versatility of the space, there was not a designated calling station. So this was pieced together with a music stand and book light placed by the monitor rack backstage. The crew was split up between two channels on a headset pack, so a full call box was not needed. Both the PA system and cue light switcher (although not visible in this image) were part of monitor tower, and are nuzzled under the FOH (front of house) monitor. It is not always common to have a FOH monitor, but this show called for it since performers traveled into the house.

Figure 6.14 is another example of a backstage calling station. Since the backstage footprint at Virginia Tech is pretty big, a standing table could be used over a music stand. In addition to the front of stage and Maestro monitor, there is screen of the cue list—this is what the light board operator is also looking at, and a monitor that reads "cue light." The only cue that was used in the show was in the pit. Instead of setting up a cue light switcher/box, it was controlled by the light board. When the cue light needed to go on/off, it was called over the headset to the board op, and through the monitor, the SM could see when it was physically on and off.

Figure 6.15 is a calling station in a booth, in the back of the balcony. Since there was a clear view of the stage, there was only a Maestro monitor setup. Directly under the Maestro monitor is the Clear Com box, which also housed a channel for the PA system, so everything went through the SM's headset. With the orchestra not being in a traditional pit below stage level, there was also some light spill on stage from their music stand lights, so transitions that took place in low light or a blackout could still be seen by the SM.

Figure 6.15   Calling station for *Roméo et Juliette* at Brevard Music Center.

As heard on headset...

When I did Brigadoon with Gulfshore Opera, we traveled to three different locations. Only one of them was a traditional theater and outfitted with items such as a proper booth, a Maestro cam and headsets. But the other two locations, one being a church and the other a high school, were not as well equipped. We were able to bring our own set of wireless headsets, and I could essentially call from anywhere as long as I had some view of the front of stage, but there was no easy way to bring around a Maestro cam and monitor. Since there were times where I needed to cue Maestro to begin the next scene, I needed a way to see him. The company bought an infrared baby camera and monitor. Although the view screen was small, it did the trick!

–DR

WHAT ABOUT THE ASM CALLING STATIONS?

The ASMs are mostly roamers backstage and for most operas, they do not remain stationary in one spot the entire time. The ASM call station consists of a music stand and a book light. Remember how we talked about keeping your score as light as possible in Chapter 3? Well, this is why! The ASM will move with their music stand and score, to different locations based on where their cues are. If stairs need to be climbed or spots are tight, they may need to forego moving the stand and just carry their score with them.

A fairly new discovery is moving away from the paper score and going to a digital score. One ASM that has made the move to digital scores is Sarah Stark. Here are some of her thoughts on digital over paper scores and why she made the switch:

> *The Alice Busch Opera Theater at the Glimmerglass Festival is notoriously narrow backstage left. Between the rail and a fire lane that must be kept clear at all times, there are only a couple places for ASMs to stand during performances. In the summer of 2017, I was an SM intern on Francesca Zambello's production of Porgy and Bess and assisted the SM team. The stage left ASM had so little space that performers knocked her score off its music stand twice. Both times, the binder rings popped open on the deck and scattered her almost-600-page score out of order. After taking a couple hours to put her score back together, she decided to run the remainder of the performances from a digital version of the score on her iPad. The next summer, when I was the SL ASM on two productions, I didn't even consider running with a paper score. When I made the switch to running from a digital score, I found myriad benefits beyond saving space backstage:*
>
> • *Keeping all my scores and paperwork (including checklists and bow sheets) in one place when working in rep*
>
> • *Avoiding the wear, tear, and repair of a physical score during a run with many performances*
>
> • *Alleviating anxiety about losing, forgetting, waterlogging, or otherwise ruining my binder*
>
> • *Using my digital score to remount or travel with productions*
>
> • *Easy breezy archiving*
>
> • *Easier on my carpal tunnel than a 400+ page score*
>
> • *In case of emergency, anyone can access my running score in the team Dropbox or Drive*
>
> *To create and run from digital scores, I use a paid iPad app called PDF Expert. In addition to creating text boxes with color-coded backgrounds (much like Post-its), PDF Expert allows me to highlight in different colors and create an "outline" to easily jump to different scenes and numbers within my document. In the past, I have also used Preview on my MacBook to prepare digital scores and the free Kindle app to read them. I always print a copy of my running score to keep backstage in case of a tech failure or malfunction. Creating and maintaining a digital score can be time-consuming, so I still use a paper score and Post-its for some productions I ASM. Like everything else, it depends on my needs and the needs of the production.*

In their own words...

The summer of 2021, The Glimmerglass Festival's 2021 season was moved completely outdoors. Since the stage and backstage was not covered at all, there was the possibility of light rain and our scores getting wet. Between the wet pages and moving around for cues, I decided to give the digital score a try. The biggest reservation I had when it came to switching over to my iPad was not being able to easily flip ahead or having the option to go back and for between two sections at the same time. Instead, I would have to swipe ahead until I found the spot I was looking for. To ease my way into the switch, I had my digital score ready for the final room run so I was not using it for the first time at tech. To make the file, I used Adobe Acrobat on my computer. Once I placed all my cues in, I transferred the PDF file to forScore, which is an app that many singers use for their scores. The nice thing about forScore is that you can tab or bookmark your scenes/pages, just as you would with your paper score, which made jumping around, or to certain sections much easier. Although I may not be running to ditch my paper score, I am definitely willing to entertain the idea of switching back and forth between the two.

—DR

Some additional pros and cons of a digital score over a paper score:

Pros:

- It is lighter and easy to carry around if you get a case with a long strap.
- Has its own backlight which you can adjust.
- Moving cues around is just as easy as picking up a Post-it and moving it to a different measure or page. All you to do is drag and drop.
- As long as the case is waterproof, you do not have to worry about it getting ruined. *So long, wet pages and ink runs from the rain!*

Cons:

- If you are outside, you have to be careful with overheating and the iPad turning off.
- You need to watch battery life if you are using an older device. Have a portable battery handy.
- Cannot as easily flip through pages.

Always have a paper copy on hand just in case! If your digital score is the most up to date over your original paper score, print out a copy and leave at the theater or somewhere backstage that you could easily get in case of an emergency.

LIGHTING AND CUING

As mentioned, one big difference between opera tech and theater tech is that we do not tech with the singers. Meaning, all the lighting that is usually done with the performers over a number of days is done with stage management, the director, AD, and light walkers. Because of this, the company will either bring in light walkers or the ASMs will light walk. A light walker is someone who will walk the blocking on stage while the lighting designer is writing and programing the cues. Typically, they are asked to wear dark clothing with a lighter option available if needed. The stage manager and/or AD will be in the house and direct the walkers where to stand or basic movements to do via a God mic or over headset. Cues will then get adjusted if or where needed during tech rehearsal with singers.

If there are spot lights, the usage of the who, what, where will come in handy, for writing and placing cues, as well as creating the spot sheet. If the lighting designer has an assistant, they will typically take care of putting together spot paperwork on their own. Most of the time, the stage manager will call spot cues as well as lighting, scenic and rail cues, but there are some instances where the assistant lighting designer or another stage manager is stationed in a separate booth or room with a monitor of the front of stage calling all the spot cues to the operators.

THE ANATOMY OF CALLING A CUE

There truly is an artform to calling cues, whether you are the SM calling cues over headset, or the ASM cuing singers onstage. There is no real common formula because it can differ from cue to cue. This is where knowing the music very well comes in handy. There are three aspects to every cue; the lead up (standby), the trigger (go), and the execution. Cues can be triggered by the beginning or end of a scene, the change of pace or emotion in the music, or even by a piece of text. Ask yourself, *how is this cue supposed to land? Should the light go out as the singer is exiting the stage, acting as their presence fading away? Should the scenery piece appear magically in the split second the singer turns in the opposite direction?* The director and designers will tell you when they want a change to happen, or what the end goal of a cue or transition should be, but it is up to the stage manager to pinpoint when and exactly *how* it gets there.

Before you start calling the show, check in with your crew on headset. Do they prefer to get a standby? Do you prefer acknowledgement or a response after you give a standby? Do you want them to repeat it back to you, or say "standing?" Do you tend to take a slight pause (breathe with the music) before giving the GO? If so, you want to give your operators a warning so they do not think you left them hanging or that you are unsure of when the cue should go. The same thing goes for when cuing singers on stage. You will have little less leeway since the score and staging does dictate when performers need to be on stage, but cues will get adjusted based on pacing, character, and comfort of the singer. Similar to how a SM may breathe with the music before giving their GO, a singer might do the same. The ASM may throw the entrance cue for the performer who may then take a beat to get themselves into character before entering the stage. If that is the case, a small adjustment may need to be made so they are making their way onto stage as directed.

TYPES OF CUES AND THEIR NAMES

Some shows may have more than just lighting cues that need to be called. Here is a list of other types of cues and how they are typically listed in the prompt book. Verbiage may change based on the stage manager or operators.

LIGHTING

Light cues can range from overhead or front of stage lights, the operation of practicals on stage, or anything else that is being controlled by the light board. In some instances, the light board will also control other cues such as projection cues, the hazer or dry ice machines, or even spot cues depending on the instrument being used for them. If that is the case, you would call all these as light cues.

How It Can Be Listed: LQ or LX.

How It Can Be Called: "Standby lights 100." "Lights GO." Also can be called "electrics."

All lighting designers are different with how they give cues to stage management. Some LDs will prepare a cue sheet and share it with the SM, sometimes ahead of time so the SM tcan add them into the call book prior to the first lighting session, while others will share it on the first day of cuing. There are other LDs who will place them directly into their score and then hand their book off to the SM to copy them. And there are those who do not write them down in a cue sheet or in a score and will give them to the SM as they write them during lighting sessions. It all depends on how the designer works. It is important that the SM calling the cues understands the cue and their purpose. If additional information is needed, such as their timing, their purpose, or what the LD is trying to achieve with said cue, do not be afraid to ask. The LD will not be offended if you do not understand what or why a cue is placed where it is.

Director: Crystal Manich				Madama Butterfly		Lighting Designer: Tláloc López-Watermann	
PSM:Hester Warren-Steijn				Opera Columbus			
Cue#	Time	Block	Page/Place	Visual or line	Description	NOTES	SCENE
1		B			House and preset	Projection: Sky whispy clouds	PRESET
2					House to half		
3			5 minutes prior to maestro entrance			Butterfly projection (in color fluttering	
4				house out	Maestro special		
5		B			Maestro to playing level		
6	10		1/1/1		Dancers enter		ACT 1
8	6		3/3/1		Goro and pinkerton enter enters	enter US stairs	
12	8		5/1/3		House turns		
14	8		Reh 8		Goro sings	Pinkerton lights up at corner of house	
16			Reh 10		Servants put stuff away		
18			11/1/1		Suzuki	More light outside US	

Figure 6.16   Lighting cue sheet for Opera Columbus' production of *Madama Butterfly*. LD: Tláloc López-Watermann.

> **In their own words...**
>
> *As a lighting designer, I put together to the best of my ability a cue list in the time before tech. It is at the final room run that this document becomes its most complete. If I can get it to the stage manager as soon as possible, then they will have a chance to add those cues to the score ahead of the first tech on stage. If at all possible it is great to have them take first pass at calling if the cues on the first piano tech, even if the cues are not all written yet. In some of the very fast tech weeks in opera this really can speed the lighting process along as I can work over that first rehearsal, even if it is before the first cueing session. I have thought for a long time, that the stage manager has a huge part in the artistic creation of the final product that goes on stage when it comes to lighting. The stage manager is able to feel how the show lives and breathes, they have been there throughout the rehearsal process. They have a deep understanding of the show and the performers. They know the music and they know the maestro and his tempo. So despite the fact that I have given them specific placements in the score for each of the lighting cues, a good stage manager is able to elevate the lighting design even more by finding the most appropriate, or sometimes even, magical spot to call the cue.*
>
> —*Tláloc López-Watermann freelance lighting and projection designer.*

SPOT

As mentioned earlier, in some larger opera houses, the assistant lighting designer, or even another stage manager may call spot cues. In the majority of regional houses, the stage manager will call these along with light cues. Sometimes there may be up to four spots for a show, and although the assistant lighting designer will make them their own cheat sheet, it is still on the SM to call their ins and outs, and any frame changes that may take place throughout the opera.

How It Can Be Listed: S or "Spot."

How It Can Be Called: "Warning spot 1 to fade up on the Captain SR in frame 1 at medium speed." "Spot 1 GO."

Since there is more information that you need to call for spots, I prefer to give warnings (this would be even earlier than a standard standby). That way, the caller has enough time to get the full call out and the spot operator has time to swap out frames (color), change their size, and prep for the action. Below are two examples, Figures 6.17–18, of spot cue sheets, one made with Spot On in FileMaker Pro and the other made in Excel.

I DUE FIGARO
FOLLOWSPOT CUE SHEET

LD: Tyler Micoleau
ALD: Mikaela Baird

9/3/2019

MSM

Head: Head only
H&S: Bottom of spot at chest
HB: Bottom of spot at belt
3/4: Bottom of spot at knees
FB: Include feet

SPOT 2
Kyle
House Left

COL FRAMES
| 1 | 2 | 3 |
| 4 | 5 | 6 |

SPOT 1
Carrie Ann
House Right

COL FRAMES
| 1 | 2 | 3 |
| 4 | 5 | 6 |

LQ	ACTION INTENSITY	CHARACTER	FRAME SIZE TIME	LOCATION NOTE	ACTION INTENSITY	CHARACTER	FRAME SIZE TIME	LOCATION NOTE
				ATTO I				
.5	OFF				Up & Out	MAESTRO	H&S 2s	IN PIT FOR BOW
20/3/1 1	OFF				Pick Up FL	ALVARO	H&S 3s	Ent SL With Cane
21/3/1 2	Pick Up FL	PLAGIO	H&S 3s	Ent SR With Glasses		ALVARO		
23/2/1 3	Fade Out 0%	PLAGIO	4s	Sneak out	Fade Out 0%	PLAGIO	4s	Sneak out
29/2/1 4	Pick Up FL	FIGARO	H&S 2s	USC Doors	Pick Up FL	FIGARO	H&S 2s	USC Doors
				Recitativo (FIGARO)				
50/1/1 5	Swap to FL	ALVARO	H&S			FIGARO		
50/5/4 6	Swap to FL	FIGARO	H&S			FIGARO		
50/5/4 7	Swap to FL	PLAGIO	H&S			FIGARO		
53/5/3 8	Fade Out 0%	PLAGIO	3s	EX SR	Fade Out 0%	FIGARO	3s	Kneel at pig he hides behind cart
				N. 2a Recitativo del Conte				
54/1/1 9	Pick Up FL	CONTE	H&S 3s	USC DOORS	Pick Up FL	CONTE	H&S 3s	USC DOORS
				Recitativo (FIGARO) 1				
64/1/1 10		CONTE			Swap to FL	FIGARO	H&S 2s	Conte X to Doors direct swap at door

12/10/2019   1:57 AM   **SPOT ON**   PAGE 1

Figure 6.17 This is an excerpt of a spot cue sheet the ALD, Mikaela Baird, made for *I due Figaro*. As you can see, this sheet lists all the information for a call. Since so much information needs to be given, you can get away with giving it all in your standby/warning. For an example, one way to call the cue at 29/2/1 would be: *Standby spots 1 and 2 to pick up Figaro head and shoulders at the upstage center door. Fade up to full in 2 seconds.*

LONG BEACH OPERA **The Death of Klinghoffer**
Created by: Cynthia Marino, SM
3.18.14

Follow Spot Sheet

Spot 1				
Cue	Color	Time	Intensity	Target
-69	1 & 2	Slow		Swap boys as they cross down stage center

Notes:

Cue	Color	Time	Intensity	Target
-69	1 & 2	Slow	↓ 0	Boy stage left

Notes: Do not follow boys all the way out, fade out early if have to
Placement: called when the first boy passes under the screen

Cue	Color	Time	Intensity	Target
-75	1 & 2	Med	↑ 100%	Captain

Notes:
Placement: called when Mamoud crosses to Captain, around 80/4/2

Cue	Color	Time	Intensity	Target
+78	1 & 2	Med	↓ 30%	Captain

Notes:
Placement: 87/2/2

Cue	Color	Time	Intensity	Target
+78	1 & 2	Med	↑ 70%	Captain

Notes:
Placement: 95/3/2

Cue	Color	Time	Intensity	Target
86	1 & 2	BUMP	↓ 0%	Captain

Notes: BUMP OUT
Placement: 99/1/1

Figure 6.18 This is another example of a spot cue sheet that was made for Long Beach Opera's production of *The Death of Klinghoffer* done in Excel and created by stage manager, Cindy Hennon Marino. There are two differences between this cue sheet and the one for *I due Figaro*. First, in the *…Klinghoffer* sheet, the light cue number that the spot cue is associated with is listed. The + and − symbols you see before some the cues indicate if the spot action should happen slightly before or after the light cue is called. The second difference is the way the time is listed. Whereas the *I due Figaro* cue sheet gives specific counts, this one lists speeds, such as medium, slow, and bump (zero count).

DECK

Deck cues are scenic or prop moves that happen on stage, or on the deck. These could be transitions or movements that crew do manually or automated. Deck cues could be called verbally or with cue lights. Figures 6.19 and 6.20 are two different deck sheets.

How It Can be Listed: DQ or "Deck" [insert movement or cue number]. If the show also has automation, you could list it as a deck cue, but if you have to differentiate because there are both deck and automation cues, then AUTO [insert cue number] would work too.

How It Can Be Called: "Standby on the deck for [insert movement or cue number]." "Standby auto cue 4" or "Standby automation cue 4."

Figure 6.19 was taken from the deck and rail run sheet for *Otello* at the Castleton Festival. In this excerpt, deck, props, and rail were all placed on one run sheet. Again, whether everything is together on one run sheet or separated out will depend on the crew and their preference. All deck cues were numbered and listed as "DQ" and called over headset by the calling stage manager. For crew members that went out on stage and had to take their headset off, the SM still gave the G-O over headset and the ASMs gave them a visual cue, similar to how they cue singers out on stage.

2013 Season		Deck and Rail Running			Dir: Lynne Hockney
Version FINAL					Cond: Maestro Maazel

Time (Placement)	RQ#/ DQ#	LS# / Description (Cue Light)	IN / OUT (Speed)	Deck	Who/ What
Act I (33:00)					
-0:15 (before downbeat)	**RQ #1**	#2/House Curtain (DS)	**OUT** (Med)		Brian M
3:40 (18/2/3)	**DQ #1**			Set stairs CS onto Jetty	Will and Brian
3:30 (18/2/3)	**Props**	Handoff to soldiers		Short Rifle Flag Short Rifle	Margaret Bert Craig
5:10 (25/2/1)	**DQ #2**	All out on stage		*Strike stairs CS*	Will and Brian
				Strike stairs SL	Vinnie and Jack
				Strike stairs SR	Josh and Craig
				Go to Places at Jetty for next DQ	All Crew
5:20 (26/2/1)	**DQ #3**			*Strike Jetty to SR/SL*	All Crew
				SR Jetty split and on-stage side moved DS, out of entrance	Paul, Vinnie, Will, Brian, Josh, Craig
	Props			Light Torches (1/2 pellet) USL/USR as offstage as possible	Brian SR, Jack SL

Figure 6.19 This excerpt was taken from the Castleton Festival's production of *Otello*. In this example, the deck, rail, and prop moves were integrated into one run sheet.

CANDIDE
Rotation Run Sheet

Director: Dean Anthony
Conductor: Michael Sakir

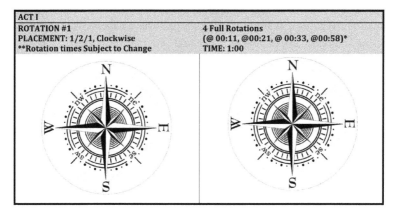

ACT I	
ROTATION #1	**4 Full Rotations**
PLACEMENT: 1/2/1, Clockwise	**(@ 00:11, @00:21, @ 00:33, @00:58)***
**Rotation times Subject to Change	**TIME: 1:00**

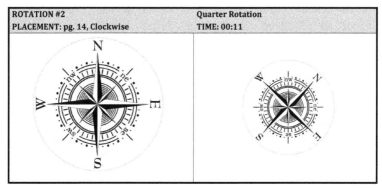

ROTATION #2	**Quarter Rotation**
PLACEMENT: pg. 14, Clockwise	**TIME: 00:11**

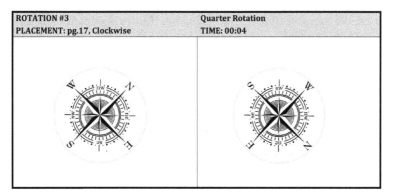

ROTATION #3	**Quarter Rotation**
PLACEMENT: pg.17, Clockwise	**TIME: 00:04**

Figure 6.20 Taken from the rotation run sheet for Brevard Music Center's production of *Candide.* This paperwork was produced and given to the automation programmer prior to tech so he could pre-program all of the turntable movements.

Sometimes, deck paperwork consist of more than just deck shifts that are done by crew. Brevard Music Center's production of *Candide* had an automated turn table as part of its set. Because of this, the deck paperwork consisted of all the rotations (Figure 6.20). It was very important to have paperwork for the turn table operator as early as possible so they could program those cues in prior to tech. Important pieces of information that is listed here are the number of rotations within a cue, the length of the turn and the direction the table should move in. With that info, the operator was able to import it into the automation computer. To make this, the graphic of the compass, which was painted on the top of the turn table, was used and rotated accordingly. The length was based on the music and the direction was based off of the staging.

SOUND

Sound cues can refer to recorded effects, live sound effects, performer mics or mics used for announcements. You will run into the usage of mics in opera, but they will most likely be area-type mics to help with balance of the singer's voice and orchestra pre-recorded sound cues may be triggered by the sound operator, either via headset or a cue light, or the calling SM will be the one pressing "GO." One more common way to run sound cues is through a program called Qlab and the simple tap of the space bar or any other pre-determined hot key will trigger the cue.

How It Can Be Listed: SQ or SX.

How It Can Be Called: "Standby sound 400." "Sound GO."

This example was taken from Brevard Music Center's production of *Street Scene*. Whereas this is a stand-alone cue sheet, sometimes sound cues are listed in the AV Run sheet (Figure 6.25 (a and b)). If there is amplification, the sound mixer will most likely not be on headset because they will be listening to the show live in order to mix. If they are also the ones running sound cues, they will take these cues themselves, or even off of a cue light if there happens to be a lot. If the sound operator is not mixing the show and happens to be on headset, then you may be calling these cues the same way you would lighting, deck, or rail cues.

TIME	SCORE	Q#	EFFECT	LOCATION	NOTES
Act I: 1:13:58					
1:20	5/2/03	SQ A	Radio of overture	House #1, 2nd floor window (SR)	Piotor will bring radio and sit outside of window
Act II: 58:21					
32:50	pg. 225	SQ B	Ambulance Arrival	Off stage left	*Mr. Buchanan! Mr. Buchanan!*
38:25	238/1/3	SQ C	Ambulance Departure	Off stage left	
43:00	pg. 243	SQ D	Baby Crying #1	UCNT (ground floor)	*Picture of it somewhere*
44:50	pg.247	SQ E	Baby Crying #2	UCNT (ground floor)	*Happy home* **_busted_** *up* through *'hush baby hush*. **Take own out Q

Figure 6.21 An excerpt from the sound cue sheet for *Street Scene*.

Since there were only small handful of cues, and they all were called at a specific place in the music, the calling SM triggered them via Qlab, since it would have been too much for the sound mixer to be stuck in a score for the full show.

RAIL

Rail cues refer to any scenery that is flying in and out, or soft goods (legs, cyc, main drape) that need to be moved or are being utilized. Even if a show does not have flying scenery, sometimes soft goods will need to fly in and out for large scenery pieces to move on and off stage. Rail cues could be called verbally or with cue lights.

How It Can Be Listed: RQ.

How It Can Be Called: "Standby Rail 4: LS 14 IN – Fast & AUTO LS 23 OUT + 56 IN." "Rail 4 GO."

Rail Cue	Who	LS #	IN/OUT	Speed	Description	Scene
PRE-SET		4	IN		Grand Drape	Pre-Show
		6	IN		Reed Header	
		7	IN		Reed Legs #1	
		10	IN		House Leg #1	
		14	OUT		Reed Wall	
		20	IN		House Boder #1	
		22	IN		House Border #2	
		23	IN		House Legs #2	
		27	IN		Emile's Terrace	
		30	OUT		Stage Proscenium	
		31	IN		House Border #3	
		32	IN		Reed Legs #2	
		33	IN		House Legs #3	
		42	IN		House Border #4	
		43	IN		Reed Border #3	
		44	IN		Reed Legs #3	
		42	IN		House Legs #4	
		54	IN		House Border #5	
		55	IN		House Legs #5	
		56	OUT		Black Scrim	
		65	IN		Show Backdrop	
1	Joe	4	OUT	4 count	Grand Drape	Top of I:1
2	Lauren	14	IN	Fast	Reed Wall	End of I:1; Deck Q #1
	Joe	27	OUT	AUTO	Emile's Terrance	
	Joe	23	OUT	FOLLOW	House Legs #2	
2.5	Joe	23	IN	Fast	House Legs #2	Shift Complete
3	Lauren	14	OUT	Fast	Reed Wall	I:2
4	Lauren	14	IN	Fast	Reed Wall	End of I:3
	Joe	23	OUT	AUTO	House Legs #2	
	Joe	56	IN	FOLLOW	Black Scrim	During transition
4.5	Joe	23	IN	Fast	House Legs #2	After STRIKE of wash machine

Figure 6.22   Rail cue sheet for Opera Roanoke's *South Pacific*.

This is an example of a rail sheet from Opera Roanoke's *South Pacific*. Prior to the cues that take place during the show, all of the line sets being used are listed with their line set number (LS#), whether or not they are IN or OUT and a description of the piece. If the SM calling is not going to give the line set numbers of each piece that is going in or out with the cue or when giving a standby (this does add to more verbiage that needs to be said, then it is a good idea to list it on the cue sheet so the operator can refer to it if needed. Another important piece of information that is listed is the speed of each cue. The speeds may not be solidified until tech (the designer and director will be the ones weighing in on this), so many times, it is the last piece of info that goes in. Another factor that tends to go into the design of how flies go in and out and at what speed is the number of fly operators that are assigned to the show. Speeds can be listed as "fast," "medium" or "slow," or with a physical count. Once the look and speed of the cue is finalized, discuss with your operators if they prefer the speed or counts listed on the run sheet.

PROJECTIONS

It is becoming more common for shows to incorporate projections into their scenery. Do not get this confused with supertitles, which SMs do not have to worry about calling. Since "projections" is such a lengthy word and quite a mouthful, the word "video" or "TAB" has been used instead. Not only does it roll off the tongue much easier, it has fewer syllables. It may not seem like a big difference now, but try spitting that out while giving three other departments their standbys!

How It Can Be Listed: PQ, VQ, TAB.

How It Can Be Called: "Video 100 GO" or "V 100 GO."

pp.	Act	m.	Action	PJ Q	Projection	LX Q	Lighting
66	1	452	With Gun shot	18	silhouette of Dr. Fowler from screen Double vision kind of video of him shooting himself	40	Only Projection and side lit Harry at SL. In Dr. Fowler house
67	1	457		19	Transition out of Dr. Fowler's	41	Fast B/O after scene to cover getting trunk out. Transition into MK Apt + Chorus DS side lit protesting DSC
67	1	460	Harry watches picketing out window. Margaret carries tea tray in	20	Transition into MK Apt. City lights down below for picketers	42	Hit Chorus at DSC in circle picketing. Tops and sides only. Establish MK Apt. Include SR Stairs and Stair top for Harry
68		471				42.5	
72	1	501	Harry watches picketing out window. Margaret carries tea tray in	21-cut	Lose City. Keep MK Apt (Resolve by m.503) Add Ethan.	43	Establish MK Apt USR Softer lit from High side top Lose focus on chorus slowly. Keep USR Stair top. Total ISO to USR

Figure 6.23 An excerpt of the projection cue sheet for The World Premiere of *Falling Angel* at Brevard Music Center. This cue sheet should not look much different than a cue sheet for lighting. It lists what the projection is/what is doing, the visual action or placement in the score it takes place on, as well as what light cue is paired with. Depending on the amount of projections there are in the show, or if there are enough people/operators, there is the option to run projections through the lightboard. Instead of calling lighting and projection cues, you would only have to worry about calling light cues. Each projection cue will then be associate with a light cue number (known as an empty cue because nothing will change within the lighting), and when that number is called, the projections cue will trigger.

CUE LIGHTS

Cue lights are not *as* common in opera since there are ASMs on either side to cue the singers on stage. Similar to monitors, if you think that you will use cue lights, bring up the request early. One cue light that is the most important to have is the one in the orchestra pit, used to cue the concert master and sometimes Maestro when to tune or start playing. Always double check that this light is setup for the first orchestra rehearsal and that you are able to control it wherever you are calling from.

If you are using cue lights for lighting, rail, or deck, you always want to vocalize via headset that you have turned on the cue light. This can be as simple as giving a verbal standby as you are turning on the light. For an example, *Standby Rail cue 4 on the red and automation 10 on the green.*

On a production of *I due Figaro* at Manhattan School of Music, there were multiple entrances on both sides that happened simultaneously. In the room, it worked with just one ASM because the singers could see her from any angle, but that would not be the same once we moved into the theater. I did not want to volunteer myself to cue singers on while at the same time calling the show, so I got creative and asked the company if it would be possible to add cue lights on either side of the stage, one in each wing, and have the ASM control them from stage right of the stage where they were mainly stationed. Not only was the company able to accomplish this, but it worked out as a great solution when running with only one ASM. Although it is not ideal, it's a great trick to keep your back pocket.

If your show does call for multiple cue lights and/or headsets, it could be helpful to put together a map showing exactly where you want them placed and their purpose for the electrician. Ideally, you would want to have this ready to hand off to the electrician or production manager at the same time as the tech request, if not sooner. The easiest and clearest way to make a cue light/clear com map is to use a ground plan from the show; that way you get both on and offstage areas (if needed). For the map in Figure 6.24a, the LD's light plot was used to show accurate placements of cue lights since they were on light booms. Different shapes and colors were used to differentiate what it was and who (SM vs ASM) was to control it. The symbol key and description of each item can be seen in Figure 6.24b.

As heard on headset…

On a production of *Brigadoon*, the orchestra pit cue light was also used to cue the Maestro when to start playing after a scene transition. Since the set was so massive and did not all fly in and out, 10–20 second pausas (short breaks between acts, usually under 5-minutes) were used to finalize any scenery changes on stage. Because the Maestro was unable to see when the transition was complete and performers were set on stage, the cue light was his signal. The light went on as a standby when everyone was close to complete, and it went off when he could start the music.

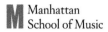

I DUE FIGARO
Cue Light & Clear Com Plot

Director: Dona D. Vaughn
Conductor: Stefano Sarzani

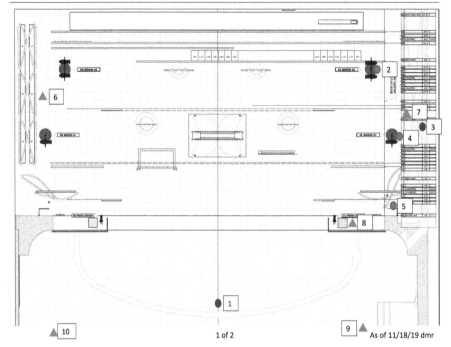

(a)   1 of 2   As of 11/18/19 dmr

#	Location	Purpose	Controlled
1	Pit	Cue Tuning/Concert Master	PSM- @ calling station
2	SL Boom #2	Cue Singer Entrances: L3	ASM- @ SR
3	SL Rail (Ladder)	Cue Rail	PSM @ calling station
4	SL Boom #1	Cue Singer Entrances: L2	ASM @ SR
5	DSL Wall	Cue Singer Entrances: L1	ASM @ SR
6	SR	Clear Com ASM	Wireless
7	Rail	Clear Com Fly men	
8	SL	Clear Com SM	Wired (*will provide their own headset)
9	HR	Clear Com Spot Op	
10	HL	Clear Com Spot Op	

SYMBOL KEY	
●	Cue Light controlled by PSM
●	Cue Light controlled by ASM
▲	Clear Com

(b)

2 of 2   As of 11/18/19 dmr

Figure 6.24 (a and b) Cue light and clear com plot for a production of *I due Figaro*.
Light plot courtesy of LD, Tyler Micoleau.

PLACING CUES IN THE SCORE

There are a handful of ways one can place cues in their score. Unlike a script, you cannot as easily place them off to one side or in the margins. The only space that is available is within the music, unless some reformatting is done. Remember the examples in Chapter 5 that demonstrated how the ASMs insert their entrances and exit cues? That is one way stage managers will put in their calling cues. Every stage manager has a different way which works best for them. Some SMs utilize different color Post-its, Post-it flags, and even colored dots. Some SMs prefer to write directly in the score above the system/measure that the cue takes place and will just draw an arrow as to where it should be called.

I found that using colored Post-it flags to insert my cues worked best when calling. They stick well and do not easily come off the page. Since they are translucent, I can place them on top of the music and not cover anything up. Just as using a pencil during staging to write blocking in so it can easily be erased and moved, the flags can just as easily be picked up and moved. Since the flags also come in different colors, it can be helpful when color coding cues. As for writing standbys and pages, I stick with $3 \times 5''$ Post-its since it gives more room to write on. The process in which stage managers place cues in their book can change based on personal preference. Ultimately, use whatever system makes the most sense and will allow you to successfully call the show. The system may even evolve the more you do it, or changed based on the show and its needs.

MAESTRO CAM

The Maestro cam is not just for the singers, but for stage management as well. When setting up the SM station at the tech table, make sure an extra monitor is available and setup with Maestro vision. It is best to get used to when and where [in the music] you will be looking at the monitor from the beginning. You do not want to go through all of tech getting comfortable watching Maestro [live] in front of you only to move backstage the day before opening and have to quickly adjust to something different. Similar to the SM using a Maestro monitor from which to call cues off, ASMs may also use them when cuing singers onto stage, watching the baton for clues such as the start of new music, cutoffs, pickups, or even tempo change. Whether you are an SM or ASM, you do not have to have a full understanding of conducting or know what all the hand gestures and waving around of the baton means in order to stage manage opera. As with all aspects of stage management, you will learn on the job, and what you do not know, you simply ask the other SMs, conductor, assistant conductor, or even pianist.

Besides a Maestro monitor being present at the calling station, some productions call for Maestro monitors to be moved around backstage. Opera has evolved over the years and singers are now given more blocking and staging to help with storytelling rather than just stand center stage and sing an eight-minute aria (what is sometimes referred to as park and bark). In order to achieve this, additional monitors are used and strategically placed so they are out of view from the audience, but in eye line of the singer. If there is an offstage chorus, the assistant conductor (or sometimes rehearsal pianist) will conduct from the wings, keeping with Maestro so everyone is together.

Monitors that are backstage are normally on rovers or moving carts. These carts are also equipped with small speakers which pipe in the orchestra. If the rovers are moving, your team will have to put together an AV Plot, which will list all the locations and times you want them to move. Diagrams make it easy for the sound or electrician op to follow, and just as you would spike furniture on stage, the same will be done with the rovers.

As heard on headset...

When I first started calling operas, I did not fully understand how valuable having an eye on Maestro was. The more shows I called, I noticed that I would call as if I were just another player in the pit. Action and music should work as one, where you cannot tell if the music is what prompts the action or the action is prompting the music. Instead of just guessing when a downbeat or cutoff will land, why not just watch the person controlling it? Not only did calling become 10 times easier, over time I became a much better musician. Calling an opera is similar to taking a strategic test; all the answers are right in front of you, you just need to know where to look and when.

—DR

In their words...

Why do conductors go back and forth between conducting with a baton vs conducting with their hands?

It really depends on the piece and the forces! Batons are easier to catch from a distance, so they are typically used with big pits and larger stages (also, if the baton will be used in performance, it should be used during staging rehearsals, even if there is no orchestra at that point). With chamber music, the baton can feel a little imperious; having no baton can create a slightly more collaborative atmosphere. Ultimately it's a very personal choice and comes down to what the musicians need.

—Kamna Gupta on conducting

AV PLOT

An AV plot is only needed if monitors are being used and moved throughout the piece. Sometimes, the theater has permanent monitors out in the audience, whether they be mounted below the mezzanine or balcony, or are fixed somehow in the wings or on the truss. If this is the case, there is no need for the paperwork, unless specifically asked for. Similar to the cue light/clear com plot, the easiest and cleanest way to make an AV plot is to use either the ground plan or light plot. To show different types of moment or angles, arrows can be used, or as seen in Figures 6.25 (a and b), text box with arrows, so they can be labeled. Cue numbers and movements will be listed below the diagram for the crew member moving them. If there are multiple movements, it helps to spike their placements as you would furniture onstage to ensure that the angle and placement is the same every time.

Tips from the toolkit...

Do not assume that monitors are always available and will be set up (besides the one that'll be at the calling station). Many times, they are easily forgotten, so bring it into the conversation early. If additional monitors are not available, it is best to know sooner rather than later, as this might affect staging.

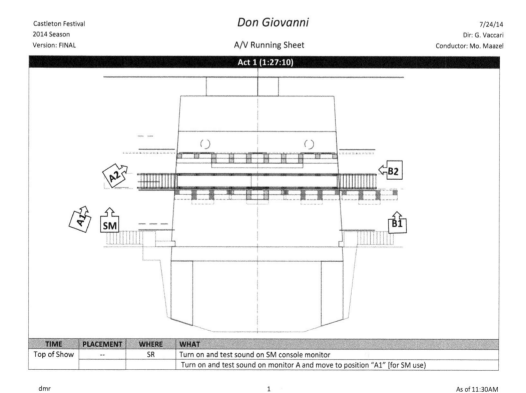

Figure 6.25 (a and b)   Here are the first two pages of the AV Plot for *Don Giovanni*.

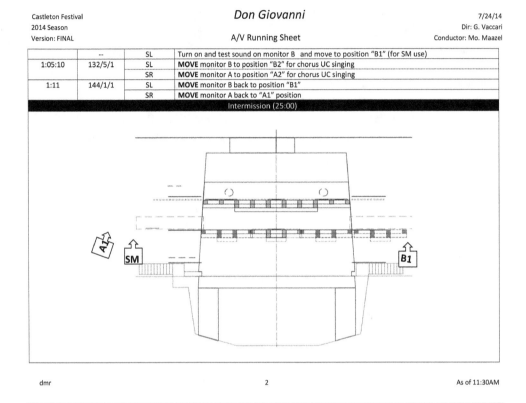

Castleton Festival
2014 Season
Version: FINAL

Don Giovanni

A/V Running Sheet

7/24/14
Dir: G. Vaccari
Conductor: Mo. Maazel

	--	SL	Turn on and test sound on monitor B and move to position "B1" (for SM use)
1:05:10	132/5/1	SL	**MOVE** monitor B to position "B2" for chorus UC singing
		SR	**MOVE** monitor A to position "A2" for chorus UC singing
1:11	144/1/1	SL	**MOVE** monitor B back to position "B1"
		SR	**MOVE** monitor A back to "A1" position
Intermission (25:00)			

dmr   2   As of 11:30AM

Figure 6.25 (b)

REHEARSAL REPORTS DURING TECH

Unless otherwise told, the stage manager will continue to put out a version of the report, although the overall style and content may change. Once in tech, the majority of the distribution list for reports will be present in the room. Typically, the creative and production team will have a short meeting at the end of the day to go over key events, discuss any changes or problem areas, and talk through the tech schedule for the next day. It is always nice to jot these notes down (although not required) or any changes that were made so there is a paper trail to go back to or a check list for the next day's work call. The SM does not need to worry about however, summarizing the overall discussion of the meeting. Whereas in rehearsal, the general section was used to keep everyone who was not in the room in the loop, now that everyone is present, this section becomes a place for announcements or full group notes. The longer the days become, the less time stage management has to put together a "pretty" report to send out. By the end of the day, the team wants to get out the door as soon as possible and try and catch some sleep before having to be back the next day. That being said, moving your report into the body of an email and bullet pointing what was discussed is just as acceptable, unless otherwise told by production.

DAYS OFF

After a long week of tech, both the cast and production crew is ready for their day of rest prior to the opening performance. This day off gives the full crew and SM team time to relax after many long hours of tech. Performing opera, especially a large role, is not only taxing on the voice, but also on the body. This is why opera performances are never back-to-back and always broken up with at least one day off in between unless they are double casted. After a day of recuperation, everyone is ready for a full house of audience! *In bocca al lupo!* When translated from Italian means "into the wolf's mouth," originally used in opera to wish a performer good luck prior to a performance.

With tech successfully completed, it is almost time for opening! In the next chapter, we will discuss performance schedules, reports, and break down the calling of the show as an SM and ASM.

CHAPTER 7

Performance

Toi, Toi, Toi, a saying that is commonly heard on opening, is an onomatopoetic imitation of the sound of spitting, done to ward off evil or cursed spirits. Nowadays, the saying has become a common good luck sentiment, such as telling someone to *break a leg!* Although we have strayed away from the "grand opera" traditions where audience members show up in ravishing ball gowns and tuxedos, opening night still has a celebratory air to it. And why shouldn't it be celebrated? Just think of the amount of work that was accomplished in a short amount of time!

In their own words...

I consider an SM the conductor of the backstage, so just like any rela-tionship, I try to put myself in the other person's shoes to determine if there's anything I can do to help make anything easier. Having a dependable SM is every conductor's biggest gift, whether the conductor knows it or not!

—*Kelly Kuo on collaboration between*
a conductor and stage manager

FINALIZING THE PRE-SHOW ROUTINES

Similar to the rehearsal period, duties are divided amongst the team in order to get everything done in a timely fashion. These duties will not stray much from what they were in the room; the costume ASM will be the one checking in with wardrobe, hair and makeup to make sure they are not only staying on schedule, but that singers are arriving on time and getting in the chair when called. The props ASM will be stationed in the theater checking off that all props are in their proper spot and that the stage is set up for top of show. The SM is in the

DOI: 10.4324/9781003047391-8

booth or at the SM console checking in with all the operators, ensuring that cue lights and headsets work, the PA system is on and works in all necessary places, and finally, being present for the backout check with the light board operator. Keeping things consistent amongst the team will ensure that things get done correctly. Now that there is an audience coming in, keeping on a schedule is key. Whereas during tech rehearsals, stage management could go out and adjust or have something fixed on stage until curtain, everything needs to be finalized before the audience walks in. (If, however, the curtain is in for top of show, you will have a little more leeway finalizing onstage presets.) The final task the PSM (or the ASM checking presets) should do is walk the stage to ensure that everything is set correctly, soft goods have been dressed, and that everything is safe. After checking in with both ASMs that everything is ready for top of show, the house will be handed over to house management to start letting audience in.

As heard on headset...

Sometimes things may look differently on stage than they do from the front of house. I assisted on a show where the stage was built with angles, which gave off an optical illusion unless you were sitting center in the audience. During a performance, the director commented that the stage right table was too far onstage from where it originally was placed, which blocked a lot of action that went on behind the bar, upstage of the table. We found out after the show that somehow spikes got adjusted by two feet. The only way to have truly noticed was to take a final look at the full stage picture before handing the house over to house management. Had it been flagged early on, someone could have gone up on stage and made the adjustment, or at least known what to look for and fix it from there. Regardless of how many times you do a show, never shortchange your preshow checks. The one time you do, the table may end up two feet off-spike!

—DR

THE STAGE MANAGER RUN SHEET

Unless something is written down, nine times out of ten, it will be missed or forgotten. This is why run paperwork is put together for crews, so duties happen when they are supposed to and in the order they need to happen in. The same goes for stage managers, both with their duties and announcements that are being made throughout the run. Unlike show run paperwork, this is for the stage manager's eyes only, so a significant amount of formatting is not needed unless preferred by the SM using it. Some stage managers like to check off the event once it has been completed, whereas others will use it as a reference page. Some stage managers are beginning to embrace the digital world and are saving everything on their phones. This is great because you do not have to worry about carrying around a hard copy, putting it down and then walking away, leaving it behind. Another plus to this, similar to the digital score, anyone can pull it up via the show Dropbox or Drive account. There are even several apps where your checklist or run sheet can be uploaded and you can physically check off the duties as they are completed. Paper backups, similar to a backup score if going digital, is always the safe way to go.

Known as the PIP, short for pre-show, intermission, and post-show announcements (Figures 7.1 & 7.2), this piece of paperwork also includes all

---

JOC 2017   Director: Dean Anthony
Street Scene   Conductor: Robert Moody
PIP   Version: FINAL dmr

60 minutes 'til TOS (6:30/1:30p)   .

"Ladies and Gentlemen of "Street Scene", we are one hour from the top of the show, one hour from the top of the show and 45 minutes 'til chorus warm up. Thank you."

- ☐ Check cast sign-in sheet, find all missing personnel (ELANA)
- ☐ Headset check
- ☐ Cue light check (orchestra pit & houses)
- ☐ Check paging com
- ☐ Check SFX levels (with Dean)

45 minutes 'til TOS (7:15/1:45p)   .
- ☐ Sugar window installed
- ☐ Check all curtains

30 minutes 'til TOS (7:00/1:30p)   .

"Ladies and Gentlemen of "Street Scene", we are 30 minutes from the top of the show and house is open, 30 minutes from the top of the show and house is open."

- ☐ Check cast sign-in sheet and hair and makeup calls, find all missing personnel (ELANA)
- ☐ Stage walk for safety check (DANIELLE)
- ☐ Turn off work lights in hallway
- ☐ All presets complete.... *LQ1*, **GO** (DANIELLE)
- ☐ Hand house over to FOH
- ☐ Radio check

15:00 minutes 'til TOS (6:45/7:45/1:45p)   .

"Ladies and Gentlemen of "Street Scene", we are 15 minutes from the top of the show and 10 minutes till places, 15 minutes from the top of the show and 10 minutes till places. Everyone to The Morrison Playhouse for vocal warm up. Thank you."

10:00 minutes 'til TOS (7:20/1:50p)   .

"Ladies and Gentlemen of "Street Scene," we are 10 minutes from the top of the show, 10 minutes from the top of the show, 5 minutes till places for Act I, 5 minutes till places for Act I. Thank you."

5:00 minutes 'til TOS (7:25/1:55p)   .

"Ladies and Gentlemen of "Street Scene", we are 5 minutes from the top of show, 5 minutes from the top of show, PLACES for Act I, PLACES for Act I. Thank you."

Ladies & Gentlemen of the orchestra to the pit

To SR: Mr. Ellege, Ms. Jaharis, Mr. Fitzwater, Ms. Jackson, Mr. Buszewski, Mr. Madden,

---

Figure 7.1 (a and b)   An excerpt from *Street Scene's* PIP. These are the first two pages, which cover all pre-show announcements up until downbeat.

JOC 2017   Director: Dean Anthony
Street Scene   Conductor: Robert Moody
PIP   Version: FINAL dmr

Mr. Rydel, Ms. Yarham, Ms. Atkinson, Ms. Hatten, Maestro Moody

To SL: Ms. Moran, Ms. Cordaro, Mr. Bair, Ms. Law, Ms. Judd, Ms. Mims, Ms. Weisman,

Ms. Helm, Mr. Thomas, Snow, Mr. Anthony

5 minutes till places: Mr. Mosley, Ms. Palmeiro

4:00 minutes 'til TOS (7:26/1:56p)
    Check for Places:

· Headset	· Stage Right
✓ LX Board – *Taylor*	✓ 10 singers
✓ Sound - *Tinesha*	✓ Maestro Moody
✓ ASM SR – *Beth*	✓ ASM- Beth
✓ ASM SL – *Jackie, Elana*	· Stage Left
	✓ 9 singers
Walkie	✓ Snow
✓ Katherine (kid wrangler)	✓ Mr. Anthony
✓ Juliet- FOH	✓ ASM- Jackie
✓ Andee- PM	✓ ASM- Elana
✓ Walt- Orch. SM	

2:00 minutes 'til TOS (7:28/1:58p)
    Confirm Places for TOS, if members missing repage.
    Dean STBY for speech

1:00 minutes 'til TOS (7:29/1:59p)
    STANDBY: LX 2-15, SFX 1
        - *Once House is given to SM* .... Speech Slider **GO,** send Dean on stage
        - AFTER SPEECH.................Speech Slider **OUT** LX 2*:* House ½, Orchestra Tune **GO**
        - *Second tune*... LX 3: House out SEND Maestro to pit **GO**
        - *End of tune*.. Mo. **GO**, LX 4: Mo. BOW

        *ANNOUNCE OVER WALKIE THAT THE SHOW HAS BEGUN. ACT I: 1:14

Figure 7.1 *(Continued)*

pages, checks, calls, and reminders that take place before, during, and after the show. This also helps with keeping consistency when making all announcements since the full script is written out. If the space you are performing in does not have a PA system, it is still a great cheat sheet to have since it will serve as a reminder when you or you ASMs should make the rounds for physical calls.

PERFORMANCE SCHEDULE AND CALLS

A daily still should still be going out to the cast and team even on performance days, whereas in theater or during long running shows, SMs are doing away with daily schedules and just sending out a weekly call. In opera, because we have (the majority of the time) shorter runs, and only a handful of performances, a daily along with the hair and makeup schedule is sent out the day prior. Calls can start as early as two hours before downbeat (or the start of music.). The earliest calls to the theater are usually hair and makeup,

PRESHOW

(11:00 am Show) (6:00 pm Show)

-70 min (9:55) (4:55)	PAGE	"5 minutes until Ensemble Warm-up on the Woodcock Back Porch."
- 1 hour (10:05) (5:05)	PAGE	"Good Morning/Afternoon everyone, welcome to performance # of The Glimmerglass Festival's production of *Il Trovatore*. 1 hour to top of show. 1 hour to top of show, please.
- 45 min (10:20) (5:20)	PAGE	"45 minutes to top of show. 45 minutes to top of show, please."
- 30 min (10:35) (5:35)	PAGE	"Half hour call to top of show. Half hour, please"
-15 min (10:50) (5:50)	PAGE	"15 minutes to top of show. 15 minutes to top of show, please." ***RADIO HOUSE 15 minutes***
- 10 min (10:55) (5:55)	PAGE	"10 minutes to top of show. 10 minutes to top of show, please. 5 minutes to places." ***RADIO HOUSE 10 minutes***
- 5 min (11:00) (6:00)	**SIGNAL** **PAGE**	**TURN OFF SOUND LIGHT – 5 MINUTE ANNOUNCEMENT** "The call is places, places please for top of show. Ms. Bryce-Davis, Ms. Castro, Mr. Kunde and Tutti Coro to Stage. Maestro Colaneri and Members of the Orchestra to the ABOT Stage. Warning on Wardrobe Q 1."
-3:00 min (11:02) (6:02)	**STANDBY**	**PRESHOW ANNOUNCEMENT and FRANCESCA**
	SIGNAL	**TURN OFF SOUND LIGHT – PRESHOW ANNOUNCEMENT**
		FRANCESCA GO – AFTER ANNOUNCEMENT
	PAGE	"The call is places, places please for top of show. Ms. Bryce-Davis, Ms. Castro, Mr. Kunde and Tutti Coro to Stage. Maestro Colaneri and Members of the Orchestra to the ABOT Stage. Warning on Wardrobe Q 1."
0:00 min	**SIGNAL**	**TURN ON – Tune Light & Sound Light**
	STANDBY	LQ 10

Figure 7.2 Here is another example of pre-show announcements created by stage manager Alex W. Siedel. Instead of adding in all the in-between check list items as in Figure 7.1, this version is strictly announcements that are made over the PA during preshow.

followed by stage crew, stage management, and operators. Hair and makeup will put together their own calls based on the first entrance sheet. Other calls that might take place before the show are chorus warm-ups, recit rehearsal, or fight calls.

ADDITIONAL CALLS DURING THE SHOW

Remember those 30-second timings that you added into your score during prep? Well, there was more than one reason for doing them. If you were able to do more accurate timings during the room run, they will be closer to show conditions, if not, the ones that you did based off a recording will be sufficient. On top of calling lighting and other technical cues (rail, spots, deck), SMs also give places calls for singers and quick-change calls to costumes, hair and

The Barber of Seville
DAILY SCHEDULE: Sunday, February 16, 2020

11:30a-12:00p	RECIT REHEARSAL: Green Room Tutti Principals *Sahr*
12:00p	STAGE MANAGEMENT CALL HAIR & MAKEUP CALLS BEGIN (see attached calls)
1:15p	COSTUME CALL TUTTI CHORUS
1:45p	CHORUS WARMUP: Green Room *Benz, Borths*
2:00p	PERFORMANCE #2 FULL COMPANY

Figure 7.3   Performance daily schedule from *The Barber of Seville*.

The Barber of Seville
Hair and Makeup Calls

	Makeup with Michele	Makeup with Mark	Hair with Roza
12:00	Cosio		Goode
12:25			Spencer (pin curls)
12:30		Coe	
12:40		Foster	Cosio
12:45	Mykkanen		
12:50		Cleland	
1:00		Allicock	
1:15	Spencer		Straight
1:20		Zhang	
1:40		Dupont	Lanter

Figure 7.4   Hair & makeup calls from *The Barber of Seville*.

makeup. Again, the tradition of calling singers to stage originated where singers would just fly in for a role. They would not necessarily know when and where they needed to be somewhere, so stage management would help guide them around backstage.

Tools you need:

- Post-its or a colored pen.
- Copy of the WWW.

  How to: Although all the information that is listed in the WWW is most likely in your book, I prefer to use it because it will be easier to skip to the sections needed rather than flipping through pages to find the next placement. I like to use Post -its —rather than writing in the margins or above systems— because it makes it easier to pick up and move if needed but also because it is eye catching. Whether you give warnings prior to a places call is a personal preference. Most calls given are typically between two to five minutes prior to their entrance but may change depending on the space that you are performing in (distance from dressing rooms), and how the group of people being called will react to the page. When it comes to technical calls such as quick changes, transitions or the end of an act, I prefer giving them a warning, usually 5-minutes, then the call to places.

  - **Step 1**: For 5-minute warnings, you will want to place them 7-minutes back from when someone is needed. The places call will be given 2-minutes prior to the actual entrance, transition, or change.

  - **Step 2:** Place your Post-it or write it in! Whether you just want to write yourself a note in shorthand (*Places: Ms. Chang-SR)* or the full script that you will announce offer the PA system (*Places please Ms. Chang to SR)* is up to you.

Other call examples:

- 5-minute warning till the end of the act and the intermission shift.
- Paging wardrobe/hair to the stage for [insert cue/quick change].
- 5-minutes till places for off stage singing SL.
- Bows

Tips from the toolkit...

It is the SM that will be giving the five minutes and places warnings to singers over the PA system. Since this may not come in over the headset, it's a good idea for the ASMs to also note when singers should be arriving to places in their prompt book. That way, if they do not show up in a timely matter, the ASM can alert the PSM to re-page them.

Figure 7.5 An excerpt from the SM's call book of *La Boheme.* In this image, you can see one way of putting in calls, both for singers and operators, by using different color Post-its.

Additional tips:

- You may have to fudge some of your pages based off of other calls (such as lighting, spots, rail, etc.) that you have to call. That is, if you need to cheat and move a singer call back a little further so you have time to call a light cue, do so.

- A crew head/supervisor might ask for you to add a specific call for them, such as a quick-change call, whether it be backstage or when a singer should be arriving to the dressing room. Although they will have the show feed in their room or work space, they may not be paying as close attention to it if they are working on other things.

- Try to add your calls into your book as soon as possible. The earlier you have them in, the easier it will be when placing in all technical cues.

- Practice saying all your calls out loud. On paper it might look like it all fits, but once you say it out loud, you may realize that you need more time in order to get everything out.

- When speaking over the PA system speak up, speak clearly, and repeat your announcement twice to make sure that everyone hears it.

- If you are unsure how to pronounce someone's last name, ask! Nothing is more embarrassing than calling someone by the wrong name or mispronouncing their name over the PA system.

OPERA AND SUBS

Due to the average short run of an opera, it is very unlikely that an additional SM will be brought in to train on a track. Although, as is live theater, there are always rare circumstances where something may come up. If that were the case, the first preference would be to try and cover duties within the team either with a PA, AD, or combining tracks, and if that still proves to not be enough or impossible, then the production manager might reach out to someone who has worked with the company before or done the opera. With companies and festivals that run in rep, there is also the possibility that an SM from another team may stand in and cover a track during a rehearsal while the SM assigned to that show is in tech for another show simultaneously. In that instance, the cover would take notes on entrances, exits, props, costumes, that take place on their side of the stage, so that when the SM does return to rehearsal they are the most up to date.

As heard on headset...

It was tech week for The Magic Flute, and we were in the middle of one of our late-night lighting sessions. Our set had 12- foot tall metal towers on casters that moved around throughout the piece. Not realizing

> *how close she was to one the metal towers, one of my assistants turned and bumped her head on a cross bar. She was rushed to the nurse to get checked out. After spending the night at the infirmary, she was not cleared to come back to work the following day, which also happened to be our final dress rehearsal, due to a possible mild concussion. Since the show could not run with just one ASM, our AD ended up stepping in, using the ASM's book and paperwork to run the show. Since her book was clear and kept up to date, the fact that someone else was running her track was unnoticeable.*
>
> *—DR*

WORKING WITH FRONT OF HOUSE

Your collaboration with front of house (also seen or referred to as FOH) will not come into play until days leading up to tech and performance week. That is not to say that you have not been in contact with them during the whole process. At some point, whether it be face-to-face or via email, a discussion should be had regarding late seating, top of show sequence, and essentially anything else that may apply to the audience experience. Your house manager or assistant house manager will be your go-to person during performances. At half hour, the stage manager will transfer the house over to them; and once the audience is in, they will in turn, return it back to the SM which signals that the show can begin.

Some front of house managers prefer a written document (Figure 7.6) of everything that was discussed at your front of house meeting so they can distribute it to their ushers, volunteers, and staff members that come in contact with audience members. This document, known as a front of house info sheet or house manager info sheet, will cover basic show facts, but also basic questions that may be asked by an audience member.

The front of house info sheet should be concise and to the point. Similar to a run sheet, you want to convey enough information without it being too wordy and make it easy for anyone to pick up and effortlessly understand the information they are being presented with. Having everything categorized into three sections rather than just handing off a list with bullet points of information will not only help with overall organization, but also make it easier for someone to quickly run down the list and pinpoint exactly what they are looking for. The sooner you can get this to the house manager, the better. They would much rather have the majority of information with some holes, than a completed info sheet right before opening. If something is not finalized, or may change, highlight it, or note it in your meeting or email. An updated copy can always be sent at a later date.

Some important notes for house managers are:

- Entrances and exits happening through the house.

- Special effects such as strobe, gun shots, haze, dry ice or, of any sensitive content that would normally be part of the opera. Signage will need to be posted at point of entry.

- Late seating and when within the piece would be the best time to bring them in. Should they be seated near the back until an intermission? Are there multiple late seating placements within the act? Maybe at the end of a big number, when applause will cover any disturbance, or during a brighter scene, when the light flow from the lobby will not be disruptive. It is also smart to think of a moment after an intermission for any late seaters that may be coming in from the bathroom.

- Length of acts and when the intermission falls. Also the length of intermission. Will it be 15, 20, or 25 minutes?

TOP OF SHOW SEQUENCE

If there was one thing I wish I knew in my early days of opera, it was the ins and outs of the top of show sequence. This sequence will begin once the house manager has passed the house back over to the calling stage manager. The same sequence will take place after intermission. Once Maestro has taken their bow, they will then stand the orchestra for a full bow. After the bow, the following act will begin. If there are more than two acts in the opera, check in with Maestro to see if they are planning to bow the full orchestra before each Act. Below, you will find a breakdown of the full anatomy of the top of show sequence.

HOUSE TO HALF

If there is a curtain speech or a pre-recorded announcement, it will happen once the house has gone to half (this term references the brightness of the lights in the audience changing). If a speech is being done live, a spot light might be added or used to isolate the speaker if a special is not available or the curtain is in. Amplification, such as a hand held mic, may also be used and will need to be cued. After the curtain speech or pre-recorded announcement, the orchestra will tune by way of a cue light. If there is an orchestra manager, usually they will alert the concert master that tune is about to start, or physically cue them via the stage manager over headset. If there is not a curtain speech or pre-show announcement, tune will take place (still off of the cue light) as house has gone to half.

TUNE

There can be anywhere from two to four tunes, depending on the size of the orchestra. The concert master will connect with the principal oboist. They will produce an "A" for the winds to tune to concert pitch and another for the strings. Tuning could last anywhere from one to two minutes. At or during the last tune, the house will go out.

Boston Lyric Opera 2017/18 Season
The Nefarious, Immoral but Highly Profitable Enterprise of Mr. Burke & Mr. Hare
Front of House Information
Last updated 11/5/17

TIMINGS:

BURKE & Hare:	90:00
Bows:	05:00

Total Running Time: 95:00

TALK BACKS
- Talk backs will occur in the black box theater next door. Patrons will be guided there by front of house staff

HOUSE OPEN
- The house will open 30 minutes before the published start time

LATE SEATING
- Speeches at top of show?
- You can continue to seat patrons until tuning starts; patrons can be seating through tuning, but please reserve for extreme circumstances only. No seating after tuning begins.
- **1ˢᵗ late seating option TBD**
  All will be cued by the stage manager over the house radios and done by the house manager.
- **Late seats are located in seats in Row L.**

TICKET STUBS & PROGRAMS:
- **Ticket stubs will be kept by Front of House Staff and given to Brianna or Becca.**
- **Programs will be stored in the coat check area for regular performances, and elsewhere for Gala.**
- There will be **one program stuffer provided by BLO staff** to be inserted in the program for all performances by usher staff.

BOX OFFICE / WILL-CALL
- **Will-Call** for all BLO ticketing will be facilitated by BLO staff at the Box Office table. BLO will set-up at 5:00PM on November 6ᵗʰ, 8ᵗʰ, 9ᵗʰ and 10:00AM on Sunday November 12ᵗʰ for both performances.

FINAL DRESS (Monday November 6ᵗʰ):
- **The stage manager will make an announcement to the audience to remain seated and refrain from talking incase we have a hold/show stop.**
- The formal program is not to be distributed at Final Dress; **BLO staff will provide a black/white handout to be passed out to patrons.**
- There will be Audience Signage noting that **photography and videography will be taking place during the performance**
- All Will-Call / ticketing operations for final dress will be run by BLO staff in the Box Office. BLO will set-up starting at 4:30PM.
- Final Dress Rehearsal is an invited dress with **general admission tickets issued by BLO. Ticket is based on Orchestra, VIP and Hype Team sections.** Ticketing for Final Dress will be labeled as follows:

Figure 7.6 (a and b)   The front of house info sheet taken from Boston Lyric Opera's production of *The Nefarious, Immoral but Highly Profitable Enterprise of Mr. Burke & Ms. Hare*, put together by stage manager, Cindy Hennon Marino. *(Continued)*

- ○ General Admission – Orchestra
- ○ General Admission – VIP (part of orchestra; this section will have signage and a BLO staff member to help reserve these seats for when patrons enter the house.)
- ○ General Admission – Hype Team (part of mezzanine; this section will have signage and a BLO staff member to help reserve these seats for when patrons enter the house)

AMENITIES
- There is no concessions
- There is coat check

AUDIENCE SIGN INFO:
- There will be photography/video during the Final Dress Rehearsal

OTHER BLO ACTIVITIES
- **PRE-SHOW ORFEO LOUNGES**: BLO will host a pre-curtain lounge for its Orfeo Society Members at Barcelona; hours are 6:00 – 7:15PM on evening performances and10:30 – 11:45AM and 2:30 – 3:45PM on Sunday.

Figure 7.6   *(Continued)*

MAESTRO ENTER/BOW

The Maestro down light, which is a special pointed down at the podium so the orchestra and singers on stage can see the conductor, will come up to full (or as close to full depending on how bright the light is) as the Maestro enters the pit and makes their way to the podium. On their way, they will shake hands with the concert master, sometimes exchanging half bows as a way of "greeting." They will then step up onto their podium, face the house and acknowledge the audience and take a bow. The ASM might also cue Maestro to the pit via the stage manager over headset.

MAESTRO LIGHT TO PLAYING LEVEL

Once Maestro has finished their bow, they will turn around, facing the orchestra. As they turn, their light will go down to playing level, which is the level it will be for the rest of the act. Maestro will then prep the orchestra and the opera will begin

You may ask, as the SM, *what is the best way to list these cues in my score?* Most likely, there will not be a lot of free space on the first page of music, so make yourself an insert that can be placed at the top of each act. Rather than having these cues scribbled off in the corner, they can be spaced out easy to read. The last thing you want is to be searching for your top of show and act cues. Since this is something that each stage manager will put together on their own, there is no right or wrong way of doing so, it all comes down to preference and what would be easiest for the caller. It can be laid out in more of a table format, shown in Figure 7.7, or in as a list.

In addition to the top of show cues, everyone who is running the show (crew) is listed at the top. This is so the SM can just go down the list and 'roll call' and do a final check in with everyone to confirm that they are set and ready to start

DIE FLEDERMAUS

Top of Act 1 Cues

-5:00:	ASMs and Board Ops on Headset **Roll Call**: SR ASM: **Jeri** SL ASM: **Meghan** Deck (not on headset): **Penelope, Micki, Elana** Deck Elec: **Mason** Light Board Op: **Maddie** Spot Ops: **Margo, Sid** Sound Board Op: **Connor**

WARNING:	Dean (SR) & Spot for p/u @ ENT Pit Cue Light ON LQ 2-8 SQ 1 Pre-Show Announcement + Dean mic STBY: Maestro+ Falke & Alfred

HOUSE TO HALF	**LQ 2, SQ1**
END OF PRE-SHOW ANNOUNCEMENT	**DEAN GO** (@ -00:30 Cue Light ON)
END OF SPEECH	**Spot OUT** **Cue Light OFF (1st Tune)** **STBY Mo.**
SECOND TUNE (HOUSE OUT)	**LQ 3** **Mo. GO (@ 2nd Tune COMPLETE)**
MAESTRO SPECIAL UP	**LQ 4**
ORCHESTRA SPECIAL UP	**LQ 5 (Mo. Turn @ Podium)**
DOWNBEAT/ TOP OF OVERTURE	**LQ 6 [WATCH]**

*START CLOCK
ANNOUNCE TO HOUSE THAT ACT 1 HAS STARTED: 44:30

Figure 7.7 Top of act cues for Act I *Die Fledermaus*.

the show. You may have also noticed something similar breakdown in the first PIP example (Figure 7.1b). Many times, what will happen, is that the SM is juggling check ins with the ASMs and crew while also following up with house management and sometime the orchestra manager. So, regardless of where it is listed, it is nice to have for reference rather than working off memory.

Tips from the toolkit...

If the orchestra manager is not present in the pit during the top of show and act sequence, make sure you touch base with the concert master so they are on the lookout for the tune cue light. More often than not, they are not paying attention when the cue light turns on and off because they are either practicing, chatting, or not at their chair. Since they are below stage level, they are not always able to see when the house lights change. Trying to grab their attention, especially when it is clear that they are not paying attention will probably be one of the hardest challenges to starting the show. One tactic that I have used is continuously flashing their cue light until I see that they (or sometimes another orchestra member will notice it and point it out) have seen it and are ready to go. A gentle reminder that when they see the light go on they should be standing by, and when it goes off they can begin to tune, never hurts.

PERFORMANCE REPORT

The performance report is for the stage manager to continue to provide daily updates and notes about the production once it has opened. Similar to the rehearsal reports, the performance reports are the official documentarians of the production. It is also a way to continue the link between artistic and technical staff.

Who's on the distribution list:

- Director
- Stage management team
- Assistant director
- Production manager
- Technical director
- Designers
- Shop heads/supervisors (scenic, props, costumes)
- Music staff
- Artistic staff
- Additional theater personnel
- House manager

There may be additional/ outside personnel based on the show or venue. Your production manager will be able to assist you with this information if it applies.

What's in it:

- Details of the day's show
- Upcoming performances

- Technical problems/issues that need to be fixed before or during the show by crew. Or, issues that came up during the show
- Info about any illness, injuries or lateness
- Front of house details as requested (sometimes the house manager will put out their own report)

  What's the purpose:

- Provide updates or make requests regarding technical issues
- Document the events of the performance
- Document run time/length of performance

Often times, you will find that your performance report is shorter than your rehearsal reports. Do not take this as any indication that you doing it incorrectly. There is no maximum or minimum to the length of your report. Similar to the rehearsal report, it is nice to add a few lines under the general or performance section to give an overview of how the performance went or what the audience responded most to.

In theater, many times one of the ASMs will start or work on the performance report backstage or in the office. Because of how active both ASMs are most of the time in opera, this is not really the norm. Similar to rehearsals, after the performance, the SM will check in with each department and ASMs for any overall notes or to follow up on any issues that might have arose from the performance. Once they have made the rounds to everyone, they can plug it into the report.

PASSING THE BATON

Opening night marks the departure of many personnel such as the director and designers. It is now one hundred percent the stage manager's show, which means it is up to the SM to keep up the artistic integrity of the show.

GIVING NOTES

It is the stage manager's task to watch the show with the director and designer's visions in mind. This can mean anything from altered blocking, changes or alterations in costumes, different use of props or scenic elements, or anything else that may impact the production. If they are still around, the assistant director will also be watching for this from the audience during each performance. Since the stage manager is the one watching the show closely, it is their job to then review all the notes that were taken and determine who they should come from and when. If they are music related, they should always go through the conductor and music staff first, and, if it is worth passing along, Maestro will talk to the singer directly. If an assistant director is present, any directorial related notes should be discussed with them. Maybe they noticed the same thing, or, if it happens to be a repeating note, maybe the AD has an idea of an alteration.

Giving notes can sometimes be tricky. When considering if you should pursue passing the note along, take these into consideration:

1. **Timing When Giving a Note:** Depending on the note, think about when the best time would be to give it. Is it something small that can be given at the top of a singer's costume or makeup call, such as a minor blocking note where they need to move over a foot to be in the light? Or is it something that the singer may need time to process and should be given at the end of the night?

BREVARD
MUSIC
CENTER
SUMMER INSTITUTE & FESTIVAL

Scheduled Curtain: 7:30p
Performance Report : #1

Date: July 25, 2019
Location: Scott Concert Hall

DIE FLEDERMAUS	Today's Call	Looking Ahead
Director: Dean Anthony **Conductor:** Mo. Michael Sakir **PSM:** Danielle Ranno **ASMs:** Jerri Barber, Meghan Crawford, Penelope Murzenski, Micki Ryan	**Thursday, July 25** 5:30p: HMU calls begin 6:30p: Pre-opera talk 7:00p: Half Hour 7:30p: Performance #1	**Saturday, July 27** 11:15a: Backstage tour 12:00p: HMU calls begin 1:00p: Pre-opera talk 1:30p: Half Hour 2:00p: Performance #2

ACT 1	INT	ACT 2	INT	ACT 3	BOWS
7:36	8:21	8:38	9:22	9:37	10:13
8:21	8:37	9:22	9:36	10:13	10:15
45:02	15:36	44:09	14:08	36:25	2:02

Total Running Time: 2:42:30

General Notes:

Trina, Henry Janiec's daughter, was in the audience tonight. She was touched when she came in and saw the portrait of her father on the set. Dean has requested, if possible, that it be carefully removed so the cast can sign it for her.

We had a great audience this evening, full of uncontrollable laughter. There was quite an uproar when Dean came out as Frosh, with his magic hat and harp bits leaving everyone in tears! Mr. Rachmuth cut his right hand on the hook when he attempted to hang his hat up. Jeri assisted him with First Aid when he came off stage. Stage Management wiped and sanitized all the props on the desk post-show.

Just a reminder, there will be a full company bow after Saturday's performance.

Technical Notes:

SCENERY:
1. Please smooth the edges of the nail for the Act 3 hat trick. It was slightly bent after Dean wiped the chalk off and may need to be replaced.
2. The greenery that fell off the ground row last night was never re-attached. Stage Management stuck it in with loose vines.

PROPS:
1. A new newspaper is needed. Mr. Rachmuth bled on it after cutting his hand on the hat hook.
2. The gold pocket watch fall apart again. It was left in the Act 1 road case.

LIGHTING:
1. Sid accidently took out the diffusion instead of the color from her spot for LQ 222.
2. There was a live move in LQ 208, the top of the Entre'Act.

Figure 7.8 (a and b)   Performance report for *Die Fledermaus. (Continued)*

BREVARD MUSIC CENTER
SUMMER INSTITUTE & FESTIVAL

SOUND:
1. Dean would like the cable to the center stage mic be taped down. The booze string got caught on it as it was being pulled up.

Lateness/Injuries/Incidents

Mr. Rachmuth cut his right hand on the magic hat hook.

-END OF PERFORMANCE REPORT-

Thanks!
Stage Management

Figure 7.8 *(Continued)*

2. **Always Show Respect:** If a designer had to give you a sensitive note, would you prefer it to be given in front of the whole team, or privately? The same goes for the singers. It may seem like something small to you, but it may mean something different to them, so try to avoid large groups. There is no harm in asking someone to "stop by and see you on their way out." Remember, the goal is not to call anyone out or embarrass them.

3. **Don't Sweat the Small Stuff:** We all have moments or off days. If the note is something small that has never happened before, file it away to "keep an eye on it" during the next performance; and if the note is repeated, then check-in.

4. **Don't Be Afraid to Ask Questions or Have a Conversation:** Remember this is a collaborative art form. Not all notes are meant to be negative and sometimes they may be questions regarding something specific from the performance. Maybe you use a specific action or hand gesture as a visual cue for lighting and the singer is now doing said gesture or action at a different time. Do not feel that it makes you any less of a stage manager by approaching them about this or letting them know what it is that *you* may need in order to make *them* look good.

5. **Add a Hint of Positivity:** As artists, we are sensitive to rejection. Regardless of what the note is, there is always a way to add a positive spin to the situation. Try to always have something positive to start or end your conversation with. Not only will the singer appreciate it, but will also be more willing and open to take the note seriously.

When giving notes, regardless of when and by whom, it is preferable to do so in person rather than by email or as a written note left in a dressing room. Verbal notes tend to come off as less cold—especially when coming from the stage manager and not the director—and open up opportunities for additional conversation to take place. With giving in-person notes, the stage manager also has the advantage of assessing the overall situation, including body language, which may alter how they approach the note with the singer to begin with.

BRUSH UPS AND COVER REHEARSALS

Unlike many theater contacts, additional rehearsal usually does not take place during the days off or during earlier sessions on a performance day. Depending on the length of the run, and if there are large breaks (days off) between performances, the music staff might request a music brush up. It is very rare that this brush up takes place in the performance space, especially if working in a union house. Rather, it will take place in a rehearsal hall, music studio, or another room in the theater with just a piano, chairs, and stands.

Depending on the schedule and length of the run, it will be the assistant director's job to rehearse covers. Many times, this will not be done with the full company, just the AD, covers, and stage management standing in for other characters in the scene. If they are lucky, they may even get a pianist. In some schedules, extra rehearsal time will be built in while the director is still in town so the covers can rehearse, and sometimes see a run of the full piece with the covers. In some companies and festivals, cover rehearsal takes place in conjunction with rehearsals, but just with the AD. So the covers will watch during principal staging with the director, and then have a separate session with the AD to work on the scenes they just saw.

One document that is made by the AD is the coro/super critical. In theater, this document is similar to a master actor tracking, used when replacing actors who are out, or when putting on a swing. This is used as a reference document in the event someone in the chorus (or even a super) calls out or is not available for a performance, and who will take over their track. Assistant director, Rebecca Herman, describes in more detail what the coro/super critical document is, how it is made and used:

> The coro/super critical document is used by the AD and SM when someone is sick or misses a performance. It is all the actions that would stop the show if they didn't happen. I tend to make a post-it flag when we are staging the first couple times that just says "crit" and who is doing the action and leave it sticking out the top of my score. Then over the course of rehearsal, as action solidifies, I look at who is around that I trust with the action, in the correct costume, or off stage and can cover that action should the person assigned be absent and note their name on the same post-it. Then, around the time we are doing a final room run or Sitz (depending on the schedule) I can easily go through my book and turn to each flag and get the document completed before the first tech rehearsal. When at a union house, substitutions are a bit more tricky and you have to be sure you haven't assigned a chorus part to a super or comprimario role as that will sometimes result in extra pay that the company was not anticipating. And if there is any singing involved, music staff must be involved in the decision.

Mo. Wood   **AUSTIN OPERA Fall 2019**   AD: rah
Dir. Faircloth   *Rigoletto*   PSM: kme

Placement	Who	What	cover
Act I (pgs.1-50)	S - Cat Treviño	Complete track: pulled off stage by DUKE, re-NTR and quick change, Questa o Quella, dance, Rigoletto/Monterone moment	Julie Silva (Page)
pg 3/5/1	S - Chris Morrow	NTR dsr with tray and goblet for the DUKE	Ryan Redfern
pgs 7 - 8	<u>S - ladies</u> 1 - L. Redfern 2 - C. Kerr 3 - V. Kelly, S. Sneed 4 - C. Treviño	Each has a moment with the DUKE, during verse 2 of *questa o quella*	No cover - just tell DUKE
pgs 9 - 11	Tutti super ladies, 4 coro men C - Evan Brown C - Carey Dietert C- Chris Auchter C - Brian Minnick	Dance (Minuetto)	Robert Veihman Julius Young *There is no cover for the super ladies*
pg 13/1/1 - 13/4/6	S - Matt Flynn	Give message to MARULLO	Chris Morrow
pg 17/5/2	C - Evan Brown	Help BORSA hold CEPRANO back "Marrano!"	Carey Dietert

Figure 7.9   An excerpt of Rebecca Herman's coro/super critical staging for *Rigoletto*.

As heard on headset…

I had to put in a Queen of the Night last minute for an opening night performance. She arrived the night before the show. The morning of the performance she had a fitting first, then 30- minutes of music with the conductor, then the director and I walked her through her blocking (and dialog!) for an hour. The show was being sung in English (not her first language). Our new singer knew the arias in English but not the same translation as we had, so we had to communicate to the super titles operator to get the new lyrics to them. I was then backstage with the new Queen of the Night after her makeup call to allow her a chance to walk the blocking on the set. At intermission once the set change was done, I coordinated with the Master Carpenter to let her get on the piece of scenery she rides as it is pushed on for her Act II entrance.

—*Rebecca Herman, Assistant Director*

EMERGENCY PLANS

Something that always gets pushed to the bottom of the "to-do" list or forgotten all together is an emergency plan. This can be weather related, such as the power going out, an issue on stage, or a medical issue in front of house. Emergencies are not just weather- or medical-based. There could be an issue with the automation or another part of scenery, or a personal issue with a singer or orchestra member. Regardless of the situation, you should always have a backup plan to avoid any panic that may arise. Some companies may have pre-written announcements or emergency guidelines in place, so always ask. If not, write up your own and have them somewhere you can quickly access them. Be sure there is a way to communicate with the audience, whether it be via God mic or through your headset piped into the house, and always check it before each show. As an ASM, always have a flashlight handy in case you need to escort singers off stage in the dark and be sure that you too are aware of the emergency plans.

Other things to think about:

- How will information be passed around if the power goes out and the headsets stop working?
- In case of an evacuation, what part will each member of the SM team play? Where are the emergency exits backstage? Will other people be involved, such as house management, ushers, or even backstage crew members?
- If the SM is unable to communicate with the audience via mic or PA system and cannot get out on stage to make the announcement, who will do it?
- Once the show is back up and running, who will communicate with whom? How will information get to the pit, front of house, and to all the operators?

Heard over headset...

During my gap year between undergrad and grad school, I served as the assistant director and assistant stage manager at a small company in NYC. I ended up calling the show because I had appendicitis and couldn't lift anything and the stage manager ran the backstage track. She had raised concerns that the main platform in the show cut corners in terms of safety, but the production manager assured her that it was fine and not a problem. During the second to last performance, the platform buckled and collapsed with the entire female chorus and female principals on stage. Luckily no one was injured but I had no idea what to do. A scene change was coming up that was supposed to happen behind the first traveler with an in-one scene happening in front of it. Instead of moving on with the in-one scene, I brought in the main and we briefly paused the

> *show to ensure everyone was ok. For the final performance, the company*
> *wanted to try and "repair" the platform and reuse it, but the stage man-*
> *ager refused to allow it, and we ended up performing with the platform*
> *pushed to the back of the stage and all the action occurred downstage.*
>
> *—Ian Silverman, Assistant Director*

BOWS

Traditionally, bows were done at the end of each act rather than at the end of the opera. Why have Scarpia, who dies at the end of Act II in *Tosca,* or Alcindoro, who only appears in Act II of *La Boheme,* wait around until the end for their bow? Directors slowly started to do away with bows at the end of each act because it disrupted the overall flow of the piece. In today's opera world, operas are being staged to avoid having to take pausas and multiple intermissions in order to keep the overall pacing coming to a halt.

Usually, it is the AD who will put together the bows and with the director's approval, publish them to the rest of the company. If there is not an AD on the project, than the director and SM will work together make them. The order in which singers will bow is based on the amount of singing per character. When you have two equal principals, for example Mimi and Rodolfo in *La Bohème,* it will be the female character who has the final call. However, if the title character of the opera is a male for example, Rigoletto in *Rigoletto,* he will receive the final call. Opera has not changed too much in that respect. What is really important, though, is that curtain calls are treated as part of the show. They must be done well or the last impression the audience will have will be unfavorable. Similar to entrances, the ASMs will give the singers a visual cue as they get a "G-O" from the SM via headset, who is watching and timing out the bows from the front of stage monitor.

When cuing bows, you want to time it out so when the current singer is rising from their bow, the next singer is entering from the wings. This might change somewhat in situations where the singers are coming through a curtain rather than the wings. If the main drape is used (this only works if it splits), one to two crew members will also be involved and will page the curtain for singers to enter. Similar to how ASM would cue singers to enter, they would also be cuing the crew to pull the curtain back. Just because the performance has ended does not mean the pacing should drop. If the opera you are working on has a chorus, it is not unlikely that the chorus master will take a bow with the full chorus, so do not forget to add this to your bow sheet! Similar to how the conductor will first take a solo bow, then one with their orchestra, the chorus master will be invited out to stage after the chorus has taken their group bow.

After the full cast takes a tutti bow (full group), the soprano will acknowledge the maestro out on stage. Maestro will take a solo bow, then acknowledge the full orchestra and take a tutti bow with them and then with the full company.

These final tutti company bows with Maestro could be one, or three. The amount will be redetermined by the directing staff. Sometimes, the ASM will be in the wings counting them down for the group.

Opera facts!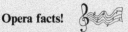

Another tradition that is still sometimes done is presenting the team and singers with opening night flowers on stage. Someone from the opera company, donor, or volunteer, sometimes with the assistance of stage management, will bring out bouquets and hand them out. This used to be only for the female singers and designers, but recently, has become more inclusive. When prepping for opening night, remember to ask the company if they are doing flowers or not because it will affect how you cue the end of bows.

OPENING NIGHT

You will see on the bottom half of the bow sheet (Figure 7.10) that there is a section labeled "opening night only." Known as the penguin bow, this is when the director comes out and bows with their full team. Traditionally, the tenor (or other lead character) will acknowledge the director out on stage. The director will take a solo bow, then bring out their team for a tutti creative bow. To finish the night off, both the full cast and creative team and Maestro will take anywhere from two or more (the number of bows will be previously agreed upon) bows. If there is a main curtain, it will be called in as the group is backing up from their final bow. If not, the stage lights will change into a post-show look, the house lights will come up and everyone will exit the stage.

Who's part of the penguin bow (not in any specific order):

- Director
- Scenic designer
- Costume designer
- Lighting designer
- Projections designer
- Props designer
- Hair/wigs and makeup
- Choreographer
- Who does not bow:
- Assistant director
- Stage manager
- Assistant stage managers
- Any other assistants (lighting, scenic, costumes, wigs and makeup, props)

GIANNI SCHICCHI
Bows

BLACKOUT
Main Curtain IN
LIGHTS UP

Mr. Swain, **Mr. Eder** enter through center curtain, bow, clear SR

Mr. Schlabach enter through center curtain, bow, clear SL

Mr. Humbert enter through center curtain, bow, clear SR

Ms. Tackett enter through center curtain, bow, clear SL

Ms. Lee Gholston, Mr. Clark enter through center curtain, **Ms. Lee Gholston** bow, **Mr. Clark** bow, clear SR

Ms. Merryman, Mr. Bunsold enter through center curtain, **Ms. Merryman** bow, **Mr. Bunsold** bow, clear SL

Mr. McKeever enter through center curtain, bow, clear SR

Mr. Banion enter through center curtain, bow, clear SL

Ms. Spencer enter through center curtain, bow, clear SR

Mr. Nevergall enter through center curtain, bow, clear SL

Ms. Willis enter through center curtain, bow, clear SR

Mr. Kerr enter through center curtain, bow center

Principals join **Mr. Kerr**- x2 COMPANY BOW

Ms. Willis step forward and welcome **Mo. Kelly** to stage

Mo. Kelly bow

Mo. Kelly acknowledge the Orchestra

*****************************OPENING NIGHT ONLY**
Tutti principals split center

Mr. Shaw enter through center curtain, bow

Mr. Watson, Mr. López-Watermann, Mr. Carty enter through center curtain

Penguin Bow
• •

COMPANY BOW

Wave and exit up center through curtain

SUBJECT TO CHANGE   As of 09/18/19

Figure 7.10 Bow sheet for *Gianni Schicchi* at Opera Columbus. Since there was not an AD on staff, the stage manager put together the bows sheet with the director.

Opera facts!

How did the design team become known as the "penguins"? Back in the earlier days of opera, and when designers were mostly male, everyone used to show up on opening night in a tux. When a line of them would walk out on stage, it was said they looked like a line of penguins! Although a tux is not always required (some of the larger houses still do), the name still holds.

Now that your show has opened, it is time to start finalizing paperwork and the prompt book. Although printed copies are needed to finalize your prompt book, many companies are keeping digital copies on file as well. In the final chapter, we will discuss how and what you should be finalizing and archiving your paperwork.

CHAPTER 8

Archiving

You made it through prep, rehearsal, tech, and performances, but the job is not over *quite* yet. Before the SM team departs, they must finalize and archive all their paperwork. To help with this process, some SMs will slowly start to archive their paperwork and clean their book during performance week. Many companies do not take into consideration a post-performance/archiving week like they do prep week, so the amount of time allotted for this is limited.

While the team is finalizing all their paperwork, they may also be in the middle of strike. Strike for stage managers can vary depending on the type of house and crew (union vs non-union) you are working with. Sometimes, the stage management team will be more hands on and assist with packing up props or help with clearing out dressing rooms. In other cases, they will only be responsible for clearing out their own areas. This would include cleaning up each individual calling station—the console or booth for the SM and backstage/music stand areas for the ASMs. You will also have to strike the callboard area, restore it back to its original look, and any signage, such as dressing room and directional signs) that were put up backstage. Stage managers might also be responsible for pulling up spike tape on stage, although this might be tricky to coordinate if the crew is jumping right into strike post-show. Coming up with a strike plan in advance to your final performance is always a good route. Run it by your production manager before distributing to your team in case they have anything to add or change. Remember the number one rule of thumb: you want to leave the space better than how you found it!

ARCHIVED CHECKLIST

To make archiving as easy as possible, it helps to make a checklist. Figures 8.1 and 8.2 are two examples of SM checklists. This checklist can then act as a Table of Contents at the front of your book. Depending on the type of show, venue, and tech/design involved, this list may be altered or edited where necessary. Also, the order in which you list everything and place it in your book is up to you.

DOI: 10.4324/9781003047391-9

[TITLE OF SHOW]
Archival Checklist

☐ Archival Checklist
☐ Rental Fact Sheet

CAST - STAFF
☐ Cast / Staff List
☐ Chorus List
☐ Supernumerary List
☐ Artist Face Page

SCHEDULES
☐ Stage Master Calendar
☐ Artist Overview Calendar
☐ Chorus Schedule
☐ Supernumerary Schedule

RUN LISTS - SCENE BREAKDOWN
☐ WWW (Who, What, Where)
☐ Scene Breakdown
☐ First Entrance Timings
☐ Critical Duties Sheet
☐ Chorus Running List
☐ Super Running List
☐ Bow Sheet

MUSIC
☐ Original Cut List
☐ Text Change & Music Cut Form
☐ Pit Plot
☐ Show Timing Sheet

REPORTS
☐ Daily Rehearsal Reports
☐ Performance Reports

SCORES - scanned
☐ SM Calling Score
☐ AD Score (scan only)

SCENERY
☐ Deck Running Sheet
☐ Rail Cue Sheet
☐ Mini Ground plans
☐ Set Renderings / Elevations
☐ Scene-by-Scene with Stage Photos

PROPS
☐ Props Running Sheet
☐ Props List
☐ Spike Map

COSTUMES - WARDROBE
☐ Wardrobe Running Sheet
☐ Costume Sketches
☐ Costume Photos
☐ Costume Plot / Inventory (Piece List)
☐ Dressing Room Assignments

WIGS - MAKEUP
☐ Wig Piece List
☐ Running Sheet (if separate from Wardrobe Run Sheet)

ELECTRICS
☐ Light Cue List / Description
☐ Follow Spot Cue Sheet
☐ Effects / Other Requirements

AUDIO - VIDEO
☐ Sound Cue Sheet
☐ Sound Running Sheet

MISCELLANEOUS
☐ Show-specific Miscellany

Figure 8.1   First example of an archival checklist.

Some SMs prefer having the score up front, as seen in Figure 8.2, whereas others have it in the middle or back of the book, as shown in Figure 8.1. If there is a header or department that was not used on the show, simply delete it.

WHY ARCHIVE YOUR WORK?

The last step is to archive all your paperwork. Updating any rehearsal paperwork that you put together because it was helpful to running the show in the rehearsal room is not as important as the run paperwork, such as, the Who, What, Where, deck/props run sheet, and wardrobe run sheet. Everything will get printed and placed in the SM book, as well as on a hard drive or folder that the company keeps electronically. Many times, this paperwork will only get used again or pulled out if the company is sending the show out on a rental, or it getting

[TITLE OF SHOW]
Table of Contents

Keys
- Cuing Key
- Highlighted cast list
- Blocking key

Score
- PIP
- Blocking/cuing score
- Curtain call sequence

Contacts
- Production staff contact sheet
- JOC contact sheet

Cast
- Cast List
- JOC Facebook
- Children Cheat Sheet
- Coro sign-in

Schedule
- Production Schedule
- Work Thru Schedule
- Tech Schedules & crew calls

Reports
- Rehearsal reports
- Performance reports
- House Management reports

Breakdowns
- Character/scene breakdown
- WWW

Props
- Prop inventory
- Prop running
- Prop tracking
- Prop list from director

Lighting
- Lighting cue sheet
- Cue light placements

Scenic
- Ground plan
- Model renderings
- Draftings
- Elevations
- Research
- Taping points (rehearsal)
- Blocking sheet blanks

Costumes
- Fist entrance
- Piece list
- Wardrobe run sheet
- Costume renderings

Makeup & Wig
- HMU call times

Sound
- Monitor Plot
- SFX cue sheet
- Headset assignments
- Radio assignments

Music/ Orchestra
- Rehearsal letter list
- Pit plot

SM Admin
- Dean's speech
- SM duties
- FOH info sheet
- Tech request
- Emergency Announcement

Figure 8.2   Here is another example of an archival checklist, but more in the form of a Table of Contents.

remounted. Sometimes, parts of a show might go out rather than the whole package, so pieces of paperwork will get pulled such as the Who, What, Where if it is just the set and props being rented, or the costume run sheet and piece list if only the costumes are being used.

There are some companies that do not want to keep the SM or AD prompt books. Either they do not have the space to store them, the production was on a rented set, or they do not plan to keep the set. If that is the case, then it is up to the stage manager to choose what to do with their score. The company may still want electronic copies of all the SM paperwork. The team should try to spend some time on cleaning and revising their paperwork, even if it is just going to be filed away. You never know who may pull it out or look at it in the future. The company might decide to remount the production or rent or build the set again; in which case, all the paperwork might be passed onto that SM team as a starting point. Unlike performers who may have video clips of their performance out in the world via the internet or on a personal website, think of paperwork as the stage manager's time capsule of their work. You never know when it will get dug up again!

WHAT TO ARCHIVE?

STAGE MANAGER

You want to clean up your book, so it is legible and easy to follow. Clean up blocking if it was just scribbled in quickly. Make sure that all your cues are easy to decipher. If you need to add a key because you have different colors or symbols for your standbys or G-O cues, be sure to add one in; that way, anyone can pick up your book and easily read it (Figure 8.3). Have the group (SM, ASMs and AD if there is one) review all entrances and exits against what is listed in the Who, What, Where and in the main blocking book. You will also want to

	Burke and Hare	Cueing Key
		chm

Symbol	Action
	Stand By Light Cue....
	Light Cue ....GO
	Stand By Projection ...
	Projection .... GO
(vis) K x DS	Visual Cue: When Knox crosses down stage
	Music Cue: take on specific beat

Letter	Character
B	Burke
H	Hare
MH	Margaret Hare
HM	Helen McDougal
K	Knox
F	Ferguson
D	Donald
J	Daft Jamie
A	Abigail
M	Madge
MP	Mary Peterson

Symbol	Action
X	Cross
DS	Downstage
SR	Stage Right
SL	Stage Left
NTR	Enter
XT	Exit

Page 1 of 1

Figure 8.3   An example of an SM cuing key for *Burke and Hare*.
Courtesy of stage manager, Cindy Hennon Marino.

print up (if you have not already) all the reports and design paperwork such as cue sheets, ground plans, and renderings. All of the running paperwork that the ASMs put together will also be printed and placed in the final archived book.

In their own words...

I always try to get a head start on my archiving because I just know how sneakily it creeps up on me! Things start to settle down once we hit final dress rehearsal, so that is when I aim to start my deep dive into score and paperwork cleaning. If it is a show I am assisting on, I will try to update as I go, or spend the 10-minutes at the end of the night when the SM is working on the report to tweak. You NEVER know who is going to pull out your paperwork in the future, so always take the time to make it pristine!

—DR

ASSISTANT DIRECTOR

You want to clean up your book, since this will be the archived blocking book. You will want to transfer over any blocking that was written on Post-its to minis so they do not accidentally come off or move. Some companies are opting to have AD books scanned so they are easier to travel with and save on space. It is also easier to send a digital copy if the production is being rented or remounted at another company. Running paperwork that was put together such as props tracking, critical chorus, or cast scene shifts should also be cleaned and updated to match the opening performance. The final step is to list in your header or footer that it is the "FINAL" version. You will want to save both the PDF and non-PDF versions of each file.

In their own words...

When it comes to archiving paperwork, the key focus is on making sure my book is as clean as possible. It depends on the company though as sometimes the AD book will not be sent with a rental/remount package and only the archival video will be sent. At the end of the day, the book is for the AD to be able to decipher. It should be clear and include as much detail as possible in case you need to revisit the production yourself in the future. So much of the stage manager's paperwork concerns what happens OFF stage: entrances and exits, presets, scene shifts, and costume changes, whereas the AD's responsibility in the archival paperwork is to detail what happens ON stage: prop tracking, critical chorus staging and placements/blocking.

—Ian Silverman, Assistant Director

ASSISTANT STAGE MANAGER

You do not have to worry about archiving your book because all of the cues-entrances, exits, transitions, prop hand offs, costume changes- will all be listed in the Who, What, Where, as well as, the SM book. Making sure your run paperwork is the most accurate is key. If there were any changes that were made between tech and performance that you did not have time to update, they should be fixed. Since much of the ASM paperwork go hand in hand, it may be helpful (and sometimes quicker) to work on some of it together. Maybe both ASMs each update their side of the stage in the who, what, where and then hand it over to the AD to check or add any final touches. When finalizing your paperwork, you will list in your header or footer that it is the "FINAL" version. You will want to save both the PDF and non-PDF versions of each file.

FINAL ADVICE

You have all the tools needed in your kit, now it is time to put it to practice. There is only so much of stage management that you can learn from reading a book. We become better at our jobs and learn new things by doing! If you are gearing up to stage manage your first opera, here are a few final pieces of advice I have to share:

- Keep an open mind. It's ok if you don't get it right the first time.

- Don't be afraid to ask questions, even if you think it's something that you should already know.

- Don't be afraid to fail; we have all done it. Just don't make the same mistake twice.

- The paperwork or email will still be there in the morning. Do not stay up all night just to finish a project that leaves you tired and not as alert for another full day or rehearsal/ tech/ performances.

- Remember how important you are in the room and that you have every right to be there! You would not have been brought on to the team if you did not have talent.

- Always try to be at least two steps ahead. When you are in prep, have your rehearsal brain on. When you are in rehearsal, have your tech brain on. And when you are in tech, have your performance brain on.

- Trust yourself, trust the music, and trust your team; they want to see you succeed too. And remember to always have fun!

Appendix

As a self-taught opera stage manager, I always found that the best way (for me) to learn was through hearing the experiences (the good, the bad, and the ugly) of others that came before me. In this appendix, you will find some "bonus material" such as an ASM journal, which gives a glimpse into the day-to-day life of an ASM working at The Glimmerglass Festival, further information about working in an IATSE house and with their crew, and additional resources to check out!

THE MAGIC FLUTE JOURNAL

By Kayla Uribe

Week 1

This week was our first week of prep. We began with safety orientations in the mornings of the first two days and prepped for our shows in the afternoons. The first thing to tackle is timing and prepping the score. On the team, the second ASM times the score, which means I did 30 second timings for The Magic Flute. Once timings were written in, I copied and distributed the score to the rest of the team. Then, I began my highlighting journey. I marked up cuts and highlighted the systems to make it easier to follow along during a show.

Another significant part of the show is meeting with other departments. We had a props meeting this week and went item by item with our props masters to clarify any questions they had and to solidify what we would be able to have in rehearsal. Even though I am the costumes ASM on Flute, I still sat in on this meeting so I would be in-the-know during rehearsals and could help out when needed. I also had a costumes meeting with the Assistant Costume Designer to obtain a piece list and discuss any significant costume changes or things that would need to be discovered in rehearsal. For example, Papageno has a feathered shawl that is free flowing and not attached to the rest of the costume at this point. Depending on how much he wears it or how much movement he will be doing onstage, it might need to be secured to the rest of his costume. I make notes of these things and flag them to watch for during rehearsal. It also helps to give these notes to the Assistant Director so they can watch out for them too and remind the director during rehearsals.

One of the final things I did on my own for prep was fill in templates with as much information as possible. Since we had a costumes meeting and reviewed the changes, I mapped out the changes in the Wardrobe Running Sheet so all I have to do when we figure out where the changes will be is copy paste them in the correct order. I did similar things for the Who, What, Where and Prop Running list for the other shows as well.

On Thursday and Friday as a team, we went to tape out the rehearsal spaces and confirm all our rehearsal materials (electrical power, tissues, hand sanitizer, etc.) were fully stocked and ready for the first rehearsal day. We pack rehearsal boxes based off a checklist to take to the rehearsal hall.

Week 2

We had our first rehearsals this week. Monday was our final prep day and we taped out the last of the rehearsal spaces and set them up. The props department transferred all props that we requested and we looked them over to familiarize ourselves with them so we could explain how they work/what they were to singers in rehearsal.

Rehearsals on Tuesday began with a music run through, as music is often the most important aspect of an opera. Once we got up on our feet, it is our responsibility to track singer entrances and exits, as well as prop and costume changes. We also cue singers for their entrances. This week was relatively light, as it is only a 90-minute opera. We staged most of the show in a week with a few chunks here and there that still need to be staged.

As per usual, prop and costume questions came in as we discovered the staging in rehearsal. The most exciting aspect was working with the giant snake puppet that is operated by 3 people! We were lucky enough to have our props master join us in rehearsal to get feedback so he could make adjustments as requested by the director and singers. Questions for costumes as far as who has pockets and could we add kneepads for singers came up as it always does, and of course some props needed replacing or fixes as they were handled by singers.

At the end of the week, I had the chance to update our WWW and double check all cues in my book. Because the ASMs this season are on multiple shows, my co-ASM will not be in rehearsals for The Magic Flute this upcoming week, so I will need to cue all her entrances, as well as my own. I borrowed her book to double check her placements and also notated them in the WWW. It is critical that this is as up to date as possible because when we move into tech, we will likely not have as much time to update our paperwork. This also helps us be as prepared as possible before we move into tech.

Week 3

This week, I was primarily the only ASM in the room as my co-ASM Sarah was needed in rehearsals for another show. Glimmerglass runs in rep, so often times, ASMs will miss rehearsals and catch up on what we missed in the show either via WWW or via email.

This week, we made several changes to the initial blocking of the show because the Artistic Director of the company, Francesca, observed rehearsal towards the end of last week and gave us notes. This changes some entrance and exit locations, which I communicated to Sarah. If there were only a few changes, I would send them to her via email, but if there were several large changes, I updated them in the WWW and then sent them to her via email, noting what the major changers were.

Many of the props are being finalized, and we continued to have a few small notes here and there, but overall, this week focused on getting ready for tech Sunday. Since I am on costumes for this show, I scheduled a costumes tracking meeting and was in communications with our Asst. Costume Designer (ACD) for any pieces list updates. At Glimmerglass, we list all pieces in our wardrobe tracking paperwork, so it's important to have an accurate and updated pieces list as close to tech as possible. This season is also a bit different because we are on a condensed tech schedule. Typically, we would not introduce costumes until dress rehearsals, but this year, we are introducing them at first tech. I created a first draft of the wardrobe tracking and printed out copies for all members of the wardrobe team to follow along with in our meeting. We went change by change to determine which dresser would assist with the changes (or if the singers could do them on their own), if hair/make up needed to be involved to ensure headpieces stayed on, and most importantly, where each change would happen (dressing room vs. backstage). After that, I made edits as needed to the paperwork based on pieces list updates, and then printed them for tech.

Week 4

As with all techs, there are always hiccups that we have to roll with in the moment. For this tech process, that hiccup was scheduling mic fittings for the singers. In addition to a mic check at the beginning of tech which we accounted for, we were informed the day before tech that every singer would need to be fitted for a mic since they are will go around the back of the singers' heads (boom mic). Since we are an opera company, we are not used to micing our singers, so this was a new addition to the schedule we did not account for. We adjusted some of our preshow calls to fit all singers in, and the morning of, I was responsible for keeping the singers on schedule. All in all, it went well.

The biggest focus on this tech was spacing and audio. Since all our shows are in the daylight and outdoors, lighting kind of takes a backseat this season. Our orchestra will also be playing in our actual theatre, so the sound will be fed to the stage via speaker system. Lining all that up with Maestro in the theatre with the orchestra and the singers onstage outside was something everyone was wary about, especially with the monitor placements. Once we readjusted blocking so all singers could make contact with at least one monitor, everyone felt pretty good about the show overall. We had a dinner break and returned in the evening for our sitzprobe with the orchestra. It was planned to be more of a wandelprobe, which was tricky because it started to rain pretty hard halfway through. Our singers were troopers though, and once we finished running through the show, we were all released early (or at least everyone that was out in the rain was).

We got the next day off from Flute since another show had to go into tech, but we were back the day after for our orchestra dress rehearsal. All costumes were finalized and we ran through the whole show pretty seamlessly. We had a few hiccups with makeup since it was much hotter today and the singers were sweating more than at tech, but we got through the show without stopping. Afterwards, we had the singers get out of costume but stay in mics for spacing and music notes. Once all notes were given, singers were released and I had to go to rehearsal for another show. We came back in two days for opening, and it all went off without a hitch!

WORKING IN AN IATSE HOUSE

By Cindy Hennon Marino

IATSE stands for International Alliance of Theatrical Stage Employees (founded in 1893 in NYC) but has grown to also now cover all forms of live theater, motion picture and television production, trade shows and exhibitions, television broadcasting, and concerts, as well as the equipment and construction shops that support all these areas. They are over 150,000 works within 12 districts and 366 Locals across not only the US but also Canada.

Each local is their own entity and determine their own Constitution and By-Laws, officers, dues, membership meetings, etc. They negotiate labor contracts in regards to wages, work rules and grievance procedures. Therefore, even though you may be working in a "Union house" the rules and procedures may be slightly different.

The best advice I can give is to ALWAYS ASK!

Here are some questions you need to ask when working in a new house/with a new local and why they are important.

Who is the Shop Steward/Head Crew? This person is your go-to. They will let you know who everyone is, their names, their department. They will also know the specifics when it comes to hours, breaks, overtime, etc. If you are ever unsure of something, this is the person who will be able to guide you in the right direction.

How are the departments broken down in this local? Each local I have worked with has had at least a Scenic, Electrics and Audio department. If that is the case, props and rigging/flymen are part of the scenic department while video can be either under electrics or audio. Many locals will also have a wardrobe department and (if not categorized with wardrobe), hair and makeup. Knowing how the departments are broken down will help inform you on how you create your paperwork (can "Scenic" crew also move props? Or are those 2 separate departments and therefore separate documents?), and who go to with information, notes or questions, and

Who are the Crew Heads? Each department will have their own Crew Head. These are the individuals you go to when you have notes or questions for that specific department. At some venues these are the only crew members you will communicate with when giving notes. At some venues they may be more relaxed and you will be able to communicate directly with the crew member a note pertains to. Again, ASK!

How do the breaks work? Crews usually work in 4-hour blocks (this can sometimes be broken down into 5 hours and 3 hours, so make sure you know what the schedule is). They will take a "coffee" break 2 hours in (15-20 mins), and a meal break after 4 hours (1 hour long). Good news is that they can often stagger their breaks during tech and performances. Since the crew is almost always needed for scene changes at intermission, they can take their 20-minute breaks during a section of the show they are not being used. The shop steward will often manage that part of it, but you need to be aware of it in case different crew members disappear at different times during the show.

Can we cross the stage during a break? I know this sounds strange, but in union houses, if the crew heads are not on, then you often cannot even step foot on the stage, or cross it. Otherwise, you incur overtime. At some venues you are allowed to use the cross over, or go thru the house. But you always need to make sure you know where those boundaries are. And make sure all performers, or anyone working on the production, knows this as well! You do not want a singer coming out to walk the stage during a crew break!

How would you like your paperwork? Yes, I know this may sound like a strange question. We were almost all trained (included in this book!) on how to create paperwork. But you need to make sure you do what works best for the crew that is looking at it because you want to make it as easy as possible for them! Do not take offense if they ask for changes. They are not criticizing your work, they may just be used to a different format or their brains may work differently than yours does, and that is ok. Often times you can ask the production manager if they have running paperwork from past shows or event templates that the crew prefers so you can start off with that and not have to make so many changes later on.

Should you create separate documents for scenic, props, flymen? Do the flymen want a very simple document that is size 40 font that they can post behind the rail to see easily? Do props crew want their run sheets in landscape vs portrait because it is easier for them to fold up in their pocket? Do they want it single sided or double sided? Do they want you to update paperwork every night and give them a fresh sheet? Or do they prefer to take their own notes? (NOTE: often they will want a new document after the first 2 days, but then keep their own notes after that). Does stage right want a separate sheet than stage left? Or do they like to see what each other does? Do wardrobe and hair and make up want to work off the same document? Or do they prefer individual run sheets? If you talk with the crew heads and hear from them what they need and want, the entire tech and performance process will be so much easier.

May I spike furniture/people? Or is that (props) crew? I swear this is different at every venue and every day! At some places you will be allowed to spike furniture based on your spike plot from rehearsal, then they will take care of it after that. Sometimes you can be there to help adjust, but they are the only ones allowed to use the spike tape. Sometimes it starts off with them doing everything, but by final dress they let you do a few things (I am probably not allowed to say that! But it is still often the case, especially if you have built a working and trusting relationship and their job is not threatened).

Are singers allowed to pick up props from the table or do they have to all be hand offs? In some union houses, no one is allowed to touch anything on the props table EXCEPT props crew. If a singer needs a prop, they literally need to hand it to them and take it back from them (catch). At some places, singers are allowed to pick up items themselves as long as a crew person is there and watching. Times they are allowed to drop off props on the table, but not pick them up. You want to make sure that you know all these rules and to *pass the information along to the singers.* Along these lines, make sure you know exactly what is allowed to be touched onstage when resetting a scene or moving back a few pages. Sometimes a singer is allowed to pick up a prop and reset it, sometimes crew has to do that. For example, if a singer picks up a cup from the desk and places it on a table on the other side of the stage, can they reset it if you need to go back and do the scene again? Or does a props crew need to go out there and reset it?

One final thing to remember is that the crew is there because they honestly love what they do. They want the show to be a success. They want everything to be as perfect as possible. They love their job and they love the arts. I know they are sometimes gruff or angry or sarcastic or quiet. But deep down they love what they do as much as you do. Remember that you just spent weeks learning this show, they know nothing about it (and they may not want to know anything about it!). But they do want to do their job to the best of the ability and they take great pride in their work. You need to treat them with the respect they deserve, treat them as part of the team, listen to them, include them, talk to them. I always love the moments when the crew pulls off an impossibly fast scene change in the Knick of time, or hits every spike perfectly. The smiles on their faces and gleam in their eyes is worth it. So even when the hours are long and everyone I stressed and cranky, remember that you are all in this together and all want the same exact thing, a wonderful production.

ADDITIONAL OPERA RESOURCES

If you are interested in learning more about the history of opera, or looking for additional resources to help with an upcoming show, such as librettos or scene by scene breakdown, check out the list below:

The Book of 101 Opera Librettos: Complete Original Language Texts with English Translations

By Jessica M. MacMurray (Editor), Allison Brewster Franzetti (Contributor)

ISBN: 978-1884822797

100 Great Operas and Their Stories: Act-By-Act Synopses

By Henry W. Simon

ISBN: 978-0385054485

Opera: Composers, Works, Performers

By András Batta

ISBN: 978-3829035712

Divas and Scholars: Performing Italian Opera

By Philip Gossett

ISBN: 978-0226304878

A History of Opera

By Carolyn Abbate and Roger Parker

ISBN: 978-0393348958

The Politics of Opera: A History from Monteverdi to Mozart

By Mitchell Cohen

ISBN: 978-0691211510

The Cambridge Companion to Twentieth-Century Opera

Edited by Mervyn Cooke

ISBN: 978-0521780094

The Cambridge Companion to Opera Studies

Edited by Nicholas Till

ISBN: 978-0521855617

A Mad Love: An Introduction to Opera

By Vivian Schweitzer

ISBN: 978-0465096930

Index

Printed in the USA
CPSIA information can be obtained
at www.ICGtesting.com
LVHW080029130124
768634LV00017B/25